Pablo Trapero and the Politics of Violence

WORLD CINEMA SERIES

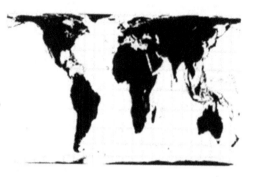

Series Editors:

Lúcia Nagib, Professor of Film at the University of Reading
Julian Ross, Research Fellow at Leiden University

Advisory Board: Laura Mulvey (UK), Robert Stam (USA), Ismail Xavier (Brazil), Dudley Andrew (USA)

The *World Cinema Series* aims to reveal and celebrate the richness and complexity of film art across the globe, exploring a wide variety of cinemas set within their own cultures and as they interconnect in a global context. The books in the series will represent innovative scholarship, in tune with the multicultural character of contemporary audiences. Drawing upon an international authorship, they will challenge outdated conceptions of world cinema, and provide new ways of understanding a field at the centre of film studies in an era of transnational networks.

Published and forthcoming in the World Cinema series:

Allegory in Iranian Cinema: The Aesthetics of Poetry and Resistance
Michelle Langford

Amharic Film Genres and Ethiopian Cinema
Michael W. Thomas

Animation in the Middle East: Practice and Aesthetics from Baghdad to Casablanca
Stefanie Van de Peer

Basque Cinema: A Cultural and Political History
Rob Stone and Maria Pilar Rodriguez

Brazil on Screen: Cinema Novo, New Cinema, Utopia
Lúcia Nagib

Brazilian Cinema and the Aesthetics of Ruins
Guilherme Carréra

Cinema in the Arab World: New Histories, New Approaches
Edited By Philippe Meers, Daniel Biltereyst and Ifdal Elsaket

Contemporary New Zealand Cinema
Edited by Ian Conrich and Stuart Murray

Cosmopolitan Cinema: Cross-cultural Encounters in East Asian Film
Felicia Chan

Documentary Cinema in Chile: Confronting History, Memory, Trauma
Antonio Traverso

East Asian Cinemas: Exploring Transnational Connections on Film
Edited by Leon Hunt and Leung Wing-Fai

East Asian Film Noir: Transnational Encounters and Intercultural Dialogue
Edited by Chi-Yun Shin and Mark Gallagher

Eastern Approaches to Western Film: Asian Reception and Aesthetics in Cinema
Stephen Teo

Impure Cinema: Intermedial and Intercultural Approaches to Film
Edited by Lúcia Nagib and Anne Jerslev

Latin American Women Filmmakers: Production, Politics, Poetics
Edited by Deborah Martin and Deborah Shaw

Lebanese Cinema: Imagining the Civil War and Beyond
Lina Khatib

New Argentine Cinema
Jens Andermann

New Directions in German Cinema
Edited by Paul Cooke and Chris Homewood

New Turkish Cinema: Belonging, Identity and Memory
Asuman Suner

On Cinema
Glauber Rocha, Edited by Ismail Xavier

Pablo Trapero and the Politics of Violence
Douglas Mulliken

Palestinian Filmmaking in Israel: Narratives of Place and
Yael Friedman

Performing Authorship: Self-inscription and Corporeality in the Cinema
Cecilia Sayad

Portugal's Global Cinema: Industry, History and Culture
Edited by Mariana Liz

Queer Masculinities in Latin American Cinema: Male Bodies and Narrative Representations
Gustavo Subero

Realism in Greek Cinema: From the Post-War Period to the Present
Vrasidas Karalis

Realism of the Senses in World Cinema: The Experience of Physical Reality
Tiago de Luca

Stars in World Cinema: Screen Icons and Star Systems Across Cultures
Edited by Andrea Bandhauer and Michelle Royer

The Cinema of Jia Zhangke: Realism and Memory in Chinese Film
Cecília Mello

The Cinema of Sri Lanka: South Asian Film in Texts and Contexts
Ian Conrich

The New Generation in Chinese Animation
Shaopeng Chen

The Spanish Fantastic: Contemporary Filmmaking in Horror, Fantasy and Sci-fi
Shelagh-Rowan Legg

Theorizing World Cinema
Edited by Lúcia Nagib, Chris Perriam and Rajinder Dudrah

Queries, ideas and submissions to:
Series Editor: Professor Lúcia Nagib—
l.nagib@reading.ac.uk

Series Editor: Dr. Julian Ross—
j.a.ross@hum.leidenuniv.nl

Publisher at Bloomsbury, Rebecca Barden—
Rebecca.Barden@bloomsbury.com

Pablo Trapero and the Politics of Violence

Douglas Mulliken

BLOOMSBURY ACADEMIC
LONDON • NEW YORK • OXFORD • NEW DELHI • SYDNEY

BLOOMSBURY ACADEMIC
Bloomsbury Publishing Plc
50 Bedford Square, London, WC1B 3DP, UK
1385 Broadway, New York, NY 10018, USA
29 Earlsfort Terrace, Dublin 2, Ireland

BLOOMSBURY, BLOOMSBURY ACADEMIC and the Diana logo are trademarks of Bloomsbury Publishing Plc

First published in Great Britain 2022
This paperback edition published 2023

Copyright © Douglas Mulliken, 2022, 2023

Douglas Mulliken has asserted his right under the Copyright, Designs and Patents Act, 1988, to be identified as Author of this work.

For legal purposes the Acknowledgments on p. xiii constitute an extension of this copyright page.

Cover design: Charlotte Daniels
Cover image: *El Bonaerense* (2002). Directed by Pablo Trapero © Photofest NYC

All rights reserved. No part of this publication may be reproduced or transmitted in any form or by any means, electronic or mechanical, including photocopying, recording, or any information storage or retrieval system, without prior permission in writing from the publishers.

Bloomsbury Publishing Plc does not have any control over, or responsibility for, any third-party websites referred to or in this book. All internet addresses given in this book were correct at the time of going to press. The author and publisher regret any inconvenience caused if addresses have changed or sites have ceased to exist, but can accept no responsibility for any such changes.

A catalogue record for this book is available from the British Library.

A catalog record for this book is available from the Library of Congress.

ISBN: HB: 978-1-3501-6338-6
PB: 978-1-3502-9015-0
ePDF: 978-1-3501-6339-3
eBook: 978-1-3501-6340-9

Series: World Cinema

Typeset by Deanta Global Publishing Services, Chennai, India

To find out more about our authors and books visit www.bloomsbury.com and sign up for our newsletters.

For my parents. And for Inge.

Contents

List of Figures	x
Acknowledgments	xiii
Introduction	1

Part One The Individual and the State

1	Neoliberalism, Violence, and the New Argentina	29
	The Violence of Neoliberalism	30
	Mundo grúa	33
	Carancho	46
2	Repression, Ideology, and the Manipulation of Power	64
	Theories of Power	64
	El bonaerense	68
	Elefante blanco	85

Part Two Violence and the Family

3	The Violence of the Arborescent Family	103
	Theories of the Family	103
	Familia rodante	109
	El clan	125
	La quietud	138
4	The Rhizome as an Alternative Family Model	152
	Rhizomes and the Becoming-Family	153
	Nacido y criado	160
	Leonera	176

Conclusion	190
Interview with Pablo Trapero	195
Works Cited	231
Films Cited	238
Index	240

Figures

0.1 The failure of the future is mediated through the White Elephant itself. *Carancho* directed by Pablo Trapero © Matanza Cine 2010. All Rights Reserved ... 12

0.2 *Carancho*'s low-key lighting is used to manifest a sense of objective violence. *Carancho* directed by Pablo Trapero © Matanza Cine 2010. All Rights Reserved ... 15

1.1 The futility of the workers' situation is evident on Rulo's face. *Mundo grúa* directed by Pablo Trapero © Lita Stantic Producciones 1999. All Rights Reserved ... 38

1.2 Claudio's sexual exploits threaten Rulo's masculinity. *Mundo grúa* directed by Pablo Trapero © Lita Stantic Producciones 1999. All Rights Reserved ... 41

1.3 Rulo's sense of isolation is emphasized as he arrives in Comodo Rivadavia. *Mundo grúa* directed by Pablo Trapero © Lita Stantic Producciones 1999. All Rights Reserved ... 45

1.4 Sosa's existence is defined by a pervasive violence that seems impossible to escape. *Carancho* directed by Pablo Trapero © Matanza Cine 2010. All Rights Reserved ... 48

1.5 Throughout the film, danger awaits just off-screen. *Carancho* directed by Pablo Trapero © Matanza Cine 2010. All Rights Reserved ... 52

1.6 The moment Sosa breaks Vega's leg demonstrates the extent to which objective violence has come to define *Carancho*'s society. *Carancho* directed by Pablo Trapero © Matanza Cine 2010. All Rights Reserved ... 60

2.1 The focus on the nondescript police station reinforces the *conurbano* as nowhere space. *El bonaerense* directed by Pablo Trapero © Instituto Nacional de Cine y Artes Audiovisuales (INCAA) 2002. All Rights Reserved ... 71

2.2 Gallo's manipulation of national symbols serves to both legitimize his actions and condemn the culture that allowed

	him to obtain power. *El bonaerense* directed by Pablo Trapero © Instituto Nacional de Cine y Artes Audiovisuales (INCAA) 2002. All Rights Reserved	76
2.3	In his violent domination of Mabel, Zapa fully assumes the Mendoza role that characterizes his police work. *El bonaerense* directed by Pablo Trapero © Instituto Nacional de Cine y Artes Audiovisuales (INCAA) 2002. All Rights Reserved	82
2.4	The combination of such potent political symbols functions as a condemnation of the State. *Elefante blanco* directed by Pablo Trapero © Matanza Cine 2012. All Rights Reserved	92
2.5	The *curas villeros* utilize the power of Mugica's memory to create a "space of self." *Elefante blanco* directed by Pablo Trapero © Matanza Cine 2012. All Rights Reserved	94
2.6	Rather than loom over the community, the White Elephant embraces the *villa*. *Elefante blanco* directed by Pablo Trapero © Matanza Cine 2012. All Rights Reserved	97
3.1	The gauchos seem to emerge from the ether, as if conjured by Emilia. *Familia rodante* directed by Pablo Trapero © Matanza Cine 2004. All Rights Reserved	113
3.2	Yanina rejects the norms imposed upon her by the arborescent family structure. *Familia rodante* directed by Pablo Trapero © Matanza Cine 2004. All Rights Reserved	115
3.3	In their confrontation, Gordo and Ernesto embody differing aspects of the same phenomenon: machismo. *Familia rodante* directed by Pablo Trapero © Matanza Cine 2004. All Rights Reserved	123
3.4	Alex is powerless in relation to his father, driving him to a kind of schizophrenic mania. *El clan* directed by Pablo Trapero © Matanza Cine 2015. All Rights Reserved	130
3.5	*El clan* presents a hierarchical structure so repressive that Alex's only means of escape is to attempt suicide. *El clan* directed by Pablo Trapero © Matanza Cine 2015. All Rights Reserved	131
3.6	The victim being held hostage in the family's bathroom functions as both a broad and specific metaphor. *El clan* directed by Pablo Trapero © Matanza Cine 2015. All Rights Reserved	135

3.7	The implied tension between Mia and her mother erupts into the open. *La quietud* directed by Pablo Trapero © Matanza Cine 2018. All Rights Reserved	143
3.8	Augusto's funeral marks the point at which the arborescent family structure begins to collapse. *La quietud* directed by Pablo Trapero © Matanza Cine 2018. All Rights Reserved	147
3.9	The sisters' quasi-incestual sex play signifies the rejection, however temporarily, of the repressive traditional family structure. *La quietud* directed by Pablo Trapero © Matanza Cine 2018. All Rights Reserved	149
4.1	The almost pure white of Santi's house gives his life pre-accident an ethereal quality. *Nacido y criado* directed by Pablo Trapero © Matanza Cine 2006. All Rights Reserved	163
4.2	Santi's scars mediate Trapero's belief that "reality is pure violence." *Nacido y criado* directed by Pablo Trapero © Matanza Cine 2006. All Rights Reserved	168
4.3	Rejecting rigid, traditional structures, Santi, Cacique, and Robert develop a kind of rhizomatic family. *Nacido y criado* directed by Pablo Trapero © Matanza Cine 2006. All Rights Reserved	174
4.4	*Leonera* eschews stereotypical women-in-prison film tropes. *Leonera* directed by Pablo Trapero © Matanza Cine 2008. All Rights Reserved	180
4.5	Julia's subtle yet significant act of rejection. *Leonera* directed by Pablo Trapero © Matanza Cine 2008. All Rights Reserved	184
4.6	Julia and Marta create a becoming-family. *Leonera* directed by Pablo Trapero © Matanza Cine 2008. All Rights Reserved	186

Acknowledgments

This book would not have been possible without the generous support of the William C. Atkinson Scholarship in Hispanic Studies that I was awarded by the University of Glasgow's School of Modern Languages and Cultures. I also acknowledge the Centre for Humanities Research of the University of the Western Cape and the Andrew W. Mellon Foundation for the fellowship award that facilitated the writing of this book.

I must also thank Andrea Enzetti, for helping to arrange my interview with Pablo Trapero, and the director himself for taking the time to meet with me despite being busy finishing editing for *El clan*.

My profound thanks to Tatiana Heise and David Martin-Jones for their invaluable perspective and guidance, and to Nathanial Gardner, Lizelle Bisschoff, Martin Botha, and Lesley Marx for their unwavering support and friendship. Thanks, also, to Suren Pilay for his advice and to Janne Rantala for his comradeship.

Thanks, also, to my parents for their encouragement and support. And, finally, to Inge, for everything.

A note on translation: where a source was not available in English, I have chosen to include the original passage as well as my translation, in order to allow Spanish- and Portuguese-speakers to compare their understanding of the information with my own. The only exception to this is the interview I conducted with Trapero, which can be found in Interview with Pablo Trapero. Though the interview was conducted in Spanish, I have included only my own English translation of it.

Introduction

In May 2014, the Argentine Episcopal Conference—the collection of Catholic bishops in the country—published a document in which it claimed that Argentina was "*enferma de violencia*"—ill from violence—and that corruption had become a "*cáncer social*"—a societal cancer. A few days after the document was made public, an article ran in the Buenos Aires–based newspaper *La Nación* in which José Ottavis, vice-president of the Buenos Aires Provincial *Cámara de Diputados*, rejected the claim, stating "la Argentina no está enferma de violencia. Sí vivimos una Argentina enferma de violencia en 1955, 1976, 1989 y 2001" ("Argentina is not ill from violence. We did, however, live through an Argentina ill from violence in 1955, 1976, 1989, and 2001.") (De Vedia, 2014). The bishops' document does not cite any statistical facts regarding crime or violence, yet it is telling that Ottavis would immediately turn to four of the most significant years in Argentina's history for his rebuttal. The four years Ottavis mentions in his response were each marked by significant and long-lasting acts of violence—1955 saw the *Revolución Libertadora*, a military-led campaign against the presidency of Juan Perón which included the bombing of the Plaza de Mayo by the Navy and Air Force and ended with Perón forced into exile; 1976 is, famously, the year that the *Proceso de Reorganización Nacional* began; and 1989 saw the collapse of the Alfonsín presidency, a decline precipitated by rampant inflation and food riots throughout the country that were so violent the government was forced to declare a state of emergency.

It is the final year Ottavis refers to, however, that has the most bearing for this study, and indeed for the current state of Argentina. The year 2001 was when the Argentine economy took the final step from threatening to collapse, as it had on numerous occasions (including 1976 and 1989), to actually doing so. Due in no small part to the visceral, immediate images, transmitted worldwide, of large swathes of the Argentine population engaging in *cacerolazos*—mass protests in which the public made their anger known by banging on their kitchen pots—the events surrounding the *corralito* of 2001–02 are, rightly, considered to be the central moment of the economic crisis Argentina suffered in the years following Carlos Menem's presidency. However, the *corralito*—a shorthand term for the measures, including bank account freezes, put in place by the government to prevent a widespread banking collapse—was in actual fact little more than a panic measure, a reaction to events which had been building for years. What ended up becoming Argentina's Great Depression, the most significant economic crisis in the history of the country, began in 1999 as a recession.

Coincidentally, that year was a significant one in the recent history of Argentine film. Juan José Campanella's *El mismo amor, la misma lluvia/Same Love, Same Rain* (1999), the first of his (so far) four collaborations with actor Ricardo Darín, was released to widespread critical and commercial success; Martín Rejtman, considered one of the precursors of the New Argentine Cinema which would emerge in the late 1990s (Andermann, 2012, p. 17), released *Silvia Prieto* (1998), the follow-up to his groundbreaking debut *Rapado* (1992); and Marco Bechis received international acclaim for his frank depiction of torture during the Dirty War with his film *Garage Olimpo/Olympic Garage* (1999). Perhaps no film from that year, however, more accurately captures the realities of quotidian life in Argentina in the post-Menem era than *Mundo grúa*, the debut feature-length film of Pablo Trapero.

Born into a middle-class family in 1971 and raised in the *partido* (county or district) of La Matanza, situated on the border between the city and province which share the name Buenos Aires, Trapero was a member of the first-ever graduating class at the *Fundación Universidad del Cine*, a private film school founded in 1991 by Manuel Antín, the influential filmmaker and former director of the *Instituto Nacional de Cine y Artes Audiovisuales* (INCAA). *Mundo grúa*, made when Trapero was only in his mid-twenties, is a portrait of average people living average lives and has become emblematic of the *Nuevo Cine Argentino* movement, which emerged toward the end of the 1990s. Where Campanella's and Bechis's works carried on the practice of using cinema to examine and confront the effects of the *Proceso* dictatorship on Argentine society (something which had begun even before the dictatorship finally collapsed in the wake of defeat in the Falklands/Malvinas conflict), Trapero (similar to Rejtman) was more concerned with Argentina's present. *Mundo grúa* in particular, filmed on grainy black-and-white 16-mm film and with a modest budget, speaks directly to the challenges facing working-class Argentines during and immediately after the Menem years, challenges that would soon spread to all classes of Argentine society. Upon its release, *Mundo grúa* was an enormous critical success—Trapero won the best director award at the first Buenos Aires International Independent Film Festival (BAFICI), a triumph described by Diego Batlle as "la reivindicación de una nueva forma de pensar y hacer cine. La consagración de la austeridad, de la credibilidad, de lo auténtico y de lo artesanal" ("the vindication of a new way of thinking about and making cinema. The recognition of austerity, of credibility, of the authentic and the artisanal") (2008, p. 150)—and the film heralded the start of a significant career, one that continues well into the second decade of the twenty-first century. Trapero has been remarkably consistent in his output ever since, averaging a new film nearly every two years. (2018's *La quietud* is his ninth film in nineteen years.) While his films have evolved considerably since the late 1990s, the events leading up to and following on from the 2001 collapse have had an enormous impact on his work and the lasting effects of that period continue to be expressed in his films. The thread that runs throughout Trapero's career, which connects films as disparate as the gritty *Mundo grúa* and the beautiful *La quietud*, is the central role violence plays in propelling his films' narratives. By following this thread throughout Trapero's body of work, it becomes clear that his oeuvre as a whole can be understood as a profoundly political statement on the state of Argentina in the opening decades of the twenty-first century.

New Argentine Cinema and Defining the Political

The evolution of Pablo Trapero's career is significant because, in many ways, he is representative of Argentine cinema generally. Hugo Hortiguera and Carolina Rocha find that, during the period when Argentina explicitly embraced neoliberalism, "the tension between local and global, past and present, reshaped the aesthetics of artistic expression and the role of mass media and other forms of cultural production" (2007, p. 3). Trapero's corpus demonstrates that many of those same tensions remained even after the nation turned away from Menem-era economic policies. The director's first film, *Mundo grúa*, was heavily dependent on two main funding sources, one domestic, one foreign—the INCAA and the Hubert Bals Fund. His second work, *El bonaerense*, was filmed at the height of the economic crisis and was so beset by financial problems that several members of the crew were forced to quit, and the director had to rely on personal loans from family members in order to finish the film. At the other end of the funding spectrum, *Elefante blanco*, released in 2012, was supported by a diverse range of sources both domestic and foreign—Patagonik; France's Canal+; Germany's ARTE; and Spain's TVE, to name just a few.

As has been noted in several studies, one of the primary subject matters of many Argentine films both before and after the crisis has been the impact neoliberalism has had on society (Page, 2009; Andermann, 2012). Trapero's oeuvre is no different, and this study will show that the violence of neoliberalism is, perhaps, the filmmaker's most central topic. Consequently, Trapero's films are inherently political in nature. Trapero is far from the first Argentine artist to focus on violence—indeed, much of the nation's cultural output has focused on the subject, from the nineteenth-century prose and poetry of Esteban Echevarría's *El matadero* or José Hernández's *Martín Fierro* to the films of Mario Soffici in the 1930s and 1940s. The Third Cinema movement of the late 1960s and early 1970s, spearheaded by Fernando "Pino" Solanas and Octavio Getino, made explicit the connection between politics and violence, and the trend has continued through to the present day, particularly in the wake of the *Proceso* dictatorship. One of the outcomes of the Argentine cultural sphere's focus on violence has been the prevalence, and importance, of the political within the country's film industry. Throughout the history of the country's cinema, stretching back to the silent film era, cinema has been used as a means of social commentary and critique; Argentine political films have, at times, foreshadowed events to come—as *Juan sin ropa* (1919) did in foretelling the events of the *Semana Trágica*—while they are more often used to reflect on the repercussions of an action or event—as any number of films produced in the 1980s did with regard to the *Proceso* dictatorship. As a result of this, political cinema in the Argentine context could, prior to the 1990s, be relatively easily defined. The archetypal political film—ranging from documentaries such as *Tire dié* (1960) or *La hora de los hornos*/*The Hour of the Furnaces* (1968) to feature films like *Tiempo de revancha*/*Time for Revenge* (1981), *La historia oficial*/*The Official Story* (1985), or *Sur*/*South* (1988)—featured a narrative whose politics were made explicit from the outset, a protagonist (in the case of feature films) who experienced some form of psychological metamorphosis or enlightenment, and offered, if not a solution, at least a semblance of denouement. Even period pieces, such as María Luisa Bemberg's *Camila* (1984) and *Miss Mary* (1986), functioned as allegories examining state oppression and social upheaval.

Although the emphasis on these types of political films continued into the 1990s, a generation emerged during that decade who offered a different perspective in their cinema. This group, which included filmmakers such as Trapero, Martín Rejtman, Lucrecia Martel, and Israel Adrián Caetano (a director whose work is frequently compared with Trapero's), is often referred to as the New Argentine Cinema. As with any cinematic trend, the understanding of what New Argentine Cinema consists of is broad, but there are certain uniformities—technically, the films were often very low budget, utilizing grainy black-and-white or 16-mm filmstock, while thematically, film narratives were characterized by a rejection of the political and allegorical retrospection that defined Argentine cinema of the 1980s (Andermann, 2012; Page, 2009). Generally considered, as a group, to have taken a less explicit approach to political commentary, Trapero goes against the general trend in this regard. Although the director's work is fundamental to any understanding of New Argentine Cinema, far from rejecting the political imperative, his films engage with. Understanding Trapero as a political filmmaker differentiates him from his colleagues in the New Argentine Cinema movement because it implies that there is a level of allegory working within his films that is generally considered to be absent from the typical New Argentine narrative. Despite Joanna Page's contention that "New Argentine Cinema often resists symbolic or allegorical interpretations" (2009, pp. 26–7), even Trapero's earliest films serve as explicit political statements, drawing direct correlations between violence, in both its subjective and objective forms, the failed economic policies of consecutive Argentine governments, and the overarching influence of neoliberalism.

Trapero's cinema, then, can be understood as political in the sense that corresponds to Mike Wayne's conception of the term. For Wayne, any film that "[addresses] unequal access to and distribution of material and cultural resources, and the hierarchies of legitimacy and status accorded to those differentials" can be considered a political film (2001, p. 1). The terms "political cinema," "radical cinema," and "revolutionary cinema" are rarely so straightforward, however, and can often mean significantly different things depending on the context of their use. In some circumstances, radical or revolutionary cinema can refer to a purely formalistic radicalism. In other circumstances, it can refer to a film that contains radical or revolutionary political content while ignoring the concept of form entirely (or, at least, significantly marginalizing it).

These two ideas are not mutually exclusive; some of the most important films from the first half of the twentieth century were important precisely because of their radicalism in both form and substance. The type of political cinema that Trapero engages with, however, is more along the lines of what Tatiana Heise and Andrew Tudor describe as "reformist cinema":

> Where a film is politically radical in its subject matter but uses the traditional cinematic apparatus of representation, we have "reformist cinema." This category encompasses most of what are traditionally counted as "political films," whether in fictional formats as in conventional "political thrillers" . . . documentary style reconstructions . . . or orthodox documentaries themselves. (2013, p. 86)

Although there was some experimentation with formal radicalism in the 1970s (Wolkowicz, 2014), much of what might be called "political cinema" in the Argentine context is focused less on making political statements through form and more on making those statements through content, with a particular emphasis on depicting issues and situations affecting society in as realistic a manner as possible. As such, it is important to clarify that, without denying the numerous other forms of political cinema which exist (indeed, Heise and Tudor examine seven different definitions of the term), within this study the use of the term "political cinema" will refer generally to this "reformist cinema" category.

Long Neoliberalism

Like many of his contemporaries, Trapero has focused most of his narratives around individuals—his films usually examine one protagonist's experiences and the notable exception to this pattern, the ensemble piece *Familia rodante*, nevertheless presents the entire family as one unit in which all the members are undergoing similar experiences at different stages of life. Political films of the 1970s and 1980s tended to provide some sort of denouement that established to the viewer that things were getting better. Trapero's films, as a rule, do not have satisfying conclusions, let alone the possibility of happy endings, and they rarely suggest that the circumstances which caused or contributed to the trauma presented in the film are going to change at any point in the future. In this way Trapero's corpus closely resembles that of his contemporaries. Yet, Trapero's films engage with the periphery in a way that does seem to carry some sort of allegorical meaning. Sometimes, these marginalized communities are presented as secondary narratives which influence the main narrative—as in the case of *Nacido y criado* or *Elefante blanco* (which examines indigenous and immigrant communities, respectively)—while other times they form the basis of the film's plot, as we see in *Leonera*, which tracks the gradual marginalization of a middle-class Argentine of European descent.

To be sure, Trapero's work is not actively political in the manner of, for example, the *cine piquetero* documentary films. Those works are heavily invested in the social movements they are documenting, whereas Trapero's films, in contrast, remain detached—indeed during *El bonaerense* Zapa comes across a *piquetero* march and simply ignores it—and his characters are far more concerned with their own person than with affecting any sort of broad-based social change. It is through the narratives themselves, however, that Trapero's films engage with the political. Jens Andermann finds that Trapero's films "uncover a deeply ingrained, corporate structure of affect guided by unofficial networks of favor and loyalty" (2012, p. 150). This is a pattern which holds throughout Trapero's career—he rarely makes bold political statements, instead letting the obvious critical implications gradually rise to the surface over the course of a film. Trapero is conscious of this, explaining,

> I view the political as one of cinema's aims, that is, for me it's intrinsic to cinema. But I don't believe in militant cinema. I think that militant cinema only speaks to a group of people who already know what they are going to hear, or only hear what they want to hear from what they are watching without any critical value, [and] probably with less aesthetic value because the ideas are more important than the aesthetic value. . . . I like political cinema, but the political that I can do is by way of an aesthetics of the political, a politics of the poetics of a film, if you will. (Interview with Pablo Trapero)

As such, Trapero's films might be considered a new form of political cinema, one which lacks the urgency of documentary film or the explicitness of Argentine fiction films of the past, but which nevertheless examines, often with a damningly critical eye, the problems affecting Argentine society in the post-Menem era.

The political nature of Trapero's films becomes especially clear when considered against the backdrop of what has been happening in Argentina since the mid-1990s. The Argentine middle class, once both a source of pride and a marker of difference from the rest of Latin America, has suffered greatly since the mid-1980s. The gradual descent of the Argentine middle class into poverty, which took place over the course of two decades, has fundamentally "altered the social structure of the country, as well as the image of it held by Argentines" (Grimson and Kessler, 2012, p. 87). This is due to a number of reasons, many of which are not relevant to this study, but the essential cause can be explained by the fact that "the interests of the middle and lower classes ceased to be the axis around which domestic policies were planned and carried out" (Rocha and Montes Garces, 2010, p. xiv). Reflecting the sense of alienation so often experienced by the protagonists of Trapero's films, the decline of the country's middle class has been "experienced simultaneously as personal dislocation and also as the disorganization of the world around" (Grimson and Kessler, 2012, p. 88). The experience of lower- and middle-class Argentines living through the neoliberal policies of the late 1990s and early 2000s was a violent one, characterized by alienation, social isolation, and exclusion, and, perhaps most significantly, a general loss of identity. This loss of identity affected not only individuals within society—Beatriz Sarlo has commented on the difficulty facing contemporary Argentines to construct any sense of self through work (2003, p. 128)—but also the foundational myth upon which the nation's identity was created. As is the case with many countries with large immigrant populations, Argentina's inhabitants had always seen the country as a place of opportunity. That belief began to crack during the 1990s and was shattered completely by 2002—

> the overriding tendency [in Argentina] was always upward and onward to such a degree that "progress" and "future" were synonymous.... In a society characterized by economic, political, and social instability, the mythical tale of collective progress functioned as a kind of collective glue: a series of generally agreed upon, stable principles that, until now, seemed to hold

things together no matter what. It goes without saying that without the inevitability of progress, this ideological nucleus falls apart. (Grimson and Kessler, 2012, p. 90)

While there were relatively isolated incidents of direct violence between citizens and the government around the time of the collapse in 2001, for the most part it is this violation of the sense of self, rather than any sort of physical violence, which most damaged the country and its inhabitants during the heyday of neoliberalism.

Although this study examines how Trapero's films contest an imposing, inherent neoliberal hegemony that permeates Argentine society, it is true that neoliberalism has only been the nation's driving political and economic model for some parts of the director's career. Trapero's early films engage directly with the then-ruling government's embrace of neoliberalist policies of the 1990s and early 2000s; however, virtually every other film in the director's corpus was made during a period dominated by the explicit rejection of neoliberalism that characterized the Néstor Kirchner and Cristina Fernández de Kirchner presidencies. While the government during this period enacted various domestic economic policies aimed at repairing many of the social fissures that emerged as a result of the neoliberalism of the Menem/de la Rúa period, the fundamental nature of the international economic system as it exists in the twenty-first century is such that even as various Latin American nations embraced a new leftism—the so-called Pink Tide, of which Argentina was a key player—the region "remains marked by economic models interwoven in global capitalism ... and social models continuously reproducing hierarchical lifeworlds and social orders" (Strønen and Ystanes, 2018, p. 5). In the specific context of Argentina, this influence was manifested in various ways—from regional issues such as a three-way conflict with Chile and Bolivia over the sale and distribution of natural gas or a highly contentious and long-running disagreement with Uruguay regarding the construction of paper mills to international economic disputes regarding sovereign debt with the so-called Vulture Funds. These external pressures often led to domestic resistance, perhaps most visibly in a pushback by the agricultural, industrial, and media sectors against Fernández de Kirchner government's protectionist policies. Anabella Busso explains that these confrontations "became a vehicle for [opposition] to the government by the urban middle classes. Thus ... a middle-class sector emerged with claims about security, inflation, and institutionality" (2016, p. 117). Trapero's films of this period reflect many of those same preoccupations; while they may have been made during a period when the government did not embrace neoliberalism, it is not accurate to say that his work does not engage with neoliberalism and its attendant (Deleuzo-Guattarian) desires. For it was these desires that drove opposition to Kirchnerism in the 2015 presidential elections won by neoliberal candidate Mauricio Macri. Similarly, the election of Alberto Fernández in 2019—marking yet another turn away from neoliberalism—serves to emphasize that Trapero's films confront not so much the specific policy decisions of a given government but, rather, what Cornel Ban has called "embedded neoliberalism," the combination of "transnational resources and domestic institutions [through which] neoliberalism ultimately becomes a contradictory, yet effectively pervasive and structural, force" (2016, p. 4).

A Hauntology of Violence

On first viewing, Trapero's work is, perhaps, not obviously political in the manner of a Solanas or a Bemberg. Writing about New Argentine Cinema generally, Gonzalo Aguilar suggests that this is not out of sync with recent films, many of which have rejected Lenin's famous question (via Chernyshevsky) of "what is to be done?" Describing contemporary Argentine cinema's approach to politics, Aguilar states "these movies show us . . . how a world operates. . . . Between indeterminacy and the recording of an operation, the new cinema establishes a different possibility of thinking the political" (2008b, pp. 123–4). Trapero's way of "thinking the political," however, shares as much with political filmmakers of the 1970s as it does with his contemporaries and, while not offering solutions necessarily, his films nevertheless share the same anger that defined so much of Argentina's political cinema historically. Indeed, it can be argued that Trapero's career represents an evolution of that concept to better fit with the contemporary sociopolitical climate. This is, perhaps, most visible in his 2012 film *Elefante blanco*. That film took place and was filmed in the slum of Ciudad Oculta, one of the numerous *villas miserias* on the outskirts of Buenos Aires. Although the building has since been demolished, in the film (as in real life) Ciudad Oculta is loomed over by the White Elephant, the enormous, abandoned husk of a building that was, when its construction began in the 1930s, originally planned as the largest hospital in Latin America. Not only does the building serve as a twelve-story testament to the political instability and economic profligacy that have characterized Argentina for decades, but by providing a haven for drug-users, gang members, and the homeless it also functions as a much more palpable reminder of the challenges facing contemporary Argentine society.

The building calls to mind the concepts of haunting and hauntology introduced by Jacques Derrida and expanded upon by Mark Fisher (among others). Where Derrida relates hauntology to the sense of "time out of joint," Fisher engages further with the concept, explaining that "[h]auntology itself can be thought of as fundamentally about forces which act at a distance—that which . . . insists (has causal effects) without (physically) existing" (2012, p. 20). Fisher goes on to explain that we are haunted by the disappearance of the future, a disappearance which results in

> the deterioration of a whole mode of social imagination: the capacity to conceive of a world radically different from the one in which we currently live. It [means] the acceptance of a situation in which culture would continue without really changing, and where politics [is] reduced to the administration of an already established (capitalist) system. (2012, p. 12)

In Fisher's conception, then, the present is haunted by "the failure of the future": our collective failure to live up to the imaginations and ideals of our past (2012, p. 12). In the most literal sense, the White Elephant that dominates the Ciudad Oculta *villa* serves as a physical manifestation of this concept (Figure 0.1).

It is also possible to view Trapero's films within the framework of hauntology, especially as it concerns the emergence of the multiform violence that has come to dominate Argentine society since (at the very least) the mid-1990s. Having made nine films over nearly two decades, Trapero's body of work documents some of the most unique moments in Argentina's history, moments that have resulted in a legacy of violence. While this violence can explode into life on occasion—the nationwide protests following the suspicious death of federal prosecutor Alberto Nisman in 2015 being one example, the occasionally violent protests in 2018 and 2020 surrounding the debate about the legalization of abortion being another—more often than not

Figure 0.1 *Carancho* (2010). The failure of the future is mediated through the White Elephant itself.

it merely simmers in the background, "insisting without existing." It is with this that Trapero's films engage: a hauntology of the failure of the future, the most immediate effect of which is the specter of violence that overshadows contemporary Argentina. By engaging with violence in this way, Trapero is making a form of political cinema that critiques the increasingly devastating effects that both national and international neoliberal economic and social policies have had on Argentine society. As such, his work stands at (or, indeed, has even created) an intersection of sorts, at the point where the observational nature of the New Argentine Cinema of the late 1990s and early 2000s converges with the committed political advocacy of Argentine cinema of the 1970s and 1980s.

Defining Violence

As mentioned previously, Trapero serves as writer, director, and producer for all of his feature films. However, it should be pointed out that Trapero is only credited as the sole writer of two films, *Mundo grúa* and *Familia rodante*, and from the very start of his career he has worked with a series of producers and co-producers. Nevertheless, Trapero serves such a central role in the creation of his works—in addition to writing, directing, and producing, he has also been involved in the editing of every film he has made since *Nacido y criado*—that, in many ways, this examination approaches Trapero's films from a traditional auteurist perspective. What this work is not, however, is an attempt to explicitly position Pablo Trapero as an auteur. Rather than focus on the sort of stylistic choices that might be found in a traditional auteurist approach to film analysis, or delve into an investigation of the role of the auteur in Argentine cinema, this book studies the function of one specific motif of Trapero's oeuvre: violence.

More specifically, this book examines the many ways in which violence is represented throughout the director's work and demonstrates how that violence functions in defining Trapero as a political filmmaker. In particular, this analysis reads Trapero's films through the lens of the (occasionally subtle) violence of neoliberalism, ideology, and the traditional family unit. In order to do so, this work engages with a varied set of theoretical perspectives that, when combined with a formalist reading of Trapero's films, help to deepen our understanding of the works in question and, consequently, the entirety of the director's corpus. There is no one specific theory that unites all of this work's analysis; the work incorporates a number of theoretical approaches, the selection of which was motivated by the content of the films being analyzed. Of particular note are Slavoj Žižek's and Hannah Arendt's analyses of violence, Steven Lukes's examination of power, and Gilles Deleuze and Félix Guattari's reconsideration of Oedipus and the family. Although Trapero's work lends itself to interesting questions of gender (particularly films like *Leonera, El bonaerense,* and *La quietud*), that is not the focus of this work. Rather, the concept that unites this book is the same one that unites Trapero's films: violence.

Despite the highly visible nature of the crisis and despite the fact that at least two of his films were made at the height of the *corralito*'s more drastic measures, the most visceral elements of the depression—the queues of people stretching around the block, hoping to pull their money out of rapidly failing banks, the spontaneous *cacerolazos* which routinely shut down streets or filled entire public squares, the *piqueteros* holding up home-made picket signs denouncing the policies of the government and the banks—are excluded from Trapero's works. Importantly, throughout his films Trapero is both constantly engaged with the depression while never explicitly interacting with it. Rather, the crisis lingers in the atmosphere of his films, inescapable yet never viewed, as present to his characters as the cityscapes and landscapes which surround them. And, just as the environment which surrounds Trapero's characters can force its way into consideration and then retreat into the background, so too the effects of the crisis come and go, at one moment present and at another seemingly forgotten. Sandwiched between protests such as the 1999 World Trade Organization riots in Seattle and the Occupy movement which emerged following 2008's Global Financial Crisis, the protests that surrounded the Argentine economic crisis were unique in just how widespread they were. What makes the period so astonishing is that the *cacerolazos* (and associated protests) of the early 2000s were one of the first moments where Žižek's concept of objective violence, a violence that so permeates society as to become invisible, was the focus not of a small, perhaps politically radical group of dissidents (as in the two examples mentioned), but of widespread anger across large swathes of the country's population. Violence, in all its forms, plays a pivotal role in Trapero's films. To understand his films, however, we must first understand what violence is, and the circumstances and events within Argentina that give rise to it.

In his examination of the word "violence" from the collection *Keywords*, Raymond Williams offers seven different definitions (or senses, as he calls them) for the concept. Williams's third sense is a key one for this study, as it describes the (possibly dramatic) portrayal of violence in various media. This sense includes both factual events—news broadcasts, for example—and fictional ones, such as films in which violence is portrayed. Further "senses" examine the concept of "violence as threat" or "violence as unruly behavior" (1983, p. 330). As Williams makes clear, these two senses of the word often go hand in hand, with the former occurring shortly after the latter. On a national level, however, this is not always the case and depends greatly on who is threatening whom—when the public is the group threatening the government with violence, as was the case in Argentina in both 1989 and 2001, then unruly behavior, in any number of different forms, quite often follows. But the events of the *Proceso* dictatorship (or the Pinochet dictatorship in Chile, the Apartheid government in South Africa, or any number of violently oppressive authoritarian regimes around the world) show that when the government is the group threatening to do violence to its own citizens it is not unruly violence which follows, but rather a highly organized, systematic violence. Williams's

Figure 0.2 *Carancho* (2010). *Carancho*'s low-key lighting is used to manifest a sense of objective violence.

essay is useful because it provides an easy-to-understand introduction to what can be a complex and multifaceted theoretical concept. As a real-life occurrence, however, violence is usually relatively easy to comprehend. When two drunkards outside a bar engage in a fistfight, we understand that an act of violence is occurring. But this sort of physical violence, the sudden eruption of ferocity that arises when an attack occurs, is as a rule quite rare in everyday life. There are, of course, exceptions to this rule—in a war zone this sort of violence can be experienced on a daily basis, while during periods of high domestic tension, such as a riot or mass protest, physical violence becomes much more commonplace. However, this direct form of violence, though not completely absent, is not the predominant form of violence which is represented throughout Trapero's oeuvre. Rather a different, less tangible form of violence is portrayed, one that, though no less affecting, is more abstract in nature (Figure 0.2). By abstracting violence from the real world and instead approaching it as a theoretical concept, however, violence becomes less readily obvious. It is this abstract, theoretical violence which Žižek, in his book *Violence*, defines as objective violence.

Žižek, as so many others who have written about the concept of violence, believes that more than one form of the thing exists. He compares "direct, physical violence (mass murder, terror)"—the type displayed in the bar fight, multiplied to any degree—and the more abstract "ideological violence (racism, incitement, sexual discrimination)" (2009, p. 9) as being two different forms of the same phenomenon, a type of violence he refers to as "subjective" violence. Subjective violence, according to Žižek, is "violence performed by a clearly identifiable agent" (2009, p. 1). This type of violence can be performed by one individual against another, or it can be performed by an abstract (but identifiable) agent against another abstract agent. One man physically assaulting another, then, is an obvious example of subjective violence, but so too is a terrorist attack or a government choosing to drop a nuclear bomb. The counterpart to subjective violence is objective violence. Žižek breaks objective violence down further, into the more theoretical "symbolic violence embodied in language and its forms," and "systemic violence . . . the often catastrophic consequences of the smooth functioning of our economic and political systems" (2009, p. 1).

Žižek is, of course, approaching objective violence, especially in its systemic manifestation, from a dialectical, essentially European framework. When considered in the context of Pablo Trapero's films, however, his analysis resonates. Take, for example, the way Žižek explains the fundamental difference between subjective and objective violence—

> [Subjective] violence is experienced as such against the background of a non-violent zero level. It is seen as a perturbation of the "normal," peaceful state of things. However, objective violence is precisely the violence inherent to this "normal" state of things. Objective violence is invisible since it sustains the very zero-level standard against which we perceive something as subjectively violent. (2009, p. 2)

This is exactly the concept that permeates virtually the entirety of Trapero's corpus—the desire to expose the "objective violence" (using Žižek's own terminology) inherent in post–Menem Argentine society. Trapero's films often include scenes of subjective violence which are, as is to be expected, capable of eliciting strong visceral reactions. Yet what most affects the viewer when watching a Trapero film is the acknowledged but never spoken uneasiness which most clearly defines the culture and society in which his characters exist. In any given Trapero film, the number of characters who seem comfortable with themselves and at ease with their surroundings is limited. Although Trapero's films do not typically present straightforward protagonist-antagonist type narratives, where they do incorporate this idea—such as in parts of *El bonaerense* or *Carancho*—it is the antagonist who seems most comfortable in his surroundings. Protagonists, conversely, seem out of place, disconnected, detached.

Žižek's definition (or, perhaps, definitions) of violence is not, of course, the only one available. Thirty years before Žižek, Hannah Arendt attempted to define violence in her book-length essay *On Violence* (1969) by comparing and contrasting it to the related concepts of power, strength, force, and authority. Arendt's definition of violence is, when compared to others, a limited one. This is largely due to the fact that Arendt considers power, strength, force, and authority to be different concepts as opposed to merely different manifestations of the same idea. In this regard, Arendt's study feels slightly incomplete. *On Violence* does not provide answers, as such, so much as it reflects on the nature of violence and whether such a thing can ever be justified. It is in this examination and reflection, however, that the work proves its value. Arendt believes that violence often emerges from rage, which is in itself a sign that change is believed to be possible—"[o]nly where there is reason to suspect that conditions could be changed and are not does rage arise. Only when our sense of justice is offended do we react with rage" (1970, p. 63). In a passage that speaks directly to the Argentine experience of the late twentieth and early twenty-first century, Arendt provides an example of both how and why a violent act might be considered justified—

> To tear the mask of hypocrisy from the face of the enemy, to unmask him and the devious machinations and manipulations that permit him to rule without using violent means, that is, to provoke action even at the risk of annihilation so that the truth may come out—these are still among the strongest motives in today's violence.... And this violence again is not irrational. Since men live in a world of appearances and, in their dealing with it, depend on manifestation, hypocrisy's conceits... cannot be met by so-called reasonable behavior. (1970, pp. 65–6)

While Arendt was writing about, and during a specific moment of, rupture (the global student protests of the late 1960s), her terminology—"machinations and manipulations," "hypocrisy's conceits"—and her writings on power (a concept that will be examined further in coming chapters) are especially relevant in the context of this work. Indeed, while Žižek's conception of objective violence underpins much of this work's theoretical framework, the alternative views presented here all provide valuable insights into understanding how Trapero engages with postcrisis neoliberal Argentina.

Neoliberalism and Ideology

Much of the violence found in Trapero's films stems at least in part from the neoliberal socioeconomic policies that have influenced Argentina so significantly since the 1990s. Indeed, the connection between violence and neoliberalism is one that is becoming more widely understood. Although ostensibly an economic philosophy, neoliberalism, and the related concept of globalization, have been shown to have a significant effect on much more than mere economic policy. Significantly, in regions that have experienced rapid globalization, as is the case with much of the developing world (Argentina included), the introduction of neoliberal policies has seemingly coincided with an increase in violence. The case of Argentina is somewhat unique, in that the country's history of political violence is well established and the Menem years, when neoliberal policies were at their most prevalent, were generally free from significant violence. However, three decades after the end of the most violent dictatorship the country had ever seen, the legacy of those years continues to have a significant role to play in Argentine society. As a result, in Argentina the type of violence that accompanied neoliberalism was not the same as it was in many other parts of the world, or even in Argentina prior to the last dictatorship. Rather than political violence, Argentine society suffered through a sort of societal collapse, experienced most heavily by the poor and middle class. Trapero's films, both on an individual basis and when analyzed as a body of work, are fairly specific in terms of focus, in that they all broadly examine the effects of this sort of neoliberal violence on Argentine society. It can be argued, then, that by using the specific medium of film—"arte de la reproducción por excelencia" ("The reproductive art *par excellence*") (Amado, 2009, p. 44)—and by focusing (primarily) on the struggles of working- and middle-class people, Trapero's films attempt to expose the seemingly non-violent for the violence it really is. This aspect has become especially important given the manner in which Trapero's films have become increasingly violent as his career has progressed.

Related to this, an aspect of Trapero's films that has become much more significant and visible over the course of his career is the centrality of ideology as a dominant force, both in terms of the role it plays in individual film narratives and its importance to the entirety of the director's corpus. As Trapero has evolved, his films have begun to engage with the violence inherent to ideology. This is, perhaps, to be expected of a filmmaker for whom violence is so important, given that, in the words of Jean-Luc Comolli and Jean Paul Narboni, "film is ideology presenting itself to itself, talking to itself, learning about itself" (1971, p. 30). As Louis Althusser makes clear, ideology (as with many of the terms used when discussing political cinema) is "a reality which needs a little discussion." Althusser is an important reference point in the study of ideology's interaction with Latin American cinema, not least because his essay "Ideology and Ideological State Apparatuses" was published in 1970, coinciding with the zenith of the Third Cinema movement. At the start of their essay "El cine como hecho político" Solanas and Getino describe film as "un hecho ideológico," an ideological action, and go on to claim that "cine, como ideología, viene a confirmar, negar o corregir los niveles de conciencia existentes en los espectadores" ("film, like ideology, confirms, negates, or corrects the levels of consciousness which exist in the spectator") (1973, p. 125). Solanas and Getino, then, view film and ideology as one and the same, which brings their understanding of ideology in line with Althusser, who states that "ideology represents the imaginary relationship of individuals to their real conditions of existence" (1971, p. 109).

This is consistent with the work Stuart Hall has done concerning the intersection of ideology and mass culture. Examining the role ideology plays in the conflict between "consensus" and "deviant," Hall finds that where once film and television were considered rather neutral media in which whatever ideological message they conveyed was merely a reflection of the social consensus, in fact they are quite influential in the very creation of the consensus-deviant dichotomy itself. Whoever controls the "means of representation," then, finds themselves in an incredibly powerful position, for,

> in orienting themselves in "the consensus" and, at the same time, attempting to shape up the consensus, operating on it in a formative fashion, the media become part and parcel of [the] dialectical process of the "production of consent"—shaping consensus while reflecting it—which orientates them within the field of force of the dominant social interests representing within the state. (Hall, 1982, p. 83)

As a result of the absolutely vital role visual media plays in shaping consensus, therefore, ideology takes on an increasingly significant importance in contemporary society. So much so, in fact, that it shifts from a theoretical concept to, essentially, something real: "[ideology] was 'real' because it was *real in its effects*" (Hall, 1982, p. 78, emphasis in original).

Some, such as Mas'ud Zavarzadeh, take this argument even further, stating that ideology, with film as a primary component, is responsible for creating society and culture. Zavarzadeh finds that

> What is assumed to be "out there," *naturally* in the world itself, or "in here," *mentally* (in the mind of the artist, reader or spectator), is in fact put "out there" or "in here" by such diverse discourses of ideology as film, novels, paintings. . . . [Reality] is "constructed" by a society's political, economic, theoretical, and ideological practices (including signifying activities such as film making and film watching). (1991, p. 92)

It is through Zavarzadeh's description of the influence ideology (generally) and film (in particular) have on social and cultural structures that we begin to understand how all forms of cinema can be used by both the State and the individual equally to attempt to shape, and even to alter our experience or understanding of reality. Indeed, the ways in which the State has done this over the course of history is the fundamental principle of Althusser's concept of the Ideological State Apparatus. With this in mind, it is easy to understand why cinema, in many ways, is the perfect ideological tool. Because films present an imaginary world that is, quite often, modelled on the world in which we live, the characters and situations offered are readily identifiable. Even when a film's narrative bears little semblance to the world as we know it—in high fantasy or science fiction films, for example—the emotions and on-screen interactions of the characters are usually easy to identify with. This, combined with the understanding of film as a "hot medium"—that is to say, one which captures the entirety of the audience's attention and in which there is virtually no opportunity for interaction between the medium and its recipient—results in an ideal channel for imparting ideology.

For the first century of its existence, film was one of the key Ideological State Apparatuses that the Argentine state had at its disposal. The studio system that produced big-budget (in relative terms) melodramas featuring idealized heroes (of which Carlos Gardel remains perhaps the most significant); the international distribution network which ensured a steady stream of foreign films presenting romanticized situations that had little to do with Argentine reality (from the early silent films such as *The Four Horsemen of the Apocalypse*

[1921] to the B-grade films imported during the *Proceso*); and the active role played by the Argentine government both in funding and, at times, censoring Argentine cinema have all meant that Argentine commercial film has been a key tool in the formation and dissemination of ideology. This phenomenon is not limited to Argentina, nor even to Latin America; as Teshome Gabriel makes clear, "[governments] in the Third World have usually sought to appropriate the medium of the cinema for propaganda favorable to their own needs" (1982, p. 1). Far from merely reflecting society's attitudes toward concepts such as violence, film, when used as an ideological apparatus, can actually shape those attitudes. Graham Matthews and Sam Goodman find that society's response to violence is influenced as much by representations of violence as by the act of violence itself, stating that these "representations . . . frame or mediate the horrors of violence in order to generate ethical and affective responses" (2013, p. 1). Xavier Aldana Reyes explains this concept even more clearly when she states, "it is precisely in their power to create meaning that images of violence become powerful ideological weapons" (2013, p. 151). Film and other (especially visual) media are powerful ideological tools precisely because they can influence both the way an event is processed and also how society, in general, approaches future violent acts. This understanding of what ideology is and how it functions is important in the context of Trapero's work because his analysis of objective violence centers on how several of the key apparatuses used in the creation of ideology are manipulated in order to allow that violence to persist in society. These range from the analysis of labor relations found in *Mundo grúa* to the role of the Catholic Church in *Elefante blanco* to perhaps Trapero's most recurring theme, the family. Trapero engages with these ideological concepts in an attempt to demonstrate the violence inherent in them (and, in some cases, propose alternatives to them). Essentially, Trapero's corpus functions as a form of deviance, creating a counter-narrative to the ideological consensus established by the very apparatuses his films scrutinize.

Connecting Violence and Neoliberalism

Chronicling the rise of violence in Latin America in the neoliberal era, Magaly Sanchez R. writes, "[r]ather than viewing violence as a personal deviation from societal norms, it is more appropriate to consider it a product of structural inequalities, a social phenomenon in which multiple actors resort to the use of violence under similar social circumstance and in mutually reinforcing ways" (2006, p. 181). Sanchez R. describes a three-step process (as it were) through which violence becomes prevalent in society—first occurs the structural violence of the inequality that arises from neoliberalism, then the radical violence of mass uprisings protesting those policies, followed by the criminal violence of a disaffected population faced with few options to escape the poverty of their reality (2006, p. 179). What Sanchez R.'s analysis makes clear, then, is that not only is the structural, systemic inequality inherent to neoliberalism a form of violence in and of itself but also that inherent violence, which is of a kind that is not immediately visible or threatening, leads to further violence. It is this further violence, the radical and criminal types to which Sanchez R. makes reference, which is manifested in the subjective violence of crime and insecurity.

Argentine society pre-collapse was certainly affected by violence, albeit a type of violence that posed less obvious physical threats to its members. What the collapse brought with it—or at least what it forced Argentine society to confront in a way it had not since the days of the last dictatorship—was the type of physical violence and insecurity that threatened bodily harm, if not death. The intensification of this type of violence within Argentine society was one aspect of what some have called the "Latin Americanization" of the country, the process by which the Argentine economic and social model lost many of the factors which had, to that point, permitted Argentina to view itself as being more similar to a European country than a Latin American one. In his book *La economia de los argentinos*, published in 2003, Argentine economist Federico Sturzenegger writes:

> durante el año 2002 muchos argentinos, pobres y ricos por igual, vivieron angustiados por la inseguridad. Secuestros, robos, muertes de policías y tomas de rehenes parecían sucederse sin cesar. De subsistir este problema, corremos el riesgo de que nuestras ciudades lentamente se conviertan en la típica ciudad latinoamericana, donde la violencia es la regla y no la excepción. (2003, p. 225)

> [during the year 2002 many Argentines, rich and poor alike, lived in a state of anguish due to insecurity. Kidnappings, robberies, police deaths and hostage-takings seemed to occur without end. If this problem persists, we

run the risk of our cities slowly becoming typical Latin American cities, where violence is the rule and not the exception.]

What is alarming about this statement is not so much the content of it—however much it may have increased post-2001, violent crime, including robberies and murders, was certainly happening before the crisis—but rather the approach Sturzenegger takes toward not only his own country but also his country's regional neighbors. Trapero's films, both before and particularly since the crisis, have functioned as a sort of counterbalance to the long-held belief, as expressed by Sturzenegger, that Argentina is somehow different from the rest of Latin America.

A Cyclical Career

Trapero's films are remarkably cyclical in the sense that he returns to ideas and narrative structures, as if compelled to process and reprocess his ideas and beliefs. Each time he returns to a subject matter or narrative, however, the second film is more explicit than its predecessor, not only concerning the connection made between violence and politics but also in its very depiction of violence. All of his films reflect this pattern in some way, as if to suggest that what was at one point merely the haunting of violence is becoming more and more immediate. In order to best illustrate this pattern, each chapter of this book will examine a grouping, usually two but in one case three, of Trapero's films. Although certain themes run throughout Trapero's oeuvre, in each chapter the group of films presented can be seen as especially complementary to one another. In each case, the films are connected by relatively obvious similarities in plot. Although the analysis of the films does somewhat follow chronological order, that is not the organizational criterion in every case.

Further, the book has been broken up into two larger sections, with each section focusing on a broad theme. Part One, entitled "The Individual and the State," examines the nature of the relationship that exists between individuals and the State Apparatus. The four films analyzed in this section all portray different ways in which the State influences and affects the lives of its citizenry. Chapter 1 examines Trapero's first film, *Mundo grúa,* and his sixth film,

Carancho. The two films, though different in many ways, are related through the fact that each one focuses, primarily, on the struggles of one man as he attempts to survive in a society dominated by objective violence. Where *Mundo grúa* is more observational, seeming to merely record the difficulties faced by Rulo as he struggles to find work in post-Menem Argentina, *Carancho* is more confrontational. Physical violence is essentially absent from *Mundo grúa*, yet it is the first thing presented on-screen in *Carancho*. Despite these differences, the two films examine the violence, sometimes visible but oftentimes not, of daily survival, and the devastating effects that can have on an individual.

Chapter 2 examines *El bonaerense* and *Elefante blanco*. Both of these films take a critical view of the State Apparatus, as manifested by the police and the Catholic Church. Although not a State Apparatus, per se, the Church as presented in *Elefante blanco* serves a very similar function, such that the critical approach toward state representatives first presented in *El bonaerense* is easily transferrable to the Church and its actions. Unlike the films from Chapter 1, the protagonists from these two films are exceptionally different from one another, a fact which is significant in how each film is understood and therefore addressed in the chapter's analysis.

Reflecting the changing nature of Trapero's work, Part Two—entitled "Violence and the Family"—shifts the focus of the analysis somewhat. Basing its analysis on Deleuze and Guattari's understanding of the Oedipal family as a site of repression, Chapter 3 examines how the families featured in *Familia rodante*, *El clan*, and *La quietud* propagate the objective violence analyzed in Part I. *Familia rodante*, in particular, is a widely misunderstood film, its family melodrama narrative masking a subversive message that is often overlooked. *El clan*, Trapero's only period piece, is based on the real-life "Clan Puccio," a well-to-do family who were secretly running a kidnapping ring, demanding enormous sums of money as ransom and then killing the victims. Set during a four-year period either side of the end of the *Proceso* dictatorship in 1982, the film focuses on the experiences of paterfamilias Arquímedes Puccio and his son and accomplice Alex, and serves as Trapero's most explicit link between violence and the political. Trapero's most recent film, *La quietud*, unites many elements of Trapero's career, and is in many ways a recapitulation of all the themes and subject matters that have defined his oeuvre to date. The film examines the claustrophobic, quasi-incestuous relationship that exists between two sisters, set amidst a broader consideration of the complex interplay of desire and rejection through which family members both support and hurt each other, often in the same moment.

La quietud also serves to introduce the fundamental concept that serves as the focus of Chapter 4. The two films analyzed in Chapter 4, *Nacido y criado* and *Leonera*, present alternatives to the traditional family structure. Using the Deleuzo-Guattarian concept of the rhizome, the chapter examines how the two films demonstrate the possibility of positive family units even for individuals who are suffering extreme hardship. *Nacido y criado* is perhaps Trapero's most personal film, reflecting his own anxieties about fatherhood and responsibility, and is perhaps the least explicitly political film in his entire oeuvre. *Leonera*, a film that the director has described as a companion piece to *Nacido y criado*, tells the story of a pregnant woman incarcerated in a prison's maternal wing. As the film focuses on a character directly under the State's control, the link between the State and violence is immediately visible. Despite this, or perhaps even because of it, the importance the narrative places on alternative family structures is heightened.

Despite their differences in narrative and setting, Pablo Trapero's films are ultimately connected through their examination of violence in all its forms. Rather than broad sweeping analyses of the actions of those in power, Trapero's films function as microhistories, providing significant insights into how the macro forces of society affect, and are experienced by, those on the micro level. When taken as a whole, Trapero's corpus paints a picture of a society that is dominated by objective violence and in which it is possible for the individual members of that society to become victims of subjective violence at any moment. By analyzing all nine of Trapero's films to date, this work is able to provide a new understanding of the director's oeuvre, one which not only tracks his evolution as a filmmaker but also locates him as a highly political filmmaker with a distinct political voice.

Part One

The Individual and the State

1

Neoliberalism, Violence, and the New Argentina

The chronology of Pablo Trapero's career is serendipitous. He produced *Mundo grúa* before the December 2001 crash; his second feature, *El bonaerense*, was in the midst of production as the worst moments of the crisis—the public protests which bordered on, and often descended into, full-scale rioting—were taking place; and the entirety of his career as a writer-director has occurred during a period in which Argentina's social fabric—including everything from the concept of *argentinidad* (Argentineness) to the way Argentines view themselves in relation to not only Latin America but also the rest of the world—has been altered fundamentally, and perhaps permanently. Trapero's films serve as a record of this particular moment in Argentina's history, documenting (from a specific perspective, of course) the ways in which the country has changed and, more specifically, the different forms of violence which both occasioned that change and occurred as a result of it.

While violence is the dominant theme around which Pablo Trapero structures his narratives, the motifs through which he examines violence vary from film to film, ranging from the family unit to the interaction between State and citizen. One motif that runs consistently through the director's oeuvre is the examination of masculinity and the male identity within an Argentine social context. In general, his portrayals of this are far from positive, a fact that is no doubt related to his fascination with violence. With the notable exception of *Leonera* and *La quietud*, all of Trapero's films focus primarily on male protagonists who have been emasculated, stripped of their agency, made to feel completely out of control or otherwise powerless. (Spanish uses the single word *impotencia* to describe this accumulation of feelings; however, the false-friend "impotence" carries perhaps too much connotation to serve as an adequate translation.) The two films analyzed in this chapter—*Mundo grúa* and *Carancho*—feature protagonists, Rulo and Sosa, respectively, who are experiencing this *impotencia* firsthand. In the case of *Mundo grúa*, the film's central narrative focuses on a character going through the process of emasculation that accompanies *impotencia*. *Carancho*, on the other hand, begins after Sosa has come to terms with his situation, and the narrative focuses on his attempts to regain what has been lost (or, perhaps, taken from him). Despite this difference, however, the films are connected by the fact that both use the lens of the Argentine male who has been reduced to *impotencia* in order to confront the inescapable, objective violence that permeates all of Trapero's films.

The Violence of Neoliberalism

While much of the violence on display in *Carancho* is highly subjective in nature, ultimately it emerges from the same point of origin as the objective violence against which Rulo and other members of the working-class struggle in *Mundo grúa*: the neoliberal policies implemented in Argentina by the Menem government in the 1990s and the attendant economic collapse of late 2001. The legacy of that period continues to affect the country today, and while the destabilizing effects of neoliberalism reverberated across the globe in the aftermath of the 2008 global financial crisis, they were felt much earlier in various parts of Latin America. Argentina was not the first Latin American country to experience economic insecurity as a result of neoliberalism, nor was the population's response to it the most violent—despite a series of riots in the aftermath of the 2001 collapse, there was no organized resistance in Argentina that could compare to, for example, the Zapatista movement that began in southern Mexico as a response to the implementation of NAFTA in 1994. However, the effect the crisis had on Argentina was incredibly profound, most significantly because of the way in which it fundamentally altered Argentine society, introducing a level of physical violence into the society which had previously been absent. (Or, at least, less prominent.) The connection between this kind of violence, which plays a vital role in *Carancho*'s narrative, and the more elusive objective violence seen in *Mundo grúa* is found in neoliberalism itself.

Simon Springer explains that neoliberalism was originally conceived from the belief that the devastation of the Second World War was brought about by "government intervention [that] trampled personal freedoms and thereby unleashed indescribable slaughter" (2016, p. 153). Consequently, he contends, "neoliberalism as a political ideology can be understood as reactionary to violence" (Springer, 2016, p. 153). While it may have been theorized as a way to prevent violence, however, in practice neoliberalism has proven to be a major contributing factor to increasing violence in societies, most appreciably because of the heightened economic (and resultant social) inequality that is commonly found in neoliberal societies. Inequality, in a neoliberal economy, derives at least in part from the belief that labor market flexibility—the ability of companies to adapt to the market as and when necessary—is of utmost importance. Guy Standing explains that labor market flexibility manifests itself in several different ways, affecting a worker's wage, his or her skillset, even employment itself. Whatever benefits this flexibility may provide for corporations looking to compete in a global market, its effects are essentially negative for the average lower- or middle-class worker: "the flexibility advocated by the brash neo-classical economists meant systematically making employees more insecure, claimed to be a necessary price for retaining investment and jobs" (Standing, 2011, p. 6).

The economic collapse Argentina suffered in 2001 provides a particularly relevant example of Standing's claim. Superficially, the Argentina of the late 1990s was a successful example of the social and economic stability offered by neoliberal policies. The Argentine government's economic plan resulted in massive foreign investment, and for the first half of the 1990s these policies seemed to have finally stabilized Argentina's historically unstable economy. That changed in the middle of the decade, however, and as foreign capital investments left the country the jobs they funded disappeared with them. Crucially, this situation affected not only the working class but the middle class, as well. Alejandro Grimson and Gabriel Kessler explain:

> The loss of earning power and jobs in the public sector, as well as in small businesses and industrial firms in the private sector . . . set the stage for displaced members of the impoverished middle class to replace the structurally poor in the unskilled jobs the latter had traditionally held during times of economic growth. Furthermore, the new low-paid jobs opened up by technology in this same period demanded skills that the chronically poor

did not have. So within the ranks of the structurally poor came a pool of older unskilled workers with no place at all now in the job market. (2012, pp. 97–8)

This new socioeconomic reality resulted in, essentially, a new social class—the precariat.

Standing describes the precariat as a social grouping that is capable of encompassing people in all walks of life, irrespective of what class they might have been considered a part of in pre-neoliberal societies. Individuals within this group are unified by several factors: "[b]esides labor insecurity and insecure social income, those in the precariat lack a work-based *identity*. When employed, they are in career-less jobs, without traditions of social memory" (2011, p. 12). It is this specific group within society to which both Rulo and Sosa belong. It is perhaps more acute in the case of Rulo, a skilled handyman and mechanic who is forced, due to a general scarcity of laborer jobs, to accept whatever work he can find. Even leaving the hub of Buenos Aires does not provide him with any sort of satisfactory resolution to his employment issues as he arrives in Patagonia and finds himself in the middle of a labor dispute. Similarly, Sosa is a skilled lawyer with a knack for relating to his clients, yet he is forced to scrape out a living working as a sort of paralegal for a corrupt firm. The precarious nature of employment in neoliberal societies, combined with the resultant systemic inequality, brings with it rising tension, particularly domestically. Significantly, inequality is an absolutely critical component in the emergence of violence in any society. The Argentina presented in both *Mundo grúa* and *Carancho* is one that has already been notably influenced by the inequality of neoliberalism. As such, Slavoj Žižek's concept of objective violence is pervasive in both narratives. However, the rise of subjective violence, which dominates *Carancho* but is entirely absent from *Mundo grúa*, can be linked to the pervasiveness of objective violence.

Masculinity in Crisis

The objective violence of neoliberalism has also affected Argentine society in more insidious ways, as well, reflecting R. W. Connell's finding that "masculinity is shaped, not in relation to a specific *workplace*, but in relation to the *labor market as whole*" (2005, p. 95). It is precisely men like Rulo—the construction workers, mechanics, and artisans whom we might perhaps expect to have the most acute sense of their masculinity—to whom Carolina Rocha refers when she writes "if men are classified according to their economic accomplishments [as they are in Argentina], the failure to attain financial success drastically erodes a man's gender identity and diminishes his sociodomestic importance" (2012, p. 11). This echoes Connell's contention that "[t]he constitution of masculinity through bodily performance means that gender is vulnerable when the performance cannot be sustained" (2005, p. 54).

Indeed, this was not merely an after-the-fact realization, either; Beatriz Sarlo commented on it *as it was occurring*, stating in 2001 that "el trabajo es un bien escaso . . . ocupa una posición completamente subordinada desde el punto de vista cultural, y no es un espacio de identificación. Hoy es difícil que un núcleo de construcción de la identidad sea alguna ocupación profesional o laboral" ("work is a scarce asset . . . it occupies a completely subordinated position from a cultural point of view, and it is not a space of identification. Today it is difficult for a professional or industrial occupation to be a nucleus of identity construction") (2003, p. 128). Rocha's analysis, coming after Sarlo's, makes it clear that the construction of identity to which Sarlo refers is not limited to a cultural one—the ability for a man to describe himself based on his profession—but also one of gender. Of the impact Argentina's neoliberal economic policies and subsequent economic crisis had on father-son relationships, Rocha explains that, prior to the 1990s, "Argentine men held domestic roles. Patriarchy legitimated men's power within families. Not only were fathers moral leaders, but they were also the breadwinners" (2012, p. 7). This relationship changed in the 1990s, however—"as men were laid off and their sources of income disappeared . . . their loss of social status and privilege translated into a diminished sense of authority in both the private and public spheres" (Rocha, 2012, p. 12). This tension is mediated in *Mundo grúa* through the relationship between Rulo and his son Claudio.

Mundo grúa

Mundo grúa tells two connected stories. The primary narrative arc concerns Luis "Rulo" Margani (Luis Margani), a working-class, middle-aged single father who, with the help of his friend Torres (Daniel Valenzuela), acquires a job working as a crane operator on a building site. Despite being a skilled handyman who spends his free time tinkering on broken-down engines, Rulo considers himself (and is referred to as such by his friends) a musician, due to having played bass in a relatively successful band in his youth. Shortly after acquiring his new job, Rulo attempts to begin wooing Adriana (Adriana Aizemberg), a woman who runs the local *kiosco* (corner shop) and who was, in her youth, a fan of Rulo's band. After working at the construction site for two months Rulo is abruptly fired, under the pretense that he is medically unfit to work. After a period of time, Torres once again lines up a job for Rulo working as a backhoe operator on a project in the Patagonian city of Comodoro Rivadavia, 2,000 kilometers south of Buenos Aires. Upon arrival in Comodoro, Rulo finds the situation even more depressing than his unemployment in Buenos Aires. Not only are living conditions atrocious, Rulo is also forced to contend with arriving in the middle of a labor dispute, motivated partly by the poor living conditions but also by the fact that the workers are not being paid on time, if at all. Finally, Rulo decides to quit and return to Buenos Aires, the film ending as he hitches a lift back home.

The secondary narrative arc focuses on Rulo's son Claudio (Federico Esquerro) who, at the start of the film, lives at home and, like his father before him, plays bass in a band. After finding him in bed with a girl one night, Rulo kicks Claudio out of his house and the son goes to live with Rulo's mother (Graciana Chironi). Claudio and his grandmother repeatedly clash, primarily a result of the fact that Claudio continues to be as lazy as before, much to his grandmother's disdain. Although most of the film focuses on Rulo, both Claudio and his narrative arc serve an important function in the film, in that they act as a counterpoint of sorts to Rulo and his experience. Where Rulo spends his nights planted in front of the television before eventually passing out on the couch, Claudio inevitably wakes his father when he comes home from partying in the early hours of the morning. Where Rulo is shown to be desperate to find work, Claudio spends his days playing arcade games with his friends, uninterested in finding any sort of job. Finally, where Rulo is interested in a long-term relationship with Adriana, Claudio engages in a one-night stand with a random girl he meets at his band's show. While secondary to Rulo's narrative, the relationship between Claudio and Rulo is an important one in the film, and Claudio provides many of the story's lighter moments.

The Precariat on Screen

Mundo grúa is, without question, Rulo's story. Although it incorporates a subplot focusing on Claudio—who seems to be following the same path as Rulo did some two decades previously—the narrative (and, indeed, the camera) only rarely (and briefly) shifts away from Rulo's experience. As mentioned previously, Rulo is a middle-aged single father of an adult child who still lives at home. His unhealthy lifestyle—he admits to smoking twenty cigarettes a day and his obesity is responsible for a number of health issues, with his doctor specifically mentioning Pickwick Syndrome—combined with his somewhat clumsy attempts to court Adriana mean that he is, in many ways, the antithesis of the image Argentina has projected of itself internationally for almost a century. As early as 1921, when Rudolph Valentino's dancing of the tango in the Buenos Aires-set international blockbuster *The Four Horsemen of the Apocalypse* resulted in a surge of popularity for the dance, Argentina has been associated with a certain suave and sophisticated panache. Even politicians helped to reinforce the stereotype, from Perón in the 1950s with his slicked-back hair and former movie-star wife Evita, to Menem in the 1990s with his perfect tan and pronounced sideburns, his expensive suits, and his penchant for associating with beauty pageant winners.

In contrast to this, *Mundo grúa* depicts frankly unspectacular characters; Rulo, in particular, represents the far-less glamorous side of Argentina, the side populated by real people living real lives. This portrayal fits into a trend that emerged in the 1990s of challenging the stereotypical portrayal of Argentina and presenting an alternate vision of the nation, and of Buenos Aires specifically. Indeed, this might be considered a defining characteristic of New Argentine Cinema, and is notable in the cinema of directors such as Martín Rejtman, Adrián Caetano, and, of course, Trapero. Caetano's films *Pizza, birra, faso* (*Pizza, Beer, Cigarettes*) (1998, co-directed with Bruno Stagnaro) and *Bolivia* (2001), in particular, share many similarities with *Mundo grúa*—the protagonists of *Pizza, birra, faso* seem like they could very easily be acquaintances of Claudio's, while *Bolivia*, like *Mundo grúa* shot on grainy black-and-white film, features an unflattering portrayal of Argentine society that meshes with what is found in Trapero's film.

The Rulo character, played by a friend of Trapero's father named Luis Margani, first appears in the director's short film *Negocios* (1995) as an employee in an auto supplies shop (based on the shop Trapero's father owned in real life). Although fictional, *Negocios* feels as if it straddles the line between documentary and fiction, and this same feeling pervades *Mundo grúa*, as well. One of the key facets of Rulo's character is his past as the bass player in a band that had a hit single in the 1970s, an aspect that was, in fact, inspired by Luis Margani's own life. In the film, the name of the band for which Rulo played bass is Séptimo Regimento (Seventh Regiment), while in real life Margani was the bassist for Séptima Brigada (Seventh Brigade). Although the audience may not know these specific details about Luis Margani (the actor, rather than the character) upon first viewing, many members of the audience (particularly in Argentina) will have been familiar with Séptima Brigada's hit song "Paco Camorra," which is also referenced in the film, perhaps the most obvious example of the work blurring the line between reality and fiction. Although all of the characters in *Mundo grúa* are fictional, the film relies heavily on the fact that the audience recognizes that the mannerisms, speech patterns, and indeed the very lives of the characters on-screen are not drastically different from the (non-) actors who play them.

The first half of *Mundo grúa* is not overtly political, focusing instead on character study and presenting the quotidian life of the working-class characters who populate the film. For more than half of the film's ninety-minute running length, the narrative seems to be, essentially, the story of one man and his surroundings. And in Rulo (and, for that matter, his son Claudio) the film presents a character of the type that could not be further from either the highly manicured image of stereotypical Argentine elegance and sophistication that had characterized Argentina throughout much of the twentieth century (and which was particularly prevalent during the 1990s), or the victim of terrible, Dirty War era government-sponsored injustices which continues to populate so many Argentine films, from *La historia oficial* to *El caso María Soledad* (1993) to *Kamchatka* (2002). Overweight, unskilled, and lacking any semblance of the *viveza criolla* (a sort of streetwise sensibility) on which so many Argentines (especially those from Buenos Aires) pride themselves, *a priori* Rulo hardly seems like the ideal character around which to base a film. Indeed, the image presented in *Mundo grúa* is that of a protagonist entirely unprepared to navigate his way through not only the future but, perhaps more significantly, his own present as well.

As the narrative progresses it becomes clear that Rulo functions as more than merely the film's protagonist. Rather, he serves as a representative of the entire precariat class, the challenges he faces in his life symptomatic of the broad difficulties being confronted by working-class Argentines throughout the country. This is made evident after Rulo loses his job on the crane (or, more accurately, is told he will not be hired permanently) and is forced to leave Buenos Aires. The mood of the film changes fairly drastically in the aftermath of this decision, for it is at this point that the narrative begins to make its social critique obvious. Although Joanna Page finds that "unemployment in [*Mundo grúa*] is hardly a social theme at all, merely the particular condition of an individual life" (2009, p. 53), once Rulo is forced to leave the stability (in the personal rather than professional sense) of Buenos Aires, unemployment and labor exploitation are shunted to the narrative's forefront. By using real construction workers and filming without a structured script, the film allows the people actually being affected by labor issues such as poor working conditions, unemployment, and worker exploitation to manifest their fears and frustrations as they would naturally. In the second half of the film, the men with whom Rulo works assume much more prominence than they do in the first half of the film. Indeed, although Rulo remains the central figure of the narrative, while he is in Patagonia the camera rarely focuses solely on him, instead including him in long and medium shots in which he is merely one of several workers (and, because he is living in a sort of dormitory community, the other people in the shots are always other laborers). The close-ups that Trapero does utilize focus on the machinery that Rulo operates, rather than on Rulo himself, suggesting a subjugation of Rulo's, and, indeed, all of the workers', identities to the work they are doing.

During Rulo's time in Patagonia, there are certain moments where Trapero focuses the camera's lens directly on Rulo, isolating him from his surroundings. These moments are significant for the way in which they contrast with the majority of scenes set in Patagonia. This contrast is most noticeable toward the end of the film, in the sequence which culminates with Rulo deciding to quit his job and return to Buenos Aires. By focusing on Rulo as an individual throughout the sequence, Trapero isolates him from his co-workers at the precise moment when they are asking for solidarity. This technique emphasizes that what might be beneficial for the collective will not necessarily be good for the individual. The first scene in the sequence is of a workers meeting, in which a large group of men are debating whether or not they can risk going on strike. Rulo appears in the scene but says nothing, listening on as the group's apparent leader exhorts his colleagues to go through with the strike. When one anonymous worker asks "si la empresa se va, ¿nosotros qué vamos a hacer? ¿Adónde vamos a laburar?" ("If the company leaves, what are we going to do? Where are we going to work?"), the leader replies,

> Acá estamos jugados todos, y todos tenemos que salir al frente para defender nuestra fuente de trabajo. Nosotros tenemos una familia por delante, y esa familia la tenemos que mantener.
>
> [We are all involved, and we all have to come together to defend our jobs. We are all family, and we have to provide for that family.]

The scene then cuts to a close-up shot of Rulo lying in bed, a pained look visible on his face despite his hand rubbing his eyes. When he finally removes his hand, the camera lingers on Rulo's face as he stares at the ceiling, taking a few deep, labored breaths, before fading to black. The next day (presumably), Rulo calls his mother and son and admits that he has quit his job and decided to come home. Rather than wait and find out what will happen between the workers and the company, Rulo decides he must leave. Where the other workers may believe some sort of satisfactory agreement will be reached, Rulo knows better; he, perhaps uniquely in the camp, has already experienced firsthand the manipulative side of corporate labor dealings, and has therefore resigned himself to what he believes to be inevitable (Figure 1.1). From past

Figure 1.1 *Mundo grúa* (1999). The futility of the workers' situation is evident on Rulo's face.

experience Rulo knows that working-class solidarity is ultimately powerless when confronted with the reality of faceless corporations.

The sense of isolation Rulo feels in Patagonia is heightened by the camera: during the meeting Rulo is at first not visible, and once he does enter the picture he does not particularly stand out, suggesting that he is in solidarity with the other workers. However, by focusing tight on Rulo's face in the following scene, the camera emphasizes both the exasperation and the sense of isolation that he feels. Watching the film now we realize that Rulo, a representative of those working-class people who were beginning to feel the effects of Menem-era economic policies long before the *corralito* impacted all segments of Argentine society, has taken the only decision possible. His personal experience, from his difficulty in finding any sort of consistent income to the general frustration he feels whenever he considers what has become of his life, foreshadows the challenges the country was to face in the first decade of the twenty-first century.

Although Rulo chooses to leave the workers rather than stay and stand in solidarity with them, it is quite clear that he is not leaving with any sense of optimism. Men like Rulo and his co-workers, though living in a "world of cranes" due to the privately funded (often with foreign capital) construction projects being undertaken throughout the country, are unable to hold down consistent jobs. Amanda Holmes describes this as a "disempowering hegemony evoked by the crane," and explains that "[t]he building boom [depicted in the film] reflected the political aspirations of the government, but not the economic reality of the population" (2017, p. 41). The effect this has on them, and on Argentine society generally, goes beyond mere economics. The nonprofessional actors that populate the film seem comfortable in their roles, not only because those roles are not drastically different from their actual lives but also because the film's relatively sparse script affords them the opportunity to react naturally to their situations. The two different networks of interpersonal relationships that Rulo maintains over the course of the film—one involving the deeper relationships of his personal life and which includes his mother, his son, his friends, and his would-be girlfriend; the other the series of relatively superficial relationships he creates in his various work environments—are both, to a greater or lesser extent, influenced by this lack of a structured script. The improvisational nature of the work is perhaps most noticeable in the numerous interactions Rulo has in his professional life, especially those in which he is not a central figure. This is most prevalent during the second half of the film, when Rulo arrives in Comodoro Rivadavia. Like so many Latin Americans who have been forced to leave their homes in order to find work, by the end of *Mundo grúa* Rulo has become a migrant laborer. From shouting into a roadside payphone as he assures his aging mother that his living accommodations are satisfactory, that he is eating enough, and that he has found work, to his reality of living in an overcrowded worker's dormitory with no running water, having to walk to work, and being so disgusted with his food that he is unable to finish it, Rulo's finds himself living a life in Comodoro Rivadavia that is, to an Argentine audience at least, unnervingly similar to that of the migrant laborers from neighboring countries (known as *bolivianos* regardless of their actual nationality) that Argentines routinely disparage.

Physical and Emotional Estrangement

The interactions between Rulo and his son Claudio make it clear that the father considers having employment to be central both to his sense of self and to his concept of masculinity. It is significant that Rulo accepts his son's immaturity virtually without question—giving Claudio money when he asks for it, allowing him to use his bass for his band's concert, and never becoming angry when he is disturbed by his son's early-morning entrances—until the moment when Rulo, returning from a date of his own with Adriana, walks in on his son in flagrante delicto, having brought home a girl from one of his band's shows. Although he ultimately relents and allows his son time to have sex with the girl, the next morning Rulo tells him he must find somewhere else to live. Rather than jealousy being the motivation for this decision, it could be argued that seeing Claudio have success in his sex life, especially when he (Rulo) has been less than successful in his own attempts at establishing a relationship, has shaken Rulo's sense of manhood. Based on many of the traditional criteria used to judge manhood, Claudio is still a child: he lives with his father and still relies on him for money, he lacks motivation and, most significantly, he makes no attempt to find work. And yet he succeeds (as it were) where Rulo fails (Figure 1.2). By kicking his son out, Rulo is not only manifesting his displeasure with his son's life choices in a possible attempt to force him to mature, he is also, perhaps subconsciously, attempting to re-exert his authority over his son and, by extension, his masculine identity.

Figure 1.2 *Mundo grúa* (1999). Claudio's sexual exploits threaten Rulo's masculinity.

The fact that Rulo has a job when this interaction occurs is a significant one, for it places him in a position of authority over his son that he might not otherwise have. Claudio mirrors his father in more ways than one. He seems to be following much the same path that his father did at a similar age, and unlike his father's generation, which came of age during a period when Argentina was still able to maintain the idea that each generation was better off than the previous one, the Argentina in which Claudio will mature into adulthood has already begun to crack. The symbolism here is clear: Argentina's promise of continual progress, of each generation improving on the circumstances of its predecessor, has proven itself to be fraudulent. Although we never learn anything about Rulo's father, at the age of forty-nine Rulo is almost certainly *not* better off than his own parents were, and where Rulo was playing in a band with a hit single when he was Claudio's age, the son is lucky to get a gig playing in front of twenty people in a dingy *boliche* (informal night club). Rulo, then, is not necessarily in a position to reproach his son, except for the fact that he has a job and his son does not; this gives him the slightest bit of leverage over Claudio. Asserting his authority seems to embolden Rulo, and he acts on this newfound sense of strength by inviting Adriana over to his house. The relationship between Rulo and Adriana is an interesting facet of the film's narrative, because in some ways it can be understood as a metaphor for the precarious situation many working-class Argentines experienced at the end of the 1990s. Although she does seem to enjoy his company, and at one point the two do share a kiss, it is clear to the audience that Adriana is not nearly as interested in Rulo as he is in her, nor does she seem particularly interested in making any sort of serious commitment to him—she consistently shifts away from his hand anytime he attempts to touch her, and she refuses to give Rulo any assurances that they will still be an item when he returns from his time in Patagonia. Rulo, however, is either incapable or unwilling to read these signs, and so continues to pursue Adriana seriously, much in the same way he continues to pursue a stable income. And, just as consistent work is difficult, if not impossible, to find, so too is a committed relationship with Adriana. Both of these things represent, essentially, stability, something that is forever just beyond Rulo's grasp.

The lack of stability in Rulo's life comes into sharp focus during his time in Patagonia. A large part of what makes Rulo's time there so affecting is the fact that this part of the film, perhaps more so than the first half, replicates the feel of a documentary to such an extent that it is difficult to decipher if what we are watching has been staged to some degree or if the scenes are entirely unscripted. The extensive use of nonprofessional actors of course accentuates this feeling, but it is not simply the presence of nonprofessional actors which creates what Page refers to as a sense of documentalism. The work's unorthodox filming and production process, combined with the decision to shoot on grainy, lo-fi 16-mm black-and-white film, lends the picture a particular aesthetic, especially for the time and place in which the film was made. In addition, Page highlights the cinematographic and editing techniques used by Trapero which provide the work with its documentary feel: "medium shots and fixed frames give the impression of a hidden camera capturing reality. Trapero has a predilection for fixed-frame two-shots, which means that cuts during scenes of dialogue are kept to a minimum" (2009, p. 50). This is prevalent in the scenes that take place in Buenos Aires, and especially in scenes set indoors. In contrast, on the worksite, both in Buenos Aires and Patagonia, Trapero uses a different filming and editing style, shifting rapidly between the machinery itself and the men working the machines, with an emphasis placed on the scale of the machinery in relation to the workers. Page claims that "the diversity of shots used throughout the film, many of them associated with nonfiction film, suggests that they are being used precisely to connote documentalism rather than simply to represent their subject" (2009, p. 50).

With their focus on marginalized characters who are quite often subjugated by sociocultural forces beyond their control, all of Trapero's films are indebted, to a certain extent, to the social realist tradition. Yet from a technical perspective, Trapero's early work fits perhaps most comfortably into the traditional understanding of neorealist cinema. Far from the polished, tightly edited films that Trapero is producing today, *Mundo grúa*—with its use of black-and-white film stock, nonprofessional actors, location filming, and its focus on the quotidian experience of working-class people—is in many ways the archetypal neorealist film. Indeed, Tamara Falicov has described the film as a perfect example of Argentine cinema's "neo-neo-realism" (2003, p. 55). *Mundo grúa*, however, also incorporates a number of specific characteristics that relate it more closely to social realism: its condemnation of the socioeconomic difficulties faced by Argentina's working class, its incorporation of documentalist imagery such as the (what appears to be) legitimate construction work taking place both in Buenos Aires and Patagonia, and, significantly, Rulo's frustrated acceptance of his situation. While Rulo does act—both his initial move to Patagonia and his decision to return home are acts of agency—his response is that of a defeated man. That sense of defeat is perhaps most obviously portrayed through Trapero's representation of the Patagonian landscape which dominates the second half of the film.

One of the features that marks *Mundo grúa* as different from other films that emerged around the same time period is the fact that almost half of the film takes place in Comodoro Rivadavia, a remote Patagonian city that the film presents as retaining an almost frontier-like atmosphere. The Argentine countryside and the men (almost invariably men) who populate it have, for much of the country's existence, represented a specific image of Argentine society. As early as the late nineteenth century, thanks to literary works such as José Hernández's *Martín Fierro*, the figure of the gaucho occupied a somewhat mythologized space in Argentina's national imagination. This feeling was entrenched further by the mass migration Argentina experienced in the early years of the twentieth century. The romanticization of the gaucho was part of a larger trend, one found not only in Argentina but throughout the Western world, of rejecting the urban. Adrián Gorelik explains that "a partir especialmente de la revolución industrial, pero incluso desde antes, la ciudad comenzó a verse como el lugar de la desorganización social y la anomia" ("beginning particularly with the Industrial Revolution, but even before then, the city came to be seen as a place of social disorganization and anomie") (2003, p. 26).

While the New Argentine Cinema of the 1990s did not necessarily glamorize the rural, it certainly rejected the urban, Buenos Aires particularly, which came to be seen as a kind of "fourthspace [where] characters are the victims of extreme violence" (Rocha and Montes Garces, 2010, p. xxviii). *Mundo grúa* does, in some respects, follow this trend. Set in the province of Buenos Aires rather than the city itself, the film provides no sense of the refinement for which the city is (rightfully or wrongfully) globally famous. However, in contrast to other New Argentine Cinema directors, and even with his own later works, while Trapero does not glorify Buenos Aires in any meaningful way he does not demonize it, either. The city certainly poses its challenges for Rulo, primarily in his difficulty in finding work, but it also offers vital comforts such as friends and family. Buenos Aires, then, can be understood as a neutral space. Rather, it is *Mundo grúa*'s presentation of Patagonia that truly stands out as remarkable. Rulo's dissatisfaction is made visible on-screen from virtually the moment he leaves the urban environment—shown standing on the side of a country road, attempting to hitch a ride as cars pass by, Rulo's solitude is made manifest by the barrenness of the landscape. Returning to Page's terminology, it becomes clear that by replicating the social realist style *Mundo grúa*'s cinematography lends an air of "documentalism" to the work's final act. So blurred is the line between documentary and fiction, both in terms of the film's depiction of the Patagonian landscape and the working conditions for the men there, that the film's overall social critique of the plight of the working class is reinforced.

In addition, the stark portrayal of Patagonia, a region famed for its natural beauty, reinforces the general feeling of pessimism that pervades the film. Although Patagonia is often presented on film in dramatic fashion, with emphasis placed on the region's snowcapped mountain peaks and enormous glaciers, in *Mundo grúa* very little of that is visible. Instead we are shown a bleak country, virtually devoid of plant and animal life, populated solely by laborers and the enormous machines they use to dig up the earth (Figure 1.3). When Rulo's friends drive down from Buenos Aires to visit him, he takes them to a dried-out lakebed that he describes as being like Chile's *Valle de la Luna*. The comparison is certainly accurate, as the black-and-white film captures the

Figure 1.3 *Mundo grúa* (1999). Rulo's sense of isolation is emphasized as he arrives in Comodo Rivadavia.

lakebed's stones and sand in a dull grey that resembles nothing so much as the surface of the moon. Throughout much of his friends' visit, Rulo is quiet and contemplative, obviously undergoing a process of realization at just how lonely his time in Patagonia has made him. The desolation of the lakebed is, perhaps, the most accurate manifestation of Rulo's sense of isolation and despair. Rather than being a *locus amoenus*, Patagonia not only crystallizes the frustrations Rulo may have felt in Buenos Aires but, in fact, may heighten those feelings, since he is now experiencing them away from the support network he has built up at home. The film's ending suggests that while working-class solidarity may not provide the solution Rulo is searching for, neither is he capable of confronting those challenges on his own.

Ultimately, *Mundo grúa*'s presentation of Patagonia fits into the film's broader portrayal of the precariat in the neoliberal Argentina of the late 1990s. Rulo heads to Patagonia in search of opportunity and instead finds nothing but desolation and isolation. Despite being surrounded by men who find themselves in similar circumstances, Rulo forms no connection with his colleagues, a fact which emphasizes just how out of place he feels. This is, perhaps, the film's most potent political statement: reflecting Trapero's desire to create a film that showed a side of Argentina that had been essentially forgotten, the Patagonia of *Mundo grúa* is filled with men who no longer have a place in Argentine society. (This is something that Trapero returns to later in his career with *Nacido y criado*.) What starts as the examination of an average man's daily life, then, becomes something much more: Rulo's time in Patagonia makes it clear that his experience is representative of the struggles felt by working-class Argentines all over the country. In this way Trapero makes manifest the objective violence that permeates the lives of the Argentine precariat, such that while neither the government nor its policies are ever mentioned, the film functions as a critique of the status quo.

Carancho makes that critique even more explicit. Indeed, in its focus on a solitary, relatively powerless man attempting to make his way through a generally hostile society, the film that *Mundo grúa* shares the most in common with is *Carancho*. The parallels between the two films range from technical aspects including grainy, high-contrast cinematography or the use of tension-building long takes to narrative similarities such as each protagonist being deeply unhappy with their employment situation or beginning an intimate relationship over the course of the film. The tensions of *Mundo grúa*, however, are heightened in *Carancho*. Where the precariat of *Mundo grúa* is essentially analogous to the working class, by *Carancho* the precariat has expanded to include the middle class, as well; in economic terms, things have not gotten better, in fact they have gotten worse. In addition, the pervasiveness of objective violence remains as central to *Carancho*'s narrative as it is to *Mundo grúa*'s, yet the film also features a level of subjective violence that, as will be demonstrated, clearly functions as a commentary on the legacy of the economic decisions taken by those in power in the years between the two films being made. Perhaps most significantly, where Rulo is presented as unprepared for what is happening to him and helpless to change it, the protagonists of *Carancho* react with rage to their circumstances.

Carancho

Carancho tells the story of Sosa (Ricardo Darín), the type of personal injury lawyer commonly referred to in English as an ambulance chaser.[1] Friendly with many of the emergency personnel he routinely encounters as he searches for new clients, Sosa is introduced to rookie EMT Luján (Martina Gusmán)

---

[1] The *carancho* is a bird of prey native to South America that, like the vulture, survives by eating weakened animals and carrion. Since the film was released the term *carancho* has come into popular usage to refer to the type of lawyer portrayed in the film. (Kairuz, 2010)

at an accident site and quickly takes an interest in her. We learn that Sosa has, in fact, lost his license to practice, though neither the audience nor Luján ever learns what he did to cause his suspension. Simultaneously, Luján is revealed to be a drug addict, locking herself in the hospital bathroom on a regular basis to inject herself in her foot or between her toes in order to prevent track marks on her arms. The film's narrative examines the two characters' personal and professional lives and shows how, as Sosa attempts to redeem himself and escape from the underworld in which he has been living, Luján gradually gets dragged down into that world, partly as a result of her relationship with Sosa.

As the film begins, Sosa works for a company referred to only as "*La Fundación*" ("The Foundation"), an ironic title considering that the company keeps the vast majority of whatever money it wins in court and provides its clients, often poor families grateful for any amount however small, with only a fraction of the money they are actually awarded. Sosa is profoundly disillusioned with his work, has an intense dislike for his boss Casal (José Luis Arias), and wants to quit The Foundation but is unable to do so until he regains his license. Sosa and Luján begin a relationship but that is quickly broken when, after an attempted scam fails and results in the death of Sosa's friend, she distances herself from him. In an effort to win her back, Sosa attempts to redeem himself by leaving The Foundation and going straight, as it were. We learn that he has already fully compensated one family, much to the displeasure of The Foundation and the detriment of his own physical well-being. Through an introduction made by Luján, and in spite of the increasing physical threat posed by The Foundation, Sosa begins helping a woman who has been involved in a traffic accident in which her brother has died. Due to his success with the case, Sosa takes on more clients and he and Luján rekindle their relationship. Sosa's professional success is short-lived, however, as The Foundation's thugs, in an attempt to force Sosa to remove himself from the court dealings, attack Luján at her hospital. This sends Sosa into a rage and he beats one of The Foundation's lawyers to death. El Perro (Carlos Weber), the crooked head of The Foundation who has connections with the local police force, offers Sosa protection in exchange for all of the money he has recovered for the various families he has been helping. Although he agrees to El Perro's offer, Sosa in fact double-crosses The Foundation by orchestrating a car accident in which he himself is badly injured and El Perro is killed. As Sosa and Luján attempt to escape Buenos

Aires with the money, an unseen vehicle slams into the side of their car as they drive through an intersection, resulting in Sosa's death and leaving Luján's fate unknown.

If, through its portrayal of the economic challenges facing the working class, the Argentina presented in *Mundo grúa* is one that hints at an oncoming crisis, the society presented in *Carancho* is one that has been struggling to come to grips with the effects of utter collapse. Upon the film's release in 2010, *Carancho* received numerous comparisons with Juan José Campanella's *El secreto de sus ojos/The Secret in their Eyes* (2009)—both feature Ricardo Darín in a starring role and can be easily summarized as crime thrillers set in the Buenos Aires underworld. However, what separates Trapero's film from many of the films with which it has been compared is its depiction of Argentina's capital. The Buenos Aires of *Carancho* seems almost postapocalyptic—dark, dangerous, a place where life seems almost impossibly difficult (Figure 1.4). In featuring a cast of characters who have suffered their own personal traumas while being set in a place that has experienced (a type of) devastation, the film's narrative brings to mind Resnais's *Hiroshima mon amour* (1959). Of that work, Cathy Caruth states, "[the film] asks what might become possible within a discourse that is not simply *about* Hiroshima . . . but within an encounter that takes place *at* Hiroshima, a discourse spoken, as it were, *on the site of catastrophe*" (1996, p. 34, emphasis in original).

Trapero's film, in contrast to Resnais's work, is more concerned with action than with discourse; however it is similar in that it asks what kind

Figure 1.4 *Carancho* (2010). Sosa's existence is defined by a pervasive violence that seems impossible to escape.

of life is achievable in a place that seems to actively discourage it. The film's protagonists could not, generally, be considered working class; Sosa is a lawyer and Luján a doctor, both professions that require a certain level of professional training beyond the reach of someone like Rulo (or even Sosa's clients). Despite the supposed benefits that their professions should provide them (including more job security and a higher salary), their daily existence seems infinitely more fraught and precarious than that of Rulo or Adriana. This is, almost certainly, a reflection of the new reality of Argentina post-economic collapse, an Argentina in which "jobs requiring skills considered middle class were created [but] the jobs were low paid and unstable, so the benefits and well-being derived from them were not as good as such jobs in the previous era" (Grimson and Kessler, 2012, p. 98). This pattern began to take shape during the 1990s, and *Carancho* presents a society where the impact of that phenomenon has become fully established. The result is a film that is deeply unsettling—containing aspects of relatively traditional film styles such as *noir* and neorealism while also incorporating an aesthetic that feels inspired by contemporary horror films, the viewer is repeatedly forced to view exceptionally traumatic and violent acts.

What Is Shown, What Is Not

Indeed, perhaps the most noticeable aspect of *Carancho* is just how violent life seems to be and, disturbingly, how that violence appears to be accepted as commonplace. A few scenes, in particular, establish the violent nature of the society presented in the film. The first of these scenes sets the tone right from the start, in a sequence of brief episodes which emphasize the violent nature of everyday life for the film's characters. The sequence consists of a collection of scenes from a typical night in the film's version of Buenos Aires, focusing primarily on the ambulance in which Luján works. The sequence begins after Sosa and Luján meet for the first time; Sosa returns home to his apartment and turns on the television. The sounds of gunfire can be heard coming from the (unseen) television set, followed by what sound like the exaggerated punches and kicks of a kung-fu film as Sosa falls asleep on the couch. The camera then cuts to Luján's ambulance speeding through the streets of Buenos Aires, its sirens blaring. A pregnant woman is shown sobbing in the back of the ambulance, Luján attempting to calm her down by assuring her that they are approaching the hospital. No blood is shown, but the fact that Luján is pressing her gloved hand below the woman's abdomen implies that this is not simply a case of a pregnant woman going into labor. The camera then cuts to Luján treating an old woman with various cuts on her face. As Luján attends to her, the woman explains that she was simply returning to her house when she was attacked and knocked to the ground. The final episode in the montage is, perhaps, the most disturbing. A man—bleeding heavily from an open wound on his head, his clothes badly torn and covered in blood, his speech and posture unsteady as if drugged—at first accuses Luján of being with the police. She attempts to explain that she is actually a doctor who is attempting to help him, and, when he finally stops accusing her, he begins to repeat, over and over again, "te amo," "I love you." He starts reaching for Luján, groping her and attempting to impose himself on her. In the confined space of the ambulance Luján is trapped and, despite the man being obviously injured and intoxicated, he is almost able to force himself upon her. Finally, Luján's partner stops the ambulance and comes to her aid, opening the ambulance door and violently dragging the man out. The audience is not shown what happens after this, but noticeably audible thuds are heard, suggesting that Luján's partner has attacked the already injured man. The sequence ends with Luján driving home and, before taking a shower, swallowing two pills of what appear to be prescription drugs.

As with the rest of the film, physical violence is present throughout the montage sequence. What marks this sequence as different is the fact that that violence is suggested—mainly by presenting its aftermath—rather than actually depicted on-screen. The violence disturbs not through shocking imagery, then, but rather through the lack of reaction these increasingly violent scenarios generate from the characters. Sosa turns on his television and perhaps the most distinctive, instantly recognizable sound of violence—a gunshot—is the first thing he hears. When he wakes up from having fallen asleep on the couch, the sounds of violence are still coming from the set. And through it all the only emotion he displays is surprised annoyance when he realizes he has fallen asleep with the television on. Even more disturbingly, Luján witnesses, and is herself subjected to, the aftereffects of seemingly random acts of physical violence and yet, while on the job, she betrays almost no emotion whatsoever other than a slight unease when the intoxicated man attempts to accost her. Even her drug use is passed over with such nonchalance as if to be mundane.

The other aspect of the sequence which unnerves is the sense that there is always a threat to the characters' physical safety waiting just off-camera. In fact, this is something that permeates the entire film. Throughout the work Trapero is meticulous in his shot framing and selection, particularly in the case of scenes involving violence. The film's first scene sets a tone that will last for the duration—Sosa is thrown out of what appears to be a funeral and savagely beaten by a group of anonymous men, the camera focusing tight on Sosa lying on the ground, while the attackers are kept entirely anonymous, nothing but their legs visible. The only noticeable lighting in the shot comes from the orange hue of sodium-vapor streetlamps that provide just enough light to adequately view the blood Sosa spits after the men have left. The film, as a whole, remains faithful to this opening scene—shot primarily indoors or inside vehicles, the cinematography creates tension by suggesting a world that is constantly imposing itself on the characters, their ambitions thwarted by a literal lack of space to maneuver. The low-key lighting creates a chiaroscuro effect that adds to the tension generated by the framing—neither the characters nor the viewer know what is lurking in the shadows, what is coming around the next turn.

Conversely, many of the interior scenes, especially those which take place at Luján's hospital, are filmed under unnatural fluorescent lights which cast an unhealthy pallor over the faces of the characters, emphasizing the cuts and scars of the film's many victims of physical violence and Luján's own addiction-induced pale complexion. In one particularly notable scene, two men are brought into the emergency room where Luján is working, both bleeding profusely as a result of knife wounds. As Luján and another doctor attend to them, the men begin to fight, one of the men attempting to leave his gurney despite being hooked up to an IV drip. The two men shove Luján and her counterpart out of the way and begin throwing punches indiscriminately at each other, until one of them runs through the emergency room's doors. Luján and her colleagues struggle to lock the doors from inside to prevent any more carnage from occurring, despite a large crowd outside the doors getting more and more agitated. Finally, two gunshots can be heard and the crowd disperses. Quickly composing herself, Luján returns to the patient who remains in the room. This scene, in particular, emphasizes several things: first, the constant threat of violence that exists in the film's world. No indication is given as to why the two men begin to fight, other than the most cursory of insults they shout at one another. As one man escapes, a group of men outside the room begin to charge at the doors, attempting to attack the man left behind. What is key in this scene, and indeed the majority of the film, is the threat just beyond the camera's view (Figure 1.5). Not so much the violence we can see as the menace we cannot. Neither Luján nor the viewer knows how many men may be trying to force their way inside, but the threat the group poses is serious enough for everyone in the room to react with panic.

The general unease which pervades the film—the sense that some unseen, unexpected danger is always mere moments away from imposing itself upon the characters—allied with the brutal depictions of violence that are shown on-screen combine to give the work, at times, the aesthetic of horror cinema. In particular, *Carancho* incorporates elements of the type of horror films that rose to popularity in the mid-2000s, dubbed "torture porn" by critic David Edelstein. Torture porn differentiates itself from other types of horror films by focusing on imprisonment as a central theme, in addition to offering realistic, and often highly graphic, portrayals of violence (Jones, 2013). In *Carancho* the characters' imprisonment is, for the most part, metaphorical rather than literal. Rather than physical confinement, Sosa and Luján are imprisoned by a society that unrelentingly barrages them with violent images and experiences. Throughout the film, violence happens not just on-screen but, perhaps as importantly, just off-screen

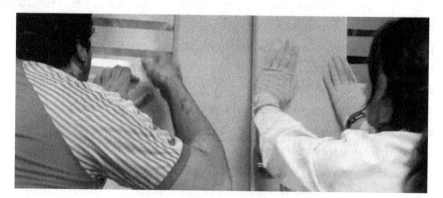

Figure 1.5 *Carancho* (2010). Throughout the film, danger awaits just off-screen.

as well. From the group of men attempting to break down the emergency room door to the black screen at the very end of the film where, in the aftermath of the horrifically violent car accident that serves as the film's final image, we hear (but do not see) the medics' attempts to revive Luján while simultaneously confirming Sosa's death, the film provides no respite whatsoever from the constant stream of violence. By portraying violence on-screen while also having it continually just out of sight, it becomes ever-present and inescapable, the symptom of a society that has broken down. How the members of this failed society cope with their situation varies. Luján reacts by attempting to remove herself, through chemical means, from her reality. Because drug addiction is relatively common, it would be easy to dismiss this as some sort of personal choice Luján makes; to do so, however, would be to ignore the constant violence to which she is exposed, and the threat of violence which is inherent to her job. It is not difficult to understand why Luján might resort to such seemingly drastic measures—she spends her nights as an EMT, exposing herself to some of the most extreme examples of traumatic injury and violence imaginable, and when not on an ambulance shift she works in a dilapidated hospital as a trainee-doctor which, as we have seen, provides little respite. She directly addresses her addiction only once, explaining to Sosa that she began using it shortly after arriving in Buenos Aires and that the drug is "lo único que me calma" ("the only thing that soothes me").

Resistance and the Middle Class

Where Luján seeks chemically induced refuge from the terrible reality of *Carancho*'s Buenos Aires, Sosa chooses a different path, focusing his rage against those who wield power over him. Although he is not rich, neither is Sosa working class. The contrast between Rulo and Sosa in this regard is an important one. Rulo is presented with all of the trappings associated with dignified poverty—he works hard, is never heard to complain about his situation (with the notable exception at the end of the film), and never attempts to present himself as anything other than what he is. Sosa, on the other hand, is educated, skilled, and has a job that requires the level of professional training he has acquired. He is evidently good at his job—throughout the film he is praised for his ability to relate to his clients and his very livelihood is dependent on ensuring that The Foundation wins its cases. And yet, despite all this, he lives in a small apartment, he drives fourth-hand cars, and, most centrally, he is legally prohibited from actually doing the job he has been trained for. Where Rulo is able to leave Buenos Aires in search of better opportunities (even if those opportunities turn out to be false), Sosa is trapped by the limitations of his job: he repeatedly states his desire to leave the city, but he is unable to do so not only because he is prohibited from practicing law but also because his current position, while providing him with enough money to survive, does not allow him to save enough money to get his license back. Throughout the course of the film, we watch as Sosa's impatience with his predicament becomes stronger and stronger until, after his boss Casal attacks Luján in order to send a message, Sosa reacts with unhinged rage, storming into The Foundation's offices and beating Casal so severely with a metal drawer that he (wittingly or unwittingly) kills him.

In these respects Sosa, while sharing many similarities with Rulo, is quite different indeed. Although educated and formerly working as a lawyer, he maintains an air of suspicion about him by admitting that he has been disbarred without ever making clear the reason why. He makes a living working for a personal injury law firm as an ambulance chaser, and is on a first-name basis with the various EMTs and paramedics who work nights. Unlike Rulo, who accepts his fate with something amounting to resignation, Sosa simmers with a barely concealed rage at his current situation. Sosa's rage reflects the rage of the Argentine middle classes in the wake of the economic crisis that engulfed the country; it is a rage that is noticeably absent from *Mundo grúa*. Both *Mundo grúa* and *Carancho* are connected by the central idea of one man attempting to survive in a society that is fundamentally structured to make survival difficult, yet their protagonists differ significantly in how they respond to their circumstances. The difference between the two films is, at least partially, a result of the different situation in which Argentines found themselves in 1999 and 2010.

Both the fact that Sosa is relegated to, essentially, paralegal functions at The Foundation and his eventual explosion of rage serve as important metaphors for the plight of, and reaction by, middle-class Argentines in the aftermath of the 2001 crash. Argentina's sizable middle class has, for virtually the entirety of the country's history, served an important role in the construction of national identity: its very existence was the thing that made Argentina different from the rest of Latin America, the thing which connected the country to the European roots of many of its citizens. Where the working class (represented by Rulo) was most affected by the economic policies of the late 1990s, it was the middle class which was perhaps hardest hit by the events surrounding December 2001. Their response to these events has been described as "unexpected" (Onuch, 2014, p. 89); where protests against the government's economic policies had, up to that point, been led primarily by trade unions and *piqueteros* (picketers usually aligned to a specific political party), the involvement of large numbers of middle-class citizens in the protests turned those protests into the *cacerolazo* for which the crisis is primarily remembered. This massive mobilization led to a kind of regime change, with the famous image of newly resigned president Fernando de la Rúa leaving the Casa Rosada via helicopter. *Carancho*'s narrative, however, questions just how lasting or effective that impact really was. Sociologist Heike Schaumberg argues that talk of Argentina having emerged from its crisis is premature, and refers to Argentina's current situation as a "crisis intermezzo," explaining that "while its political and economic dynamics are different to the era prior to the 2001 uprising, it is nevertheless circumscribed by the evolving global crisis" (2014, p. 144). The difficulties and challenges faced by *Carancho*'s protagonists present this very argument in cinematic form. By featuring a lawyer and a nurse, two quasi middle-class protagonists who personify both the frustrations of the middle class during the crisis and their subsequent impoverishment in postcrisis Argentina, the film highlights the fact that for many people (and especially those from the middle class, a background from which Trapero himself emerged) circumstances have not improved.

Margani versus Darín

The difference between Sosa and Rulo is further emphasized by the actors who play them. Where Rulo is played by a nonprofessional actor who is, for all intents and purposes, playing himself, Sosa is portrayed by Ricardo Darín, perhaps the most popular Argentine actor of the twenty-first century. Although Luis Margani continued his acting career after *Mundo grúa*'s success, when the film was first released he was a complete unknown, both within Argentina and internationally. Darín, conversely, is a highly prolific professional actor who, by the time he featured in *Carancho*, was not only extremely well known domestically but also, due to his starring roles in internationally popular films such as *Nueve reinas/Nine Queens* (2000) and (especially) *El secreto de sus ojos*, as well known an actor internationally as Argentina has produced in several decades. This difference is an important one, since both films manipulate the stature (or lack thereof) of their main actors. Rulo is played by an actor that the audience has absolutely no familiarity with. As such, the audience has no expectation of what could or should happen in the story, and, perhaps more importantly, Rulo is able to fully embody the social type (or types)—down-and-out laborer, middle-aged single father—that he is playing on-screen. By casting Darín to play Sosa, however, Trapero is tapping into the audience's preconceived ideas of not only what kind of characters Darín typically plays—he has been described as the screen embodiment of the "middle-class Argentine everyman" (Zamostny, 2015, p. 146)—but also the kinds of films in which he typically stars. This brings to mind Richard Dyer's concept of "star theory," in that the audience approaches Darín's films with a certain "foreknowledge" based upon, amongst other things, their preconceived expectations of the actor (1999, pp. 107–9). As a kind of surrogate for the average Argentine, then, Darín-as-Sosa's increasingly violent response to his circumstances suggests that the rage his character feels is the reflection of an anger that pervades broad swathes of Argentine society.

This contrasts drastically with Luis Margani's portrayal of Rulo, a character who seems virtually incapable of committing a violent act. Indeed, even after being fired from his crane job—the only point in the film when he loses his temper—he never resorts to any sort of physical violence. This is as much a reflection of the actor playing him as it is the character. The differences between Margani and Darín, as actors and public figures, are precisely what allows each man to accurately depict the specific social type their respective characters are supposed to signify. Although their characters represent different social and economic strata, Rulo and Sosa find themselves in fairly similar circumstances to one another. Their individual responses to those circumstances are reinforced, at least somewhat, by the actors who play them. Although social types often positively represent society's dominant values, occasionally "there may also be other types that express discontent with or rejection of dominant values" (Dyer, 1999, p. 52). Both Rulo and Sosa belong to social types which are discontented with society's dominant values. Rulo, upon his forced displacement to Patagonia, finds himself isolated even if, as demonstrated by his sitting in on the meeting, the other workers in the labor camp accept him as a comrade. As a member of the working class who is so desperate for work that he is willing to travel hundreds of kilometers in search of a stable income he should, ostensibly, be invested in ensuring the laborers receive proper treatment. But he is not, instead feeling so profound a sense of disconnect that he decides to quit the job and return home.

The conversation he has with a friend as he is about to leave Patagonia underscores just how alienated Rulo feels from his own circumstance. After reminiscing about his days as a musician he laments his current state of affairs, telling his friend,

> ahora con el quilombo que tenemos del laburo y todo esto, ya prácticamente ni me acuerdo de estas cosas, viste. No estoy con el ánimo de andar contando estas cosas que pasaron . . . como está la cosa uno anda bajoneado. Te digo la verdad, no estoy con esa. . . . Tipo, me gusta joder, me gusta divertir, y con estos quilombos ¿qué voy a andar bien?
>
> [Now with the disaster we've got with work and all that, I almost can't remember those things, you know? I don't really want to go around talking about those things that happened . . . the way things are now it brings you down. I'll tell you the truth, I've not got that. . . . Like, I like to party, I like to have fun, and with all this crap how can I be happy?]

These are virtually the last words Rulo says in the film, and they represent the moment he finally seems to crack, the moment when his sense of alienation gets the better of him. His words are doubly moving because we are aware that Margani is very likely reminiscing about a moment from his own actual lived experience, and the feelings of frustration he expresses are almost certainly not confined to the "Rulo" character he is playing on film. Writing about the particular quality the (non-)actor brings to *Mundo grúa*, Aguilar states, "Margani carries on his face the traces of the labor—that is, as we have analyzed, the promise of a narrative . . . this use [of the face] establishes a documentary connection with the real" (2008b, p. 221). Whatever Margani's face does convey, the thing it pointedly does *not* carry with it is any sort of conditioned response on the part of the audience. In *Carancho* Darín, the megastar, portrays Sosa as alienated, his goals and norms (which, due to Darín's fame and past roles, the audience understands as being fundamentally middle class) contrasting with those of the people (El Perro and The Foundation) who exert control over him. Conversely, Margani's anonymousness further heightens the sense of alienation that Rulo both feels and projects.

Response to Violence

The differences between *Mundo grúa* and *Carancho* stretch beyond the popularity (or lack thereof) of each film's primary actor. Indeed, although the two characters share certain similarities, they differ significantly in how they each respond to the many challenges with which they are confronted. Their responses are, perhaps, based on their individual characters, but they are also highly conditioned by the societies in which they live. Although both films take place, primarily, amongst the working class and lower middle class in the vast urban sprawl of Greater Buenos Aires, Sosa's experience is so drastically different from Rulo's as to be practically unrecognizable. It would not be accurate to claim that the difference between *Mundo grúa* and *Carancho* is the difference between a peaceful society and a violent one. Rather, *Carancho* is a much angrier film. None of Trapero's films to that point are so filled with rage (to borrow an important word from Arendt's book) against both the systemic violence already examined in *Mundo grúa* and the more direct physical violence which emerged in the postcrisis years. Whereas most of Trapero's films prior to *Carancho* address violence in relatively subtle ways, *Carancho* is, first and foremost, a violent film, and must be understood as such. Although couched in the terms of a relatively traditional narrative structure, the film's subject matter is, ultimately, violence. The film includes straightforward examples of the rationally irrational violence which Arendt claims is inspired by moments of rage; but it also, and much more disturbingly, includes numerous representations of a sort of violence which might be considered to be the product of the Žižekian concept of objective violence. *Carancho* is set in an objectively violent society, one that seems to cater to the corrupt and leaves the majority of its members feeling entirely powerless. The oppressiveness of this type of society is what leads characters to sacrifice their own bodies (and, in some cases, their lives) in an attempt to feel as if they are able to exert some modicum of control.

Of Trapero's first four films, *El bonaerense* is perhaps the most graphically violent, in that we see a chaotic gun battle between the police and a group of (mostly) unseen criminals and, toward the end of the film, a character is murdered. However, there are no acts of physical violence in Trapero's first film. *Mundo grúa*'s various characters may struggle through life but it is a struggle that is, apparently, free from the risk of physical attack or assault. There is, however, a constant tension that emerges almost from the moment the film begins. The violence Rulo experiences is the type of violence termed "symbolic violence" by Pierre Bourdieu: "a gentle violence, imperceptible and invisible even to its victims, exerted for the most part through the purely symbolic channels of communication and cognition ... recognition, or even feeling" (2001, p. 2). This violence is so subtle that its manifestation is found not in direct confrontation, as we see in Trapero's later works, but rather through the hint of a possibility. As much of the film takes place on construction sites, and Rulo is in constant interaction with heavy machinery, the film simmers with the threat of an industrial accident, the sort of unexpected eruption of violence that cannot be accounted for. It is, perhaps, significant that the possibility of violence present in *Mundo grúa* is not a violence that emerges due to strained interpersonal relationships, as we see in *Carancho*, but rather a violence that exists simply as a result of Rulo's insecure employment situation; as if Trapero is emphasizing the precarious existence of the Argentine working class, at risk of losing their jobs at any moment, and at risk of losing much more while on the job.

This contrasts with the world presented in Trapero's subsequent films significantly. Indeed, physical violence has become a fairly consistent motif throughout much of Trapero's latter works. *Leonera*, made in 2008, serves as a sort of point of departure, in that it includes more representations of graphic violence than any of his previous works. It is with *Carancho*, however, that Trapero's films take a new direction, one in which physical violence is not hinted at but, rather, depicted with excruciating persistence. Where the camera looks away at the moment of acute trauma in a film like *Nacido y Criado*, in *Carancho* the gaze is unflinching, forcing the viewer to experience the horrific events vicariously along with the characters themselves. No scene is so traumatic as the moment when the audience is shown the planning, execution, and aftermath of one of Sosa's insurance fraud cons. Trapero himself has called this scene "the heart of the film" (Interview with Pablo Trapero). Indeed, from the perspective of understanding the pervasive and devastating effects of violence, it is perhaps the most important moment in the film. Although the scene is somewhat confusing at the start, it quickly becomes apparent that Sosa and his friend Vega are planning to run an insurance scam by first injecting Vega with anesthetizers, breaking his leg, and then walking in front of a moving vehicle (driven by an accomplice). In a moment that might feel more appropriate to one of the previously examined "torture porn" films, we watch as Sosa injects his friend Vega with drugs, Vega props his leg up, and Sosa then smashes a 9-kilogram sledgehammer down onto his friend's tibia (Figure 1.6). Vega's screams of agony, which Sosa quickly attempts to muffle so as not to alert any passers-by, suggest the drugs did not have the intended effect. A violent scene becomes even more traumatic when, moments later, Vega stumbles out onto the road and, as planned, a car slams into him, sending him flying into the street.

The scene is presented frankly and without any suggestion of moral judgment—shot in one three-minute-long continuous take, the camera never wavers from the action, there is no non-diegetic music that might imply a specific emotion, merely a banal conversation between the two men followed by Vega's screams—and it is incredibly affecting, capable of drawing a physical reaction from the viewer. Trapero's use of the long take is fundamental to the scene's intensity. The aesthetic he creates is not one of beautiful violence but, rather, one that emphasizes just how brutal violence actually is. He does so by making no attempt at all to stylize the violence in the scene, by refusing to allow the viewer to look away, and by forcing the viewer to act as a real-time witness. The sequence of violent actions occurs so quickly, one after the other, that the psychological texture created by the film is one of vulnerability.

Figure 1.6 *Carancho* (2010). The moment Sosa breaks Vega's leg demonstrates the extent to which objective violence has come to define *Carancho*'s society.

In this way, the viewer is no different from the characters themselves. There is nowhere to escape—even looking away from the screen at the moment Sosa breaks Vega's leg will not provide solace from Vega's screams. It is this reality, the inescapable violence in which these characters live, that leads them to attempt their scheme in the first place. Throughout the entirety of *Carancho*, any attempt by the film's protagonists to exert agency in their own lives is thwarted. The characters themselves, however, continue fighting against this situation until their literal dying moments, even if they themselves know that they are bound to fail.

The con the two men are attempting to pull off will not provide them with enough money to alter their lives in any meaningful way, but it will allow them to feel like they have somehow gotten the better of a system which routinely gets the better of them. In *On Violence*, Hannah Arendt writes, "rage and violence turn irrational only when they are directed against substitutes . . . [Violence] becomes 'irrational' the moment it is 'rationalized', that is, the moment the re-action . . . turns into an action" (1970, pp. 64-6). The two men's con demonstrates both of the ways Arendt believes violence becomes irrational—the violence Sosa and Vega commit is irrational not only because it has been thought through and planned out in a rational way but also because it has been committed against a substitute (in this case themselves) rather than the actual agents responsible for their repression. The two men believe that they have everything under control—they need money, after all, and what easier way to get it than by using Sosa's law skills and Vega's willingness to sacrifice his own body? Žižek's invisible objective violence has become so ingrained in the two characters' psyches that they fail to envision anything going wrong. The absolute irrationality of their actions, however, becomes readily apparent (to Sosa, at least) when, while on his way to hospital, Vega suffers a heart attack and dies. What was meant to be a quick and easy scam to earn a bit of money turns into an unmitigated disaster, and highlights how completely powerless Sosa and people like him really are in the face of objective violence. What makes this scene so disturbing is not merely the unrelenting sequence of violent actions presented, but the motivation behind those acts. The oppressive system in which all of the film's characters exist, and from which they are unable to escape, has caused them to become so desperate that they believe their only option is to sacrifice their own well-being. Even the acts of subjective violence—the physical violence shown when Sosa breaks Vega's leg, or when Vega allows himself to be hit by the car—are merely manifestations of the broader violence which permeates society. The link between poverty and violence is undeniable, and Trapero seems to be making an explicit point— the increase in both poverty and violence is having (or, perhaps, has had) a devastating effect on Argentine society. This is most discernible by the fact that almost every single act of violence or immorality found in *Carancho* is committed by someone who, prior to the crisis, would have been considered a member of that central pillar of *argentinidad* that is (or, perhaps, was) the middle class.

Carancho, then, is consistent within a pattern that has emerged amongst Argentine filmmakers of Trapero's generation, which Ignacio López-Vicuña describes as,

> [films] structured around both narrative inevitability and an overarching sense of being trapped in a situation with no solution. By showing the ways in which [characters] are cornered, [these] films expose the injustice of the neoliberal model's consequences for Argentina, displaying at the same time an ethics of defiance against the current order and irreverence towards nation discourse, which has lost credibility as more people are pushed to the margins. (2010, pp. 146–7)

Where Sosa and Rulo fundamentally differ is in their responses to being pushed to the margins. Rulo, perhaps because he still believes in the "upward and onward" ideal of Argentine society, seems to accept his continual marginalization with a certain amount of resignation. A decade later—a decade during which whatever remained of the Argentine ideal was wholly stripped away through a series of social and economic crises—Sosa reacts violently against those he believes to be his oppressors. In doing so, he embodies the rage of the former middle class, the same middle class that feels emboldened to take to the streets and protest government incompetence and corruption through the numerous *cacerolazos* that have occurred since the December 2001 protests that received so much coverage. This is not something unique to Trapero's oeuvre. Carolina Rocha contends that many of the so-called New Argentine filmmakers have examined how "violence is largely perpetrated to eliminate those who stand for moral values and respect for the law" (2010, p. 94). *Carancho* would, at first, seem to be an exception to this; although not completely innocent, Sosa's quest for redemption seems legitimate, and when he finally does explode in anger the violence is committed against his corrupt, immoral bosses. At least in one sense, then, morality and respect for law appear to triumph. The film's final moments, however, imply that Sosa's attempt at resistance, his moral stand, is ultimately for naught. Sosa's victory over El Perro is but a small, momentary mercy. Much like the look of despair etched on Rulo's face as he makes his way back to Buenos Aires at the end of *Mundo grúa*, the car accident that ultimately kills Sosa must be read as a message that resistance is futile in the face of such a violent, corrupt society.

2

Repression, Ideology, and the Manipulation of Power

Moving beyond a highly focused examination of violence, the two films analyzed in this chapter incorporate another concept that is central to Trapero's work: power. Violence and power are certainly related and any examination of objective violence must, to an extent, also be an examination of power, as well. The two films studied in this chapter—*El bonaerense* (2002) and *Elefante blanco* (2012)—focus on individuals who are, to a greater or lesser degree, within the power structure itself. The films take on the Buenos Aires Provincial police force and the Catholic Church, respectively, each examining an institution that is fundamental in the creation of what Althusser calls the State Apparatus. Where resistance was a theme which connected Rulo and Sosa, the two films examined in this section offer two very different protagonists, with two very different goals, their only connection being their positions within the State Apparatus.

Theories of Power

While violence is the concept that unites Trapero's corpus, it is power that serves as the central theme of the two films analyzed in this chapter. Similar to violence, power can be understood in many different ways, some of which are far more nuanced than others. Max Weber writes, "we define power as a person's or group's chance to enforce their own will through an action by a *Gemeinschaft* (community), even against the resistance of others involved" (2015, p. 41). Weber explains that power arises in various ways, ranging from economic to legal to social factors, and finds that it is honor, rather than power, that determines the social order. *Stände*—status groups or, in their most extreme form, castes—are what emerge as a result of this social order. The creation of *Stände* is closely associated with both power and honor, for "stratification by *Stände* goes hand in hand with a monopolization of ideal and material goods or opportunities" (2015, p. 52). Power, then, can be understood as a building block of the social order in which we live.

Continuing this basic logic, Hannah Arendt proposes a fairly straightforward definition of power, stating, "[power] corresponds to the human ability not just to act but to act in concert. Power is never the property of an individual; it belongs to a group and remains in existence only so long as the group keeps together" (1970, p. 44). Although she does differentiate between the two, Arendt links power closely to violence—creating what Paul Ricoeur calls the "conceptual pair power-violence" (2010, p. 19). This "power-violence" is particularly interesting in the context of *El bonaerense* and *Elefante blanco*, for both films focus on power structures—the State, the police, the Catholic Church—and in both instances those power structures make fairly generous use of violence. Critically, however, Arendt emphasizes that power and violence can, and indeed do, exist independently of each other. The example Arendt uses to make her point is a particularly relevant one when considering the two films examined in this chapter. Arendt writes, "the superiority of the government has always been absolute; but this superiority lasts only as long as the power structure of the government is intact—that is, as long as commands are obeyed and the army or police forces are prepared to use their weapons" (1970, pp. 47–8).

Steven Lukes expands on Arendt's approach, introducing three "dimensions" of power. The first two dimensions focus on power's influence over decision-making and what Lukes calls "nondecision-making," that is "the ways in which decisions are prevented from being taken" (2005, p. 25). It is Lukes's three-dimensional view of power, however, that provides the most pertinent understanding of the concept in the context of this study. Lukes summarizes this view of power by stating, "A may exercise power over B by getting him to do what he does not want to do, but he also exercises power over him by influencing, shaping, or determining his very wants" (2005, p. 27). This view of power is much broader than the first two views of power Lukes proposes, and has less to do with personal interaction than with the way societies are established and maintained, as Lukes explains: "the radical [view of power]

... maintains that people's wants may themselves be a product of a system which works against their interests" (2005, p. 38). As with Williams who, in his essay from *Keywords*, provides various different definitions for the concept of violence, in *Power* Lukes (in opposition to the work of Bachrach and Baratz, whom Lukes cites extensively) differentiates between several of the different words that can be, and often are, associated with power. Where Bachrach and Baratz (and, by extension, others) utilize the single term "power," Lukes breaks down the general phrase into five separate concepts: "[the] typology of 'power' ... embraces coercion, influence, authority, force and manipulation" (2005, p. 21). Although these definitions refer primarily to one- and two-dimensional views of power, the terminology links Lukes's study of power with Althusser's study of ideology and Žižek's study of objective violence.

Because they both center on questions of ideology, parallels can be drawn between Lukes's three-dimensional, radical view of power and the Žižekian concept of objective violence. The two concepts overlap in their consideration of the importance of personal agency in creating, maintaining, and exerting violence and power. Lukes acknowledges that one of the difficulties with the three-dimensional view of power is how to distinguish between outcomes resulting from the exercising of power (individual agency) and those that are the result of "structural determinism." Ultimately, he arrives at the conclusion that "[t]o use the vocabulary of power in the context of social relationships is to speak of human agents ... [W]ithin a system characterized by total structural determinism, there would be no place for power" (2005, pp. 56–7).

The echoes of this can be seen in Žižek's writing, especially in the context of objective violence. Although Žižek certainly does place an emphasis on the very "structural determinism" that Lukes minimizes the importance of, he also acknowledges that the denial of agency is one of the key factors that allows objective violence to continue unchecked. Writing about culpability with regard to different forms of violence, Žižek states,

> Responsibility for communist crimes is easy to allocate: we are dealing with subjective evil, with agents who did wrong.... But when one draws attention to the millions who died as a result of capitalist globalization, from the tragedy of Mexico in the sixteenth century through to the Belgian Congo holocaust a century ago, responsibility is largely denied. All this seems just to have happened as the result of an "objective" process, which nobody planned and executed. (2009, p. 12)

Žižek contends that while those who propagate objective violence, those who allow the violent status quo to remain, might claim that it is simply the result of "structural determination" (that is, a by-product of social structure), in fact objective violence must be considered as an example of (three-dimensional) power being exercised. Indeed, the manner in which the objective violence of contemporary society is, generally, accepted as normal might be considered the most prevalent example of Lukes's radical view of power, something Lukes himself hints at when he writes,

> Is it not the supreme and most insidious exercise of power to prevent people . . . from having grievances by shaping their perceptions, cognitions and preferences in such a way that they accept their role in the existing order of things, either because they can see or imagine no alternative to it, or because they see it as natural and unchangeable, or because they value it as divinely ordained and beneficial? (2005, p. 28)

This paragraph, in particular, calls to mind the Repressive and Ideological State Apparatuses of Althusser's "Ideology and Ideological State Apparatuses."

Contrasting Ideological State Apparatuses (ISAs) with the (Repressive) State Apparatus (RSA), Althusser differentiates between the diverse kinds of apparatuses used by the State in order to maintain control. Althusser claims that the State Apparatus, to which he adds "(Repressive)" in order both to imply the violence associated with this concept and to emphasize its difference from the ISAs, is made up of all the different official forms of visible State control—"the Government, the Administration, the Army, the Police, the Courts, the Prisons, etc." (1971, p. 96). Althusser finds that the State "functions by violence," even if that violence is nonphysical, as in the case of administrative repression (1971, p. 96).

ISAs, on the other hand, are pluriform, and consist of institutions that are more difficult to singularly identify, institutions such as religion, family, media, the arts, sport; in short, the Ideological State Apparatuses are made up of all the institutions that make up culture and society. Some of those institutions are highly personal—a State's population can practice any number of diverse religions, and even amongst members of the same faith no two individuals will engage with that religion in the same way. Other ISAs, such as the mass media, are less personal, and are created to engage with the maximum number of people possible. Where the State, in its repressive guise, functions by violence, the unifying principle for all ISAs, whatever their other differences, is that they function by means of ideology (1971, p. 97). Trapero's work mediates the Repressive State Apparatus in various ways, with significant emphasis placed on the dictatorship and, as is the case for both *El bonaerense* and *Elefante blanco*, the police force. Alternatively, the director's examination of Ideological State Apparatuses centers heavily on two ISAs in particular: the family (the foundation upon which Trapero's cinema is built) and the Catholic Church, the most important State Apparatus (of either category) in *Elefante blanco*.

El bonaerense

El bonaerense tells the story of Zapa (Jorge Román), an unemployed locksmith living in a small rural town who, much like Rulo in *Mundo grúa*, seems completely devoid of any inkling of street-smarts. As the film begins, Zapa is recruited by his boss Polaco (Hugo Anganuzzi), seemingly unwittingly, to crack the safe of a shop that Polaco and his accomplices are robbing. Though successful in this, Zapa's naiveté is put on display when, the next day, the police arrest him due to the fact he is the only person in town capable of cracking the safe and all his accomplices have disappeared. His uncle, a high-ranking official in the Buenos Aires Provincial police force, arranges for Zapa to join the police, despite lacking both the desire and the skills necessary to be a capable officer. (The film's title is a play on both the demonym for someone from Buenos Aires province and the informal name for the "*Policía de la Provincia de Buenos Aires*," known in Argentina as *la Bonaerense*.) Zapa leaves his hometown and heads to the suburban outskirts of Buenos Aires, where he enrols in the police academy and attempts to acclimatize to life in the big city. While still a cadet he begins an affair with Mabel (Mimí Ardú), a female officer teaching at the academy. As part of his practical experience training, Zapa is assigned to a small station in the neighborhood of La Matanza, where his primary duty consists of cleaning up after the other officers and being generally ignored. Before long, however, his lock-picking ability earns him the attention of Gallo (Darío Levy), one of the station's more experienced officers. Gallo—bald, a thick moustache covering his upper lip, his voice rarely descending below a yell—is the opposite of Zapa in almost every respect, embodying the stereotype of police machismo and violent authority to which Zapa so noticeably does not conform. (It is surely not a coincidence that the word *gallo* carries both the literal meaning of rooster and the slang meaning of a big, tough man.) The film's narrative alternates between Zapa's experiences in the academy, where he is a poor student and seems incapable of grasping even the most rudimentary demands of police work, and his experiences in the station, an environment in which his training is of so little practical use that his deficiencies go more or less unnoticed. Despite Zapa's obvious flaws as a would-be police officer, under Gallo's guidance he comes to be accepted amongst his peers and, when Gallo takes over command at the station, Zapa assumes a second-in-command role. As Gallo's most-trusted lieutenant, Zapa oversees the widespread extortion racket that Gallo has set up throughout the precinct, much to the disgust of Mabel, who eventually breaks off their affair. Despite his frustration at this rejection, Zapa seems comfortable with the modicum of power he has acquired; this situation changes, however, when Polaco suddenly appears in La Matanza and attempts to recruit Zapa for a heist he is planning. While initially agreeing to the job, Zapa in fact approaches Gallo, who devises a plan to double-cross Polaco. During the heist Gallo kills Polaco, much to Zapa's surprise, and then shoots Zapa in the leg, justifying the assault by claiming it will make the killing look like self-defense. Zapa is horrified by this and, despite receiving a commendation for bravery, requests a transfer. The film ends with Zapa returning to his hometown having been promoted to local police chief.

With its combination of *Nuevo Cine Argentino* styling and social and political critique, *El bonaerense* has proven to be particularly fertile ground for film studies analysis, and is perhaps Trapero's most closely analyzed film. Joanna Page and Jens Andermann both dedicate significant portions of their respective surveys of Argentine film to the work, while Gonzalo Aguilar has published a booklet-length Spanish-language critical study of the film. Finally, and most pertinently for this study, James Scorer has written a wonderful chapter on the film for the *New Trends in Argentine and Brazilian Cinema* collection edited by Cacilda Rêgo and Carolina Rocha. Scorer's analysis of the film touches on many of the same concepts as found in this chapter, and there is some overlap between the two analyses. This work differentiates itself from Scorer's study, however, with its specific focus on power and how it is mediated throughout the film.

El Conurbano

Although they share the same name, the distinction between the Autonomous City of Buenos Aires, Argentina's capital and largest city, and the province of Buenos Aires, a separate governmental entity which includes cities such as Quilmes, La Plata, and Bahía Blanca and which is almost twice as large as neighboring Uruguay, is an important one. An estimated 10 million of the roughly 13 million people who live in Greater Buenos Aires (an area that includes both the city and its provincial outskirts) live in the province, making it one of the largest population centers in South America. *El bonaerense* takes place in Buenos Aires province; more specifically it is set in the *conurbano* (conurbation), the common name for those provincial regions that border the city of Buenos Aires and are home to the large majority of the province's population. The *conurbano* is a fundamental part of the Buenos Aires megalopolis, yet it is also governmentally distinct, and both culturally and geographically isolated—to the north and west, the boundary between the city and the province is delineated by the Avenida General Paz freeway (a road so wide that it is clearly identifiable in satellite images of the region), while the Rio de la Plata and the Matanza-Riachuelo River delimit the city to the east and south, respectively. Conversely, there are no obvious distinctions that might signal the *conurbano*'s borders (whether cultural or geographical) with the interior of the country; rather the *conurbano* seems to simply dissolve into the *pampa húmeda* of Buenos Aires province. Within Argentina, therefore, the *conurbano* can be understood as a sort of liminal space, excluded from both the romantic sophistication of the city of Buenos Aires, from which it is conspicuously divided, and also the folkloric nobility of the Argentine pampa, into which it bleeds out.

Vast numbers of people live in the various zones of the *conurbano* and work in the city, yet the distinction between those who live in the province and those who live in the city is so marked as for there to exist two different demonymic adjectives in Spanish: a resident of the city of Buenos Aires is referred to as a *porteño/a*, in reference to the city's port, while residents of the province are referred to as *bonaerenses*. As José Natanson explains it,

> Aunque alberga a casi un cuarto de la población nacional y condensa exacerbados los tres hechos malditos de la clase media argentina (pobreza, inseguridad y peronismo), el Gran Buenos Aires carece de una identidad

propia.... Con algunas contadísimas excepciones ... el conurbano no se recorta como una geografía con entidad propia sino apenas como una extensión aspiracional de la capital. (*Le Monde diplomatique*, 2015)

[Although it is home to almost a quarter of the national population and it condenses in exacerbated form the three cursed realities of the Argentine middle class (poverty, insecurity, and Peronism), Greater Buenos Aires lacks its own identity.... With only a very few exceptions ... the *conurbano* does not stand out as a geography with its own identity, but rather as a mere aspirational extension of the capital.]

This representation of the *conurbano* as a nowhere place is readily apparent in *El bonaerense*. Although it is made clear that the police academy where Zapa trains is located in the *partido* (county) of La Matanza (not coincidentally, Trapero is from the same part of the *conurbano*, having been raised in the San Justo neighborhood of La Matanza partido), the majority of the film is set in an unidentified suburban space, with much of the narrative centering on a small police outpost located next to a highway overpass (Figure 2.1). Often presented in wide-establishing shots, the office is the only point of geographical reference to which the film consistently returns. The *conurbano* as presented in *El bonaerense* is so lacking in distinguishing landmarks or geographical identifiers that it could take place in virtually any suburban

Figure 2.1 *El bonaerense* (2002). The focus on the nondescript police station reinforces the *conurbano* as nowhere space.

outskirt of any major city anywhere in the country. That lack of a unique identity is perhaps the *conurbano*'s defining feature. Trapero has explained that he desired to make a film that examined this particular aspect of the region's (lack of) identity:

> Ese era el proyecto original: contar la vida del conurbano a través de alguien que iba y venía entre la provincia y la capital. . . . Entonces pensé: ¿qué es tristemente lo más simbólico de la provincia y el conurbano? La policía. (Aguilar, 2008a, p. 62)

> [That was the original project: tell the story of the *conurbano* through someone who came and went between the province and the capital. . . . So I thought: what is, sadly, most symbolic of the province and the *conurbano*? The police.]

Indeed, in place of a particular cultural movement or overwhelming geographical landmark, over the course of the past twenty years the *conurbano* has come to be defined, as much as anything, by its police force.

"*La Bonaerense*"

The reason the police are so symbolic of the *conurbano* is due to the fact that the Buenos Aires province, and the *conurbano* in particular, has one of the highest crime rates in the country. Since the 1990s the rise of crime and insecurity that Argentina has experienced generally has been perhaps most keenly felt in the province, as explained by Mercedes S. Hinton who states that while the heightened crime rate in the city of Buenos Aires "shook most people to the core," the "lawlessness was far worse . . . in the *conurbano*" (2006, p. 20). Perhaps the most damning aspect of the circumstance in which the province found itself was the fact that the Provincial police force, rather than combating crime and reassuring the public, seemed to be contributing to the problem: "[far] from fulfilling their roles in a democracy, namely to provide assistance and psychological reassurance, to deter crime, and to give auxiliary support to the rest of the judicial system, the [Provincial] police struggled on each count, actually exacerbating the perception as well as the reality of public insecurity" (Hinton, 2006, p. 22). Trapero's film accurately portrays not only the flawed chain of command that existed within the organization but also the fundamentally corrupt culture of the force at the time of the film's production and release. Such was the corruption of the Provincial police in the late 1990s and early 2000s that Marieke Denissen describes the police force as being "a mafia that [functioned] as part of the state" (2008, p. 79). Despite attempts at restructuring, the late 1990s and early 2000s were a particularly contentious time for the Provincial police, with police violence and corruption reaching levels not seen since the final years of the *Proceso* dictatorship. By focusing on the Buenos Aires Provincial police, then, Trapero's film carries added significance for domestic viewers, a significance that might be lost to external audiences.

The fact that *El bonaerense*, a film which casts a damningly critical eye over the second-largest police force in Argentina, was filmed as the country itself was crumbling both economically and (for a brief moment) socially is significant. In many ways, the economic corruption and financial mismanagement in the government as a whole that was exposed by the crisis echoed the maladministration that had been rampant throughout the Provincial police force for years. Indeed, the police force and the crisis itself are connected through the person of Eduardo Duhalde, the man appointed president of Argentina in January 2002. In 1997 it was Duhalde who, as governor of the Buenos Aires province, declared that the Provincial police were "la mejor policía del mundo" ("the best police force in the world"). This comment was met with widespread derision, especially in light of the fact that Argentine police, generally, have a deep-seated reputation as being "*gatillo fácil*"—trigger happy—and the police forces of the Buenos Aires province, in particular, have the country's highest rate of police violence per capita (Denissen, 2008, p. 64). Both Duhalde and Carlos Ruckauf, the man who succeeded him as the Buenos Aires Provincial governor, preferred what Denissen refers to as a *mano dura* (heavy-handed) approach to policing. Because of this, the reforms that began in 1997 had little actual effect on police violence. By 2001, then, whatever attempts at reforming the Provincial police that had been undertaken had essentially failed, with the result that, from an organizational point of view, the force was in as bad a shape as it ever had been.

This fact reflected, to a certain extent, the state of the government itself. Indeed, the Argentine government and the country's police have maintained a complicated, intertwined relationship since at least 1880, when the ministry of the interior assumed control over the Buenos Aires police force (Hinton, 2006, p. 30). The close association between police and government was perhaps most notable during the *Proceso* dictatorship, a period when the Argentine Army and the various paramilitary organizations backed by the country's armed forces (most significantly the *"Triple A"*—the *Alianza Anticomunista Argentina*) intensified the already brutal interrogation techniques that the police force had been using for decades. Although the most heinous crimes perpetrated by the dictatorship, such as those that took place at the *Escuela de Mecánica de la Armada*, are associated with the military, the police were nevertheless actively involved in the government's repression of the civilian population throughout the seven-year-long regime. Hinton explains that the police's role in assisting the dictatorship, while "a shameful episode whose consequences still resonate," is merely one example in the long history of influence the State has exerted over the police, stemming as far back as the creation of the force itself: "the [police] institution has in fact been manipulated politically, by both military and civilian regimes, throughout its history" (2006, p. 29).

Police Repressive State Apparatus

The government's tacit acceptance (to not say encouragement) of *gatillo fácil* tactics, both during the dictatorship and in more recent times, calls to mind Althusser's analysis of the Repressive State Apparatus. The importance the police, as a cog of the Repressive State Apparatus, place on violence is visible throughout *El bonaerense*. It is visible when the officers celebrate Christmas by gratuitously firing their weapons into the air, emptying the clips of their machine guns and pistols in a drunken revelry; and again the next morning when officers from Zapa's station, still drunk from the previous night, fight with and eventually shoot and kill a group of similarly drunken civilians. And it is visible in the shootout with unseen perpetrators in which Zapa partakes toward the end of the film, his (literally) aimless shots posing as much, if not more, of a threat to his fellow officers as anything coming from their adversaries.

These episodes demonstrate the State's relationship to violence—in "Politics as Vocation," Weber finds that "the state is the only human *Gemeinschaft* which lays claim to the monopoly of the legitimated use of physical force" (2015, p. 136). This monopoly is perhaps most visible in the various extortionate protection rackets the officers run from their small station house, hinting at the vast network of abuses of power committed by officers throughout the force across the *conurbano*. These protection rackets make visible the way in which the State monopolizes power by allowing certain crimes to occur, so long as the authority of the State is respected. James Scorer explains that this sequence in the film "[illustrates] that the police's apparent 'independence' is only possible precisely because of its fundamental tie to the state: [the police] can only act with impunity because its violence is ultimately sanctioned by the state" (2011, p. 166). When individuals attempt to resist this State-sanctioned monopoly on violence, the police resort to more visible forms of violence to ensure their position and control. And, while much of the narrative is centered on displays of police violence, in the character of Gallo the film acknowledges the important role ideological manipulation plays in maintaining State control.

The scene which best exemplifies this occurs roughly halfway through the film, and marks a turning point in the protagonist's conversion from Zapa, the civilian, to Mendoza, the police officer. Following the burnout of the previous station chief, Gallo is promoted. To mark the occasion, Gallo gives a speech to his new subordinates in which he outlines his vision for the future. The shot's mise-en-scene highlights the importance the police force places on ideological manipulation—dressed impeccably in his formal police uniform, flanked on either side by the national and provincial flags, Gallo is standing in front of a wall adorned with various police-related banners and memorabilia, the centerpiece of which is a painting of José de San Martín, the Southern Cone counterpart to Simón Bolívar and the father of the Argentine nation (Figure 2.2). All of these symbols are meant to create a feeling of righteous authority, suggesting that the police are merely carrying on the work of the nation's most revered hero. Scorer suggests, however, that the more accurate parallel would be Facundo Quiroga, or even the then-president Duhalde (2011, p. 167). Like those men, Gallo imagines himself a caudillo, an attitude that is particularly visible in the way in which he exerts power over his colleagues. Up to this point in the film, Gallo has played a relatively minor role; he is shown as an intense, dedicated cop who has enough sway within the department to ensure he can look after his fellow officers—when Zapa mentions that he has not been paid in three months it is Gallo who manages to secure the trainee an advance, just as he is able to secure Zapa a discount on the firearms he purchases after graduating from the academy. His taking over the station seems, if one were to judge Gallo's words alone, to be a good appointment. The true extent of Gallo's corruption becomes evident, however, in the very next scene.

Figure 2.2 *El bonaerense* (2002). Gallo's manipulation of national symbols serves to both legitimize his actions and condemn the culture that allowed him to obtain power.

Already profoundly ironic considering the reputation of the Provincial police, Gallo's speech is proven to be downright fraudulent when he sends Zapa and another colleague around to the various informal businesses in the area—a scrap metal yard, the transvestite prostitutes outside the *boliche*—to collect protection money. Although the people are at first hesitant to give their money to Zapa (as opposed to his colleague), the other officer explains "de ahora en adelante, Mendoza va a pasar por acá periódicamente, y tiene que arreglar con vos." ("From now on, Mendoza is going to come by every now and then and he'll settle with you.") Both the speech itself and the events which immediately follow it, however, are clear examples of how Lukes's concept of three-dimensional, radical power can be manipulated and made manifest. Although he is in fact exceedingly corrupt, Gallo presents himself as a sort of true believer in the ideals of police work, both as an officer and, especially, when he becomes station chief. What becomes clear over the course of the film, however, is the fact that Gallo is absolutely in control of his actions and surroundings at all times, and is manipulating his colleagues accordingly. In a sense, Gallo has created a sort of Weberian *Stand* within the larger police force. Weber explains that "the honor of the *Stand* is predominantly expressed by a specific lifestyle that is imposed on anyone who wants to belong to that social circle" (2015, p. 49). By ensuring that all of the officers within his *Stand* are implicated in the various extortion schemes he has set up, Gallo is able to exert considerable power over almost every other character in the narrative, for if they do not engage with this "lifestyle" they will be excluded from the *Stand*. Gallo's first speech as station chief is the moment when his strategy of ensuring radical power comes to fruition—he has maneuvered himself into a position where he is capable of controlling the thoughts and desires of those around him. This is particularly true in the case of Zapa-cum-Mendoza (as the corrupt officer refers to him), who has now become part of Gallo's inner circle, an enforcer of the police muscle that allows illegality so long as it is adequately compensated for.

Whatever authority or morality is suggested by the symbols shown during Gallo's speech is immediately undermined by Zapa's actions (under orders from Gallo) in the following scene. The portrait of General San Martín looking intently over Gallo's shoulder, however, hints at something beyond the mere corruption and disingenuousness of one individual officer, or even of the police force as a whole. Žižek writes of "the notion of the illegitimate origins of power, of the 'founding crime' on which states are based, which is why one should offer 'noble lies' to the people in the guise of heroic narratives of origin" (2009, p. 98). By connecting Gallo with San Martín—a man who is viewed as a founding father of not only Argentina but also Chile and Peru—and then immediately exposing Gallo as a fraud, the film's implications become clear: *El bonaerense* is not merely scrutinizing the actions of the contemporary police force, it is scrutinizing the very foundations, the "noble lies" upon which the nation, indeed the entire region, has been built. Trapero has said as much in interviews, explaining about his worldview:

> Perhaps this is the view of a person who was born in a country that is the product of violence. Latin America was the product of the slaughter of many people. There was one colonization, another colonization, and another . . . [Our] history is built on slaughters of different types, some very bloody, some less so, some very explicit, others less explicit, some direct, others hypocritical. (Interview with Pablo Trapero)

In a variety of ways, *El bonaerense* reflects both the institutional rot and, especially, the violent *mano dura* policing for which the Provincial police had become infamous. On an institutional level, at no point in the film are the Provincial police ever presented as anything other than entirely compromised. The two scenes analyzed in this section, however, suggest that the film's primary critique is not aimed merely at the police, but rather at the entire Repressive State Apparatus. The portrait of San Martín seen during Gallo's speech, then, becomes even more significant—by directly connecting a corrupt and violent police force to the country's most revered national hero, the film implies an historical legacy from which the systemic violence of present-day Argentina has emerged.

Zapa

It would be wrong, however, to suggest that the corruption and immorality exhibited by members of the police force is solely a by-product of what Lukes would refer to as "structural determination." Explaining the role individuals play in exerting power, Lukes writes, "to identify a given process as an 'exercise of power,' rather than as a case of structural determination, is to assume that it is *in the exerciser's or exercisers' power* to act differently" (2005, p. 57). From Zapa's politically connected uncle to the random, unjustified acts of violence committed by various officers throughout the film, the Provincial police are shown generally to be corrupt at every level. However, there are scattered throughout the film moments where individual members of the police force act in a lawful or moral way—Zapa's arrest at the start of the film is entirely justified, while Mabel's eventual rejection of Zapa is caused both by her personal dislike for Gallo and her ethical stance against the style of policing he represents. These actions, particularly on the part of Mabel, show that while corruption and systemic violence may be ingrained in the structure of the Provincial police force, individuals within that structure *are* capable of acting independently. What we see in *El bonaerense*, then, is not merely a systemically violent system but also people, influenced by that corrupt system, exercising power in such a way that the violence is propagated. By following Zapa's evolution from small-time burglar to Officer Mendoza of the Buenos Aires Provincial police force, the film presents a study of how one person is not only manipulated by the power structure above him but also, in turn, exercises power over others and ensures the perpetuation of a repressive system.

Zapa's rise through the police ranks is indicative of a larger societal issue that is highlighted consistently throughout Argentine cinema of the last two decades—the ineptitude and corruption of the State both during the Menem administration and in the aftermath of the collapse. Trapero has admitted that this was a fundamental aspect of the narrative, while also suggesting that Zapa's innocence at the beginning of the film is, in fact, a ruse—"at the beginning you feel sorry for Zapa, coming from the countryside, an innocent. But he's not like that; he's a dangerous person, he's the kind of person I'm afraid of in life, always giving the impression that [he is] suffering, but actually self-indulgent" (Matheou, 2010, p. 277). A certain cognitive dissonance emerges when the realization is made that, however untrustworthy or dangerous Zapa may be, he fits comfortably into the world of the police. The film functions, then, as a sort of twist on the traditional cop drama where a dirty cop with a good reputation gradually has his web of lies detangled in a highly public manner (*a la* Abel Ferrara's *Bad Lieutenant* (1992) or Antoine Fuqua's *Training Day* (2001)—a film to which Trapero's film was compared in the *New York Times*). Rather, a known criminal is gradually accepted into the police force, his unlawful past, dangerous nature, and illegal actions serving not to hasten his demise but to encourage his acceptance. Horacio González describes this process as "la historia de un hombre que es tomado por un aparato pedagógico machacador y es devuelto herido a la comunidad, comunidad que vive de una falsa ilusión de unidad" ("the story of a man who is taken in by a grinding pedagogic apparatus and returned, injured, to the community, a community which lives due to a false illusion of unity") (González, 2003).

Much like Luis Margani, his counterpart from *Mundo grúa*, Jorge Román, the actor who portrays Zapa, was a relative unknown when *El bonaerense* was released, a fact which allows the audience to completely invest themselves in the character. With his dark complexion, hangdog face, and subdued voice, Zapa is entirely unremarkable. Despite his artless exterior, however, Zapa is surprisingly multifaceted, as complex a character as any to be found in Trapero's corpus. A naïve, even incompetent, petty thief when first introduced, he gradually transforms into an equally incompetent corrupt police officer, albeit one who is highly dangerous. Although he is hardly capable of protecting himself, his relationship with Gallo places him in a situation where he is able to exert a certain amount of authority. The film chronicles both Zapa's physical movements—from a small, rural town in the vast western expanse of Buenos Aires province to La Matanza, a district that abuts the border between the province and the federal district of the city of Buenos Aires—as well as the changes he undergoes as he delves further and further into the life of a police officer in the sprawling urban space of Greater Buenos Aires. It is not entirely accurate to describe Zapa's evolution as a descent into depravity or immorality—he begins the film as a thief, after all—but the portrait Trapero creates of his subject and his surroundings is hardly a flattering one.

When Zapa first arrives in the city he is visibly shaken by what he encounters. Not only does he appear to be completely out of step with the pace of life in an urban center, but he also appears to be incredibly innocent. It is this same innocence which allows him to be so easily taken advantage of, forcing him to leave his small town in the first place. The longer Zapa remains in the city, the more comfortable he feels in his role with the police department, the less likeable a character he becomes. When the audience first encounters Zapa, he is presented as essentially harmless, his only real crime being, as with Rulo in *Mundo grúa*, a complete lack of the *viveza criolla* on which many Argentines pride themselves. It is through a series of corrupt agreements that Zapa transforms from petty thief into full-fledged police officer—his uncle arranges for his criminal charges to be dropped; although too old to enter the police academy his age is falsified by the station chief; despite still being a trainee Gallo covertly provides him with a pistol, which is the ultimate symbol of police authority (Gallo even states plainly *"un policía sin arma no es policía"* ["a cop without a gun isn't a cop"]). As if to signify his newfound ease in this new world, his name changes—rather than his nickname, Zapa, his police colleagues refer to him by his surname, Mendoza. This is, of course, to be expected in a hierarchical system such as the police force, but the change in name seems as symbolic as it is practical. It is only when interacting with his girlfriend or people from his past that the name Zapa is used. This is significant at the end of the film, when Polaco, his former accomplice, suddenly appears and attempts to both reconcile with him and present him with a job (in the criminal sense). Polaco believes he is speaking with a known quantity, Zapa the easily-taken-advantage-of thief, when in fact he is speaking with a much more sinister and untrustworthy character: Mendoza the corrupt police officer. By the time the film ends the Zapa from the start of the narrative seems to have disappeared for good, replaced by Mendoza.

Zapa-cum-Mendoza's rise through the Buenos Aires Provincial police force, a rise facilitated (if not made entirely possible) by rampant corruption, mediates not only the way in which the Žižekian concept of objective violence functions but also the way in which power, in all its manifestations, is exercised within an already corrupt structure. Zapa's quiet, reserved personality is, essentially, a tabula rasa upon which those higher up the chain of command project their demands and desires; he never does anything to stand out from his peers, and even shows himself to be fairly incompetent when it comes to the actual demands of police work, legitimate or corrupt. Yet his very compliance ingratiates him to those with a measure of power, so that he continues to move up the ranks. His is not a case of failure leading to promotion so much as it is inaction leading to promotion. As he evolves from Zapa into Mendoza, his own power (and its limits) begins to take shape. Zapa's power is comparatively primitive; it is a type of power that manifests itself in what Lukes would describe as coercion: using the "threat of deprivation," Zapa (in his role as Mendoza, corrupt police officer) is able to exert influence on others and ensures that the prostitutes and night club owners make decisions that contradict with their own interests. But his power never stretches beyond this most basic, one-dimensional state. Of course, this form of power pales in comparison to that exerted by Gallo, primarily because it lacks authority and, perhaps more importantly, it is free from manipulation. While Zapa may want for the basic abilities of a police officer, he is smart enough to realize that by acquiescing to the power of those above him, particularly Gallo, he will be accepted into the power structure itself. Once this occurs, his deficiencies as an officer are inconsequential, for he is a member of Gallo's *Stand*, and so able to exercise power over those outside of that structure.

Zapa's evolution into Mendoza is perhaps most visible in the complicated, passionate, and (at times) violent affair he maintains with Mabel. The relationship begins just as Zapa has first earned the trust of Gallo, and from that point on the times when Zapa and Mabel are seen together on-screen generally serve to punctuate moments in Zapa's ascent through the force (or, alternatively, his incorporation into the Repressive State Apparatus). The first time Mabel and Zapa interact in any way is during a class she is giving as part of Zapa's basic training. Although ostensibly the authority figure, Mabel realizes the class (including Zapa) is taking neither her nor her lesson seriously. The next time Mabel appears is immediately after Zapa has received the pistol from Gallo, and the behavior of both man and woman has changed significantly—sitting with some other cadets, Zapa notices Mabel walking into the academy with her arms full and immediately runs to help her, an offer she politely declines despite his insistence. A few scenes later the situation is reversed: Zapa is shown leaving the academy one evening when Mabel approaches him and insists on giving him a lift home even after he initially declines her offer. The scene then quickly cuts to a tight shot of the two sitting in her car; they fondle each other for a few moments before Mabel climbs on top of Zapa, straddling him and pulling up her dress. At the end of the scene, having returned to the driver's seat, she pulls him to her shoulder, patting him and giving him a kiss on the top of his head. The fact that Mabel is the one who initiates the relationship is significant; at the start Mabel is firmly in control—she invites Zapa into her car, she climbs on top of him, she pulls up her dress—but as Zapa transforms into Mendoza, the balance of that control shifts considerably.

The contrast between the first and last times Zapa and Mabel are shown having sex on-screen is drastic. In addition to functioning as a sort of mirror image of the previous encounter, the scene is a key moment in Zapa's character development, showing the manner in which he exercises the modicum of power he has achieved (Figure 2.3). The first sex scene is presented as a moment of intense mutual lust, with neither character able to keep their hands off the other. Zapa has just begun his career in the police (in fact, at the point in the film when this occurs, he is still a trainee) and, as a police instructor, Mabel is the more powerful of the two. By the end of their relationship, these circumstances have changed. Not only is Zapa a full-fledged field officer, he is also a part of Gallo's inner circle, something which Mabel vocally opposes. Indeed, so opposed is she to his increasing complicity with Gallo that Mabel is

Figure 2.3 *El bonaerense* (2002). In his violent domination of Mabel, Zapa fully assumes the Mendoza role that characterizes his police work.

even hesitant to allow Zapa into her flat, in direct opposition to their first sexual encounter, when she invited him into her vehicle. Both from a narrative and a cinematic perspective, the two scenes are highly similar—in each instance Mabel can be heard begging Zapa to stop, in each scene one of the characters is obviously in control over the other, and in each scene the framing is tight and claustrophobic. Yet where Mabel's pleas are part of an "erotic, sexual game in which she clearly takes the lead" in the first scene, in the second they are the pleas of a woman who is legitimately fearful, engaged in an act that "[borders] on rape" (Scorer, 2011, p. 169). With shots that linger on Mabel's naked breast as it falls out of her shirt, and on Zapa's face as she fellates him, the tight framing of the first scene emphasizes the unbridled lust exhibited by the two characters in the initial stages of their relationship. In contrast, the framing of their final sexual encounter, while equally claustrophobic, lends an entirely different feeling to the scene. The camera focuses almost exclusively on Zapa, with Mabel entering the shot only when pulled or pushed into the frame by him. The camera shows Zapa's face throughout much of the scene, while Mabel's face is almost always obscured by her hair, or covered by Zapa's hand, or out of the frame entirely. In an inversion of the previous sex scene, after Zapa finishes he lies down on the floor next to Mabel, gently kissing her back and shoulders; when we finally see her face, it is flush with trepidation.

The violence of this scene is shocking not only in comparison to the earlier sex scene but also when compared to Zapa's behavior throughout the film, both before and after this scene takes place. Scorer believes that the scene demonstrates the point where "[t]he violence that Zapa has learnt in the supposed controlled and separate sphere of the police ... becomes [his] means of engaging in human relations" (2011, p. 169). It must also be understood, however, as the moment when Zapa's personal agency in his own corruption is affirmed. Throughout the film, Zapa is presented as fundamentally lacking power: he is a terrible cadet while at the police academy, he is Gallo's lackey while in the field, and when confronted with the more violent aspects of police work he poses a greater threat to himself and his fellow officers than he does to his adversaries. Indeed, even outside of his work environment Zapa is shown to lack assertiveness: he puts up no resistance to his uncle's initial suggestion that his only way out of jail is to join the police force; Mabel makes the first move at the start of their relationship; and he doesn't even secure a permanent place to live until Gallo sets him up with an estate agent. For most of the film, then, Zapa appears superficially to lack any real agency in his life, instead allowing things to happen to him without ever putting up any real resistance. It is this same passivity that leads, at least in part, to his incorporation into and complicity with the Repressive State Apparatus of the police. Once part of the system, however, and under the guise of Mendoza, he begins to exercise a modicum of power. This is first demonstrated in the scene which immediately precedes Zapa and Mabel's final sexual encounter. In a demonstration of his one-dimensional, coercive power, Zapa is shown extorting a bar owner for money and, when the bar owner plays dumb, Zapa mentions Gallo's name, an act which causes the man to acquiesce to Zapa's demands.

What makes these two scenes (the extortion scene and the subsequent sex scene) so jarring is the fact that they are virtually the only moment in the entire film where Zapa exerts agency and forces a situation. The tone for the final sex scene is set by the scene which precedes it. Zapa's threat to call Gallo if an agreement with the bar owner cannot be arrived at suggests that Zapa is acting alone in this case, without Gallo's explicit knowledge (even if he does have the boss's tacit support). This is the first time that Zapa is shown choosing to do something of his own accord, and it is an act of corruption. The sex scene that follows implicates him yet further. Throughout most of the film, Zapa's relationship with Mabel is characterized by its warmth: swamped with work on Christmas Eve, Zapa takes a moment to call and leave a message on Mabel's answering machine; at a later point in the film he is shown playing table football with her son; in celebration of his upcoming graduation from the academy she takes him shopping for items he will need as an official member of the force, including a bulletproof vest. The final sex scene, however, lacks any of this warmth. Rather than caring, or even sexual desire, Zapa projects an image of violent domination, as if Mabel is merely another person who he can extort for personal gain. Despite his passivity throughout much of the film, these scenes demonstrate that Zapa is not lacking in agency. He has made a conscious decision, and it is one that allows him to exert power over another, just as Gallo exerts power over him.

Crucially, this decision, a choice which affects not only his professional life but also his personal life as well, is one which carries with it significant consequences. Those consequences are borne out in the final twenty minutes of the film. First, Mabel rejects him entirely, dismissing him by saying "que te consuele Gallo" ("let Gallo console you"). More seriously, his decision to approach Gallo for advice on how to deal with Polaco leads directly to Polaco's death. The film's denouement highlights the fact that the power Zapa achieves is basic, one dimensional. In order to exercise power, Zapa's only recourse is to use what Lukes would call "force," that is the removal of any option of noncompliance. In the case of the bar owner, this works: once Zapa mentions Gallo, the man knows there is no chance he will get out of paying the bribe and so he agrees to it. In his relationship with Mabel, however, the limits of Zapa's power are laid bare. No matter how much he protests, once she decides to move on from him he cannot force her to change her mind.

This stands in stark contrast to his relationship with Gallo. Gallo's power over Zapa is three dimensional in nature—Gallo provides Zapa a little bit of power, brings him into his *Stand*, and in doing so ensures that any future decisions Zapa takes will be ones which implicate him further into the Repressive State Apparatus of which Gallo forms a part. It is only once Gallo has murdered Polaco that the true nature of the RSA is exposed in its entirety, horrifying Zapa and causing him to reconsider his loyalty to his boss and, by extension, the police force generally. By that point, however, he is too complicit in the workings of the RSA to extricate himself, realizing that any attempt to discredit Gallo will simply lead to his own downfall, a situation in which he is unwilling to place himself. This is, ultimately, the most disquieting aspect of *El bonaerense*: it exposes the role individuals and their decisions play in sustaining a corrupt organization. Furthermore, by presenting its protagonist as an Argentine everyman, the film's condemnation extends beyond the realm of the individual—the film's protagonist is a nobody who could be anyone in Argentina. Zapa is not noteworthy, he is not special, and yet he is at least partly responsible, as a result of the choices he makes, for the continuation of systemic objective violence within society.

Elefante blanco

Where *El bonaerense* ends with Zapa confronting the realities of death for what appears to be the first time, *Elefante blanco* begins with the film's two protagonists confronting death, perhaps fittingly for a work that focuses on the actions of two Catholic priests. The nature of these confrontations, however, could not be more different from each other or what is seen in

El bonaerense—a middle-aged Julián (Ricardo Darín) is introduced lying on a CT scanner, his face covered with the type of mask used to pinpoint the location of brain tumors. Nicolás (Jeremie Renier), on the other hand, is introduced crawling through jungle vegetation in the middle of the night as a group of armed soldiers ransack a village and execute its inhabitants. Julián is next seen traveling up a river and through dense jungle, finally encountering Nicolás in a field hospital and whispering to him in French. After a period of recovery, the two travel to Buenos Aires where Julián has been assigned to work in Ciudad Oculta, a *villa miseria* (slum) on the city's outskirts. As Nicolás acclimatizes himself to his new surroundings, he (and, by extension, the viewer) learn more about the challenges confronting the residents of the villa—drug use is rampant (particularly *paco*, a form of crack cocaine); shootouts between rival gangs pose a constant threat to the security of the villa's residents; and living conditions are horrendous, with even the church flooding whenever it rains. Julián explains to Nicolás that a series of new houses are being built but, as with virtually everything in the villa, the project is beset with problems: the workers are not being paid and take out their anger on Luciana (Martina Gusmán), a social worker who liaises between the municipality, the construction company, and the residents of the villa who are working on the project. In addition, we are introduced to Monito (Federico Barga), a boy from the villa who, despite his addiction to *paco*, is interested in improving himself and seems to be a favorite of Julián and the other priests.

After a gang shootout leaves a drug runner dead, Nicolás enters a zone of the villa controlled by one of the gangs in an effort to return the boy's body to his family, despite the protests of Luciana and several priests. Although he is successful in returning the body, he is severely rebuked by Julián, who explains that by interacting directly with the gangs Nicolás has threatened the entire social project that the Church has been constructing in the villa. During their argument, Julián makes veiled references to his cancer and hints that he is grooming Nicolás to take over the parish. The conflicting views that Nicolás and Julián have regarding the church's role in the villa, combined with the attraction Nicolás feels toward Luciana, causes the priest to have what appears to be a crisis of faith and he soon begins an affair with Luciana. The situation in the villa begins to deteriorate along with Julián's health—one of the drug kingpins is arrested during a police raid and Cruz (Walter Jakob), one of the social workers in the villa, abruptly resigns. Much to Julián's horror, Cruz is found murdered shortly after his resignation; it is revealed that he was, in fact, an undercover police officer. Most ominously, with their aggravation regarding the nonpayment of their salaries having reached boiling point, the workers on the housing project protest and refuse to work until they are paid. The protest turns violent when the riot squad enter the villa, with police first using tear gas and eventually resorting to firing live bullets. As the various clergy members attend to the wounded, Monito appears wielding a pistol, having been shot in the leg. He admits to Julián that it was he who killed Cruz and that the police are now looking for him. Julián and Nicolás attempt to smuggle Monito out of the villa in order to take him to the hospital, but are stopped by a police officer. The boy attempts to escape and a Mexican standoff develops, with the officer pointing his pistol at Monito and Nicolás while Julián points Monito's pistol at the officer. In the ensuing chaos Nicolás is shot and Monito, the officer, and Julián are all killed. The film ends with Nicolás, having cloistered himself in a monastery, returning to the villa with Luciana in order to attend the community's homage to the slain Julián. The film's final image shows Nicolás sitting at his mentor's table, silently contemplating his rosary.

Ciudad Oculta and the Catholic Church

As with *El bonaerense*, *Elefante blanco*'s title contains a dual meaning that speaks to the film's content. Quite literally, the title refers to one of the primary buildings in which the film was shot. The work was filmed on location in various villas, primarily in Ciudad Oculta (the common name for the area officially known as Villa 15), a villa that is one of the largest in Buenos Aires and home to anywhere between 15,000 and 30,000 people. As Julián explains to Nicolás early in the film, the villa was centered around an enormous abandoned building, the white elephant of the title. Construction on the building began in the 1930s and was intermittently abandoned and resumed, a victim of the whims of the numerous changes of government that the country experienced throughout the twentieth century. Imagined as the largest hospital in Latin America when the project began, the *Elefante blanco* (as the building was commonly known) was at the time little more than a modern ruin. The building was completely demolished in 2018, and a year later the Ministry of Human Development and Habitat of the City of Buenos Aires moved its headquarters to a new building on the site.

On a symbolic level, the title represents several different aspects found in the film. The dictionary definition of a white elephant is "a possession that is useless or troublesome, especially one that is expensive to maintain and difficult to dispose of" (*Oxford English Dictionary*). In this sense, then, the title might be a condemnation of the general public's attitude toward the villa itself. Indeed, as the film makes clear, the villa is so difficult a place to maintain that the Argentine state has all but given up trying. Rather than a representative of the municipality, it is Luciana, a social worker who serves a variety of roles throughout the villa, who engages in dialogue with the construction workers, and what little money the municipality does provide for the project is so delayed that the men are on the verge of striking, despite the fact that they are building the very houses in which they will live. Virtually the only representatives of the State seen at any point in the film are the police, and their presence only serves to increase tensions in an environment that is already riven with conflict.

In contrast to *El bonaerense*'s *conurbano*, where the corrupt police force actively engages in extortion and fraud, the villa in which *Elefante blanco* is set is, for all intents and purposes, a *zona liberada* (liberated zone), a place where criminals have negotiated with law enforcement to, essentially, create a police-free area (Denissen, 2008, p. 238). The police make only infrequent appearances, and when they do, it is reminiscent of a blitzkrieg: the force encircling the entire villa in their riot gear, entering the area with their weapons drawn, and then leaving as quickly as they appeared. As the chants of *hijos de puta* which welcome every police appearance in the area attest to, many in the villa consider the police to be as dangerous as the drug-fueled gangs that dominate the area, if not more so. In this particular case, therefore, abandonment seems to be the State's preferred option for how to deal with the villa and its residents.

This state of affairs brings to mind the Weberian concept of *Gewalt*, that is violence or force. Weber states that "it is only possible to define the modern state with respect to the one specific means innate to every political organization: the physical force that includes the capacity to be violent [*Gewalt*]" (2015, p. 135). Furthermore, Weber believes that if there "were social entities which were unaware of the concept of *Gewalt* as a means [especially with its implications for the use of violence], then the term 'state' would cease to exist" (2015, p. 136). In a reverse sort of way, the reality of the villa proves Weber's point—it is not so much that social entities (in this case, the rival gangs) in Ciudad Oculta have become unaware of the implications of *Gewalt*, but rather that they have become *exceedingly* aware of those implications, and have manipulated *Gewalt* to their own will. The gangs use physical force just as readily as the State and, perhaps most importantly, it is accepted by villa society even more than State-sanctioned force. Weber states that "all organizations or single persons have the right to physical force only to the extent that the state permits it" (2015, p. 136); however, in the villa the gangs are responsible for determining what is acceptable and what is not. As a result, the State, which supposedly has a monopoly on the use of physical force, has lost the one thing that gives it any sort of power. This is precisely what allows Ciudad Oculta to become (essentially) a State-less *zona liberada*. Within the villa it is the preponderance of *Gewalt* which has caused the State to abandon its citizens.

One institution that has not abandoned the villa, however, is the Catholic Church. The Church is perhaps the final white elephant to which the film's title refers. Indeed, it might be argued that the fact that the Church serves as the film's central thematic element is in itself surprising. Although the Catholic Church remains a significant cultural identifier that unites disparate Latin American societies (Edgerton and Sotirova, 2011, p. 36), the position of the institution in Argentine society is rather distinct. Like virtually all of Latin America, Argentina is an ostensibly Catholic nation; however, Anna Edgerton and Ina Sotirova explain that "only 20 percent of Argentines are actively practicing" (2011, p. 39). Argentina is not unique in this regard, as studies have shown that identification with Catholicism is declining across Latin America (Pew, 2014, p. 4). Much of this is down to the rise of evangelical Christianity throughout the region in the twenty-first century; however, the tension between Argentine society and the Catholic Church goes back much further. The decline of the Catholic Church in Argentina is generally considered to have begun in the 1980s, and is closely linked to the stance the Church took during the *Proceso* dictatorship. Indeed, in his study *La iglesia católica en la política argentina*, Jose Maria Ghio explicitly condemns the Church, going as far as to state that, "la parte medular de la jerarquía católica participó en los preparativos del golpe de estado" (the core of the Catholic hierarchy participated in the preparations for the coup d'état) (2007, p. 222). This is noteworthy because it contrasts so starkly with the actions of the Church in other Latin American countries that suffered similar dictatorships. Whereas in neighboring countries like Chile and Brazil the Church attempted to protect individuals and, where possible, maintain a record of human rights abuses committed by the government, Gustavo Morello explains that in Argentina no such arrangements were made, either by the Argentine Bishops' Conference or by any major diocese (2015, p. 4). Ghio makes it quite clear that, on an institutional level, the Catholic Church was highly complicit with the military government during the *Proceso* dictatorship, and this collaboration has done significant damage to the Church's reputation and status in Argentina; as such, while many Argentines may identify themselves as culturally Catholic, in practice the Church has little impact on the day-to-day experience of the majority of the nation's population.

This decline is consistent with the decline of the religious ISA throughout many parts of the (especially Western, formerly Christian) world and, while it may be true in society broadly, in the case of Ciudad Oculta (at least as it is represented in *Elefante blanco*) not only is the Catholic Church the dominant ISA, it may very well be the *only* one. Althusser lists several different ideological apparatuses that function in concert with one another, chief amongst them the family ISA, the religious ISA, and the educational ISA (to name those ISAs with which Trapero's films most directly engage). Throughout *Elefante blanco* the Church and its representatives are shown engaging not only in the activities with which the institution would normally be associated—leading mass, baptizing children, presiding over funeral services—but also in all sorts of activities which would normally be the purview of other ISAs. The absence in the community of both the educational and family ISAs are particularly noticeable, with the priests standing in not only for the absent school system but also, perhaps more significantly, for the families which so many of the villa's residents, and Monito in particular, are lacking.

It is important to clarify here that the film makes a significant differentiation between the Church hierarchy, isolated as it is from the realities of the villa, and the *curas villeros* (slum priests) who *are* actively involved in their communities. While Trapero's film is quite sympathetic in its depiction of the representatives of the Catholic Church who devote their lives to serving the Ciudad Oculta community, it portrays the Church hierarchy in a far-less flattering manner; Beatriz Urraca, for example, describes Julián as Trapero's "only protagonist of heroic proportions," while simultaneously referring to the "massive, unalterable power structure of the Church" (2014, p. 367). One of the primary narrative threads that runs throughout the film is the disconnect that exists between the quotidian experience of Julián, Nicolás, and the rest of the *curas villeros* and the level of investment (both financial and otherwise) the Church hierarchy is prepared to commit to the villa. This disconnect mirrors the disconnect that existed between the Catholic Church's actions during the *Proceso* dictatorship and the actions of individual priests at that time. Despite the Church hierarchy's complicity with the dictatorship, individuals within the Church structure were not spared the horrors of the era, suffering along with the population en masse.

State Violence and Death

The connection between the two institutions—Church and State—is mediated through the character of Cruz. Although Cruz plays a relatively minor role in the film's narrative, he (or, more specifically, his death) is vital in establishing the film's critique of objective violence. When Cruz is first introduced, he is made out to be a church layman assisting the priests in Ciudad Oculta. When Nicolás decides to enter the headquarters of one of the two drug dealers operating in the villa in order to retrieve the body of a slain drug runner, it is Cruz who shows him the way and helps him to return the corpse. The next time Cruz appears, he is shown explaining to Julián that he has decided to quit working in the villa, and asks the priest for forgiveness. Throughout this scene Cruz's mannerisms suggest fear and resignation—his voice quivers, his face twitches, and he ends his conversation with Julián by saying "lo único que espero es que un día me perdone" ("I only hope that someday you will forgive me"). As he says this, far-off police sirens are heard and the scene cuts to a police raid of the villa, in which one of the two drug lords working in Ciudad Oculta is arrested.

Although the connection between Cruz and the raid is not immediately obvious, shortly after this scene he is found dead in the upper floors of the abandoned hospital, and his identity as an undercover police officer is made known to the priests. As a slain police officer, Cruz's remains are given a formal public viewing, which Julián, Nicolás, and Luciana attend. Although the film's three main characters converse briefly, the camera pans away from them, instead contemplating the scene around Cruz's casket. Two police officers in formal dress stand guard over the casket, behind them on the wall above Cruz's body is a crucifix, and several other officers pay their respects and offer support to Cruz's sobbing wife as she caresses her deceased husband.

The shot then cuts to an overhead close-up of Cruz's face, which is covered as the lid to the casket is put in place. The casket is adorned with a silver image of a crucified Christ, visible for a moment until it is, in turn, covered by an Argentine flag and a formal police dress hat (Figure 2.4). The three symbols shown on the outside of the casket are, in themselves, entirely political in nature—the crucifix is perhaps the most potent religious symbol in the world; flags are visceral representations of State authority; and the dress hat is an instantly recognizable symbol of the military and law enforcement. Combined together, given the context of both *Elefante blanco* and Argentina's history, the three symbols become accusatory: Cruz's death, like so many before him, is the by-product of the functioning of the State Apparatus in both its repressive and ideological manifestations.

More pointedly, the composition of the shot further enhances the critique implied by the connection of the three symbols. The camera for the overhead shot is located at the top of Cruz's casket facing down toward his feet, so that Cruz's head enters the shot from the top of the frame. As such, his face (while visible) is upside down; more significantly, the image of the crucified Christ that adorns the casket lid is also upside down, replicating the inverted Cross imagery that is often associated with anti-Christian sentiment. This sequence replicates the film's opening image, in which Julián, lying on a scanning machine table, is slowly introduced from the top of the frame, his face upside down. Just as Cruz's face is covered entirely by the casket, Julián's face is obscured by the mesh mask put in place for

Figure 2.4 *Elefante blanco* (2012). The combination of such potent political symbols functions as a condemnation of the State.

his brain scan. By replicating the construction of Julián's brain scan scene so closely during Cruz's funeral, Trapero seems to be foreshadowing not so much Julián's death—this being almost a foregone conclusion from the moment the film begins—but rather the manner of his death at the hands of the police. Cruz, a member of the Repressive State Apparatus, is killed by an unidentified resident of the villa in an act of rebellion against the State. When Monito admits to Julián that it was he who murdered Cruz, Julián's first instinct is not to hand him over to the authorities but rather to protect him and attempt to smuggle him out of the villa. Julián's death is inevitable not merely because he has brain cancer, but because he attempts to prevent the State from exacting its revenge for Monito's act of defiance. Ultimately, Julián takes his rebellion to its logical (at least in the objectively violent world of the villa) conclusion and shoots the police officer threatening to kill Monito; the officer shoots him back, killing him and ensuring that the State's dominance is, *a priori*, maintained.

Mugica and the Power of the Alter

Both throughout his life and even in the moment of his death, Julián struggles against the subjective violence (or *Gewalt*) of the State. In its stead, he and his fellow *curas villeros* exercise a different kind of power, a power that is less obviously connected to violence, and which has been earned through the work of those who came before. As explained earlier, many of those priests were made to suffer as a result of their work, and *Elefante blanco* is explicitly dedicated to the memory of one such victim of State violence: Carlos Mugica, a *cura villero* (slum priest) who worked primarily in Villa 31 and was assassinated in 1974 under controversial circumstances. Mugica was a member of the *Movimiento de Sacerdotes para el Tercer Mundo* (MSTM), a left-wing group of priests within the Argentine church who championed radical beliefs, such as liberation theology and the Argentina-specific theology of the people (*teología del pueblo*). His commitment to these beliefs is the very thing that led to his murder. Mugica was murdered in 1974, an assassination widely believed to have been carried out by the *Alianza Anticomunista Argentina* (Morello, 2015, p. 62). Acting in the years immediately prior to the start of the *Proceso* dictatorship, the *Triple A* was a paramilitary unit that carried

Figure 2.5 *Elefante blanco* (2012). The *curas villeros* utilize the power of Mugica's memory to create a "space of self."

out politically motivated murders and whose leaders were all high-ranking government officials.

Not only is the film dedicated to Mugica's legacy, it is also an explicit homage to him. Geoffrey Kantaris postulates that *Elefante blanco* locates Mugica in "el meollo de una lucha simbólica por lo que podríamos llamar la legitimidad 'onteológica' (en el sentido heideggeriano)" ["the center of a symbolic struggle for what we might call 'onteologic' legitimacy (in the Heideggerian sense)"] (2016, p. 88), while Aguilar finds that Trapero uses Mugica's legacy as a means of anchoring the film's politics (Aguilar, 2015). Hugo Vezzetti contends that, through its evocation of both his life and death, *Elefante blanco* recovers ("recupera") Padre Mugica's legacy (2014, p. 183) and, in its violence, Julián's death is certainly reminiscent of Mugica's. References to the murdered priest abound in the film: in scenes that were filmed in Villa 31 itself, various people in the villa pay their respects at a wall covered in the plaques and painted-tile murals typical of Argentine cemeteries, all of which are in Mugica's honor; a new priest is ordained on the anniversary of Mugica's death, an event during which enormous images of the fallen priest can be seen throughout the villa (Figure 2.5); and at the end of the film, when the residents of Ciudad Oculta come together to celebrate Julián's life, the calls for justice include both the fictional Julián and the real Mugica.

This remains the case in *Elefante blanco*—in everything from their backgrounds, nationalities, and education levels Julián, Nicolás, and the rest of the *curas villeros* are distinct from the residents of the villa, yet they live amongst them and experience many of the same quotidian hardships. When gang violence erupts on the villa's streets, Nicolás and Luciana are forced to take cover along with everyone else in the vicinity; similarly, when the police invade the villa to apprehend one of the drug kingpins, Julián allows residents to shelter in the Church's space and prevents the police from entering. This scene, in particular, demonstrates just how central the Church and its representatives are to the life of the villa. However, where the functionally powerless State engages in shock tactics to enforce its will, the representatives of the Catholic Church in the villa community are confronted with the challenge of exercising a form of power that is completely independent of violence. Many of the conceptions of power so far included in this chapter might seem to suggest that such a form of power cannot reasonably be expected to exist; even Lukes's "radical" view necessarily implies that the wants of a person or society are subject to the violence of manipulation by an external force. Understood in this way, the Church and its representatives in Ciudad Oculta are fundamentally powerless. Byung-Chul Han, however, provides an understanding of power that offers insight into how seemingly powerless individuals such as *curas villeros* can, in fact, exert significant control. In his description of the concept, Han writes, "complex interdependencies mean that there is reciprocity of power. If the *ego* needs the cooperation of the *alter*, a dependence of *ego* on *alter* is the result. . . . Even the very weakest can turn their powerlessness into power by making skillful use of cultural norms" (2019, p. 4, emphasis in original).

Han describes power as creating "a vast *space of self*" (2019, p. 6), going on to explain that within that space both the powerful and the powerless enjoy a great deal of freedom, which is a further defining feature of power—"[i]t is precisely freedom that distinguishes power from violence or coercion" (2019, p. 8). What *Elefante blanco*'s narrative portrays, then, is the way in which the Church representatives in the villa attempt, through a demonstrated commitment to the villa's residents, to create a space in which they—both the *curas* and the residents—are able to exert something resembling power. This power is entirely free from the influence of violence; instead of threatening those under (or outwith) their control with the threat of violence if they do not obey—as do both the drug dealers who run the villa and the police who sporadically invade it—the *curas villeros* offer freedom. That is, they offer a space in which those who choose to enter do so of their own will. Viewing power through Han's understanding of the concept, we can see that the power of the Church, the power of the *curas villeros*, resides in this very space. This is not always immediately evident, however, as demonstrated by *Elefante blanco*'s final act, when construction of the housing development stops and the residents of the villa storm the abandoned lot. Although the residents occupy the space peacefully at first, the State reacts with violence, sending riot police as a show of force. The presence of the State's repressive apparatus—a police force that the villa residents understand as being specifically tasked with committing violence against them—increases the tension of the moment, escalating it to such a degree that the police storm the area and begin forcibly clearing people out, which in turn leads to a riot breaking out. The riot and its aftermath lead directly to the death of both Monito and Julián, perhaps leading us to believe that power does, indeed, reside only in the hands of those who are capable of enforcing it through violence, that a power free from violence is, in fact, an illusion.

The film's second-to-last scene, however, is an incredibly profound reaffirmation of the type of power that Han describes in his work. After a period of silent contemplation at a cloistered monastery outside of the city, Nicolás returns to Ciudad Oculta and participates in a march and candlelight vigil commemorating the now-deceased Julián. As members of the community march through the streets they chant out, "Viva el Padre Julián! Justicia para el Padre Julián! Viva el cura villero!" ("Long live Padre Julián! Justice for Padre Julián! Long live the slum priest!") Most of this scene is shot from a medium distance, allowing the audience to view the plurality of the crowd taking part in the march. However, after Nicolás stops, seemingly in an attempt to both collect and control his thoughts, the camera frames his face tightly in close-up. As he turns to look at the would-be hospital, the camera gradually zooms out, revealing the abandoned husk of the *Elefante blanco* of the title. Paradoxically, however, the enormous, potentially foreboding building—a building that serves, quite literally, as a monument to the failure of the State—takes on a different meaning in these final moments. Far from functioning as a site of violence, the building seems to wrap Nicolás in a sort of embrace, an embrace that is emphasized by the warm light that illuminates the priest's face,

Figure 2.6 *Elefante blanco* (2012). Rather than loom over the community, the White Elephant embraces the *villa*.

emanating from the candles being carried by the community that he marches alongside (Figure 2.6). It is in these moments that Nicolás—and, by extension, the audience—finally understands the power Julián and Mugica before him were attempting to harness, a power that creates space and freedom rather than the fear and violence that characterizes the Repressive State Apparatus.

The solidarity demonstrated by the residents of Ciudad Oculta in two disparate situations—the riot and candlelight vigil functioning as two extremes of possible forms of protest—is emphasized by Han in his analysis of power relations, where he describes the interplay between the powerful "*ego*" and the subordinate "*alter*." Han writes,

> It is . . . a sign of the *ego*'s power that the *alter* follows the selection made by the *ego* despite attractive alternatives being readily available to him or her. But the freedom that the *alter* enjoys through the broad space of possible actions does not necessarily increase the power of the *ego*. It may even be destabilizing . . . If a decision is not fully accepted by the subordinates, the superior loses . . . influence because the influence on decision-making does not coincide with the influence on what is *actually* put into practice by the subordinates. (2019, p. 11)

Throughout virtually all of *Elefante blanco* the residents of Ciudad Oculta are presented as the *alter* within the complex network of power relations that exist within the villa. They are portrayed as subordinate to the power of the State, subordinate to the power of the two rival gangs that terrorize their space, and subordinate to the broader, national-level social mechanisms that maintain systems of generational poverty. In the film's final act, however, they demonstrate precisely the destabilizing potential that Han contends the *alter* is capable of exerting. The resistance against the State's attempts to clear the construction site is the more obvious example, for it is a case of meeting subjective violence with subjective violence. But it is the candlelight vigil and march in Padre Julián's honor that is, perhaps, the more significant event in relation to the loss of influence that the *ego*—the State, in this case—has experienced. This is so because of how the community responds to Julián's death, a death that might, at first glance, appear to be much less explicitly political than was the historical Mugica's. Julián dies as a result of a confluence of desperation, chaos, and madness. This contrasts significantly with Mugica's murder, which was neither an accident nor random; his assassination was an attempt to silence his message of social justice. Even in the moment, Mugica's death was a scandal; from the perspective of the Repressive State Apparatus, however, killing Julián is entirely justifiable—he fired on a police officer, who defended himself in kind. Despite this, the community in the film rallies around Julián's memory in the same way that real-life communities in various *villas* around Buenos Aires have rallied around Mugica's memory. Rather than allow the circumstances surrounding Julián's death—his potential killing of a police officer—to overshadow the deeds of his life, the community demonstrates that they understand that the fallen priest sacrificed himself for his flock, in the same way Mugica willingly endangered himself through his dedication to social justice in a time when such commitment was extremely dangerous.

The violence that befalls Julián at the end of *Elefante blanco* connects the film with *El bonaerense*. Both films' protagonists experience violence at the hands of the very State Apparatus they either explicitly (in the case of Zapa) or tangentially (in the case of Julián) form a part of. In both circumstances, the films' denouements recall Arendt's statement that "violence appears as a last resort to keep the power structure intact" (1970, p. 47). By murdering Polaco and then shooting Zapa, thereby implicating him in the cover-up, Gallo ensures that Zapa is in a compromised position for the rest of his career. Although the event profoundly alters Zapa's view of both his own and Gallo's roles in the police department, by the end of the film Zapa has become too complicit with the police force's corruption to rebel against it in any meaningful way. Whatever his misgivings, Zapa (or, perhaps more accurately, Officer Mendoza) is now a fully entrenched member of the Repressive State Apparatus. Julián, on the other hand, rejects his position within the Ideological State Apparatus, and in doing so ensures that the apparatus itself will take whatever steps necessary to maintain its power. By murdering Julián, however, the State works against itself—the priest's violent death ensures that he becomes a martyr for the residents of Ciudad Oculta, and anti-State sentiment in the villa, already a place where the Repressive State Apparatus has only a minimal presence, is further embedded in the community's collective memory. This echoes Arendt's warning that "[rule] by sheer violence comes into play where power is being lost. . . . To substitute violence for power can bring victory, but the price is very high; for it is not only paid by the vanquished, it is also paid by the victor in terms of his own power" (1970, p. 53). The film's penultimate scene, of the entire Ciudad Oculta community coming together to commemorate Julián's sacrifice, echoes this sentiment. The scene makes it clear that murdering Julián has not strengthened the State's power within the villa, and in fact has most likely weakened it, if only from an ideological standpoint. Despite the respect the residents of the villa held for Julián, however, no representatives of either the Church hierarchy or the State itself are visible in the scene. And that, perhaps, is the film's most damning critique: while Julián's sacrifice is highly significant for those who are powerless, it means little to those in power. Like Cruz, like Zapa, like so many of Trapero's characters, Julián is merely another victim of the objective violence of the State.

Part Two

Violence and the Family

3

The Violence of the Arborescent Family

The nuclear family plays a role in every one of Trapero's films, so it is not possible to make any generalities about how he approaches the concept; in some of his films—*El bonaerense*, for example—the protagonists' families are present but do not necessarily figure in the narrative in any meaningful way. However, this is by no means always the case, and in the three films studied in this chapter Trapero examines the concept of family with the same wary eye with which he scrutinizes the State in other films. Far from being a safe and nurturing space, *Familia rodante*, *El clan*, and *La quietud* portray the family not only as an institution in which the effects of objective violence are felt acutely but also as a site in which hostility and conflict are generated, thereby ensuring the continuation of violence. This is consistent with how Trapero approaches the State Apparatus in his other films and, in keeping with Althusser's writings on the concept, this portrayal signals a reading of the family as politics. Indeed, despite their differences, the films analyzed in this chapter must be considered amongst Trapero's most potent political statements.

Theories of the Family

Unsurprisingly, considering its centrality to the human experience, the family as a social construct has been the focus of an enormous range of critical analysis. Perceptions of how the family functions and how it influences individuals have shifted over time, yet one thing that has remained constant is the acceptance that the family plays a fundamental role in the shaping of culture and society. This is especially true with regard to the family's relationship with violence. Since at least the late nineteenth century the family, both as a sociological concept and as an organizational structure, has been understood as an agent which is capable not merely of propagating repression but, in fact, of generating it, as well. Althusser sets the framework for this through his analysis of the family ISA, while Michel Foucault and Deleuze and Guattari examine what makes the family ISA violent, and how we can understand the violence created by the family. Throughout his analyses of the State Apparatus, Althusser emphasized the particular importance of three ISAs in the subjection of individuals—the religious ISA, the educational ISA, and the family ISA. While the significance of the religious and educational ISAs has shifted over time (the religious ISA losing much of its dominance as the educational ISA has increased in importance), the constant, from the Middle Ages through to contemporary society, has been the family.

The function of the family ISA is central to Althusser's concept of interpellation, the process of recognition through which an individual is made into a subject. The formation of ideology, the creation of an environment in which interpellation occurs, is predicated on the idea that "*individuals are always-already subjects*" (1971, p. 119 emphasis in original). This is so as a result of the basic functioning of the family unit, which places individuals within an ideology even before birth: "[b]efore its birth, the child is therefore always-already a subject, appointed as a subject in and by the specific familial ideological configuration in which it is 'expected' once it has been conceived" (1971, p. 119). Beyond merely playing a role in the creation of ideology, the family is fundamental to it—through the normal functioning of the family the requirements necessary for ideology to exist are (often unwittingly) sustained.

Family and Control

Moving away from an explicit Marxist understanding of the family, Foucault analyzed the concept of family in its relation to power. For Foucault and others, the family is a structure which is manipulated in order to exert control and exercise power over individuals. Foucault's analysis of the family, found primarily in *The History of Sexuality, Vol. 1*, states that "the family cell" was originally a site in which "deployments of alliance" were encountered, with the concept of alliance being described as, "[a] system of marriage, of fixation and development of kinship ties, of transmission of names and possessions . . . built around a system of rules defining the permitted and the forbidden, the licit and the illicit" (1990, p. 106). Foucault contends that, while alliance was the dominant social construct for much of history until the nineteenth century, it was gradually replaced by sexuality, the deployment of which now governs not simply familial relationships but large swathes of human interaction generally. Foucault defines sexuality as "a great surface network in which the stimulation of bodies, the intensification of pleasures, the incitement to discourse, the formation of special knowledges, the strengthening of controls and resistances, are linked to one another" (1990, pp. 105–6). The family unit is an especially critical focal point for the deployment of sexuality, as sexuality has come to depend on the deployment of alliance in order to propagate itself: "[the family's] role is to anchor sexuality and provide it with a permanent support.... The family is the interchange of sexuality and alliance" (1990, p. 108). Sexuality is fundamental to any exercise of power, and the family plays a critical role in both introducing and maintaining sexuality as a social construct.

Although Foucault does not devote significant attention in his work to the concept of the family, it nevertheless figures prominently in his analysis, for it is within the family that the deployment of sexuality takes hold. Foucault describes the family as "an agency of control" (1990, p. 122), and contends that though the family may have originally emerged as a result of the deployment of alliance, the deployment of sexuality has emphasized the family structure even more: "family was the crystal in the deployment of sexuality.... By virtue of its permeability, and through that process of reflections to the outside, it became one of the most valuable tactical components of the deployment" (1990, p. 111). This is of particular importance for an analysis of Trapero's cinema because relations of sexuality, as with relations of alliance or any other relationship, are an integral feature of power and control, themes with which Trapero engages consistently.

Foucault also locates the family within the context of disciplinary and sovereign power. Sovereign power represents a more obvious type of power, a kind centered around one dominant individual such as a king or, in the context of a nuclear family, the *pater familias*. Disciplinary power stems less from one instantly recognizable individual, emerging rather from a web of social and cultural constructs that, to an extent, mirror Althusser's Ideological State Apparatuses. Of the family structure itself, Foucault finds that "the family is a sort of cell within which the power exercised is not... disciplinary, but rather of the same type as the power of sovereignty" (2006, p. 79). There are two points that must be made regarding this statement. The first, a counterpoint of sorts, is that the family structure to which Foucault is referring is implicitly understood as a traditionally patriarchal understanding of the family, with an all-powerful father figure, a mother who is subordinate to her husband, and children who are subordinate to both parental figures. This understanding of the family excludes alternative family units, and so has perhaps lost a certain relevance as alternative families have become more mainstream. The second important point is that while the family structure may be a site in which sovereign power is exercised, the family generally has become one of the most significant spaces of disciplinary power in contemporary society. Just as Althusser finds that the family ISA is fundamental to the creation and continuation of ideology, so Foucault finds that the family—as a site in which relations of sexuality are introduced and deployed—is critical to establishing control over individuals. This is implicit in *The History of Sexuality, Vol. 1*; it is made explicit in *Psychiatric Power*, where Foucault contends,

> Inasmuch as the family conforms to the non-disciplinary schema of an apparatus (*dispositif*) of sovereignty, I think we could say that it is the hinge, the interlocking point, which is absolutely indispensable to the very functioning of all the disciplinary systems. I mean that the family is the instance of constraint that will permanently fix individuals to their disciplinary apparatuses (*appareils*), which will inject them, so to speak, into the disciplinary apparatuses (*appareils*). (2006, p. 81)

The internal structure of a family, then, allied to the family's importance to the disciplinary apparatus generally, aids in the subjection and repression of individuals. In the words of Foucault's disciple Jacques Donzelot, "[f]rom being the plexus of a complex web of relations of dependence and allegiance, the family became the nexus of nerve endings of machinery that was exterior to it" (1979, p. 91).

Family as a Source of Violence

Deleuze (often, but not always, working in tandem with Félix Guattari) offers a broadly similar but alternative understanding of the family unit. Deleuze and Guattari even make use of similar terminology to Foucault, with the term "alliance" found in both Foucault's and Deleuze and Guattari's works. While the Foucauldean understanding of "alliance" is closely related to the nuclear family structure and refers to the ties of kinship which connect family members, however, this concept more closely resembles the Deleuzeo-Guattarian "filiation," with "alliance" in the Deleuzeo-Guattarian sense referring to the system of interpersonal networks outside the family unit. This altered vocabulary is indicative of the difference in thought that exists between Foucault and Deleuze and Guattari regarding the concept of the family. Deleuze and Guattari approach the family from a more neutral perspective: it is not the family itself that is repressive, rather it is the manipulation of the family (or any other sort of interpersonal relationship) by repressive forces that converts the family into a site of repression. This can be seen in Deleuze's essay "The Rise of the Social," written as the foreword to Donzelot's *The Policing of Families*. In that essay, Deleuze describes the family as "simultaneously the occasion of an unburdening of the liberal state and the target or charge of the interventionist state: not an ideological quarrel, but two poles of one strategy on the same line" (1979, p. xiii). The duality of the family concept is particularly important in Deleuze and Guattari's *Anti-Oedipus* (1977).

In the preface to that book, Foucault provides an alternate title for the work, coining it "an *Introduction to the Non-Fascist Life*" (1983, p. xiii). Foucault believes that *Anti-Oedipus* is a treatise directed against "the fascism in us all, in our heads and in our everyday behavior, the fascism that causes us to love power, to desire the very thing that dominates and exploits us" (1983, p. xiii). From a Foucauldean perspective the family, with its roots in the deployment of alliance, is an archetypal example of the sort of social structure based around "subdivision and pyramidal hierarchization" (1983, p. xiii), and as such is something that must be rejected in favor of openness and independence. Where Foucault, in his rejection of "pyramidal hierarchization," defines the family structure as a site that is inherently fascistic, Deleuze and Guattari focus instead on the concept of oedipalization, the process through which the Oedipus complex is introduced into social structures, thereby converting them into agencies of fascism and repression. Significantly, for Deleuze and Guattari the family is not inherently fascistic. Deleuze and Guattari themselves state plainly that

> It is not a question of denying the vital importance of parents or the love attachment of children to their mothers and fathers. It is a question of knowing what the place and the function of parents are within desiring-production,

rather than doing the opposite and forcing the entire interplay of desiring-machines to fit within the restricted code of Oedipus. (1983, p. 47)

Rather than the family specifically, then, what Deleuze and Guattari are concerned with is the concept of "desiring-production," and how desire is restricted in the family structure through Oedipus. Both "Oedipus" and "desiring-production" (along with its foundational concept, desire) are fundamental to Deleuze and Guattari's understanding of the family; as the translator's note to *Anti-Oedipus* explains, the term "Oedipus" is used in many different ways and with different meanings throughout the text—"[Oedipus] refers . . . not only to the Greek myth of Oedipus and to the Oedipus complex as defined by classical psychoanalysis, but also to Oedipal mechanisms, processes, and structures" (1983, p. 3). In all of these meanings, however, what does not change is the concept's interaction with (and repression of) desire; Deleuze and Guattari spend much of *Anti-Oedipus* examining this interaction within the context of the family structure.

Deleuze's understanding of desire differs from that of other philosophers. Where traditionally desire has been associated with lack, Deleuze instead associates desire with production. This contrasts sharply with Oedipus, which is in constant conflict with desire: "[Oedipus] is a contemporary form of social repression that reduces the forms desire takes—and thus the connections desire makes—to those that sustain the social formation of capitalism" (Lorraine, 2005, p. 195). Indeed, the conflict that exists between desire and Oedipus, within not merely the family but society generally, is a crucial one, for desire has revolutionary capacity: "[i]f desire is repressed, it is because every position of desire, no matter how small, is capable of calling into question the established order of a society. . . . there is no desiring-machine capable of being assembled without demolishing entire social sectors" (Deleuze and Guattari, 1983, p. 116). This makes the family a (potentially) crucial battleground against repression. For Deleuze and Guattari, Oedipus is merely the most readily identifiable form of psychic repression, the primary instrument used to combat desire. We can see, then, how the (Oedipal) family is used to foment repression—

> Psychic repression is such that social repression becomes desired. . . . Strictly speaking, psychic repression is a means in the service of social repression. . . . Psychic repression is delegated by the social formation,

while the desiring-formation is disfigured, displaced by psychic repression. The family is the delegated agent of psychic repression, or rather the agent delegated to psychic repression. (Deleuze and Guattari, 1983, p. 119)

Psychic repression corresponds, to a certain extent, with Althusser's ISAs, in that just as ISAs work unconsciously to create "always-already subjects," so psychic repression, and particularly Oedipus, manipulates desire, leading to individuals desiring repression: "Oedipalisation is a form of social repression that funnels the productive capacity of the unconscious back into the constricting channels of Oedipal desire" (Lorraine, 2005, p. 196). It is not so much that the family itself is fascistic or repressive, but rather that the family represents the repressive nature of an inherently fascistic society.

Familia rodante

Just as the philosophers studied in this chapter share broadly similar perspectives on the family but arrive at their conclusions using significantly different approaches, so the films examined in this chapter make similar statements concerning the family but do so in noticeably different ways. Coming immediately after *El bonaerense*, an obviously political film that received widespread critical acclaim in numerous countries, *Familia rodante* was viewed by some as lacking the gravity of the director's earlier films (Andermann, 2012). Trapero's third film is not explicitly political in the manner of his first two films—rather than focus on economic policies or government manipulation of power, the film provides a close reading of the forced interactions of a specific family. Far from distancing itself from national allegory, the intrafamilial bickering that characterizes much of the film's narrative (and which at times escalates to actual physical violence) is a potent manifestation of the quotidian objective violence that has been the central target of Trapero's critique throughout his entire career. Unlike his first two films *Familia rodante* has no central protagonist, instead examining the effect the increasingly tense environment in which the characters find themselves has on several generations of the same extended family. As such, the film allows viewers to, in effect, witness the process of subjugation and oppression that occurs gradually over the course of a life. In particular, the many interpersonal relationships that are portrayed throughout the film allow *Familia rodante* to mediate the Deleuzo-Guattarian understanding of the family as a construct that represses desiring-production and causes the family to function as a site where repression is created.

The great majority of those relationships occur within the titular "rolling" family on which the film focuses. While no character could be considered the film's protagonist, the family matriarch Emilia (Graciela Chironi) can perhaps be viewed as the narrative's catalyst. The film begins on the morning of her birthday; she is shown living a comfortable, albeit somewhat solitary, retired life—she spends most of her time in her garden watering her plants and feeding her cats and chickens. Her extended family—her two daughters and their husbands and children—come over for a birthday dinner and, during the dinner, Emilia announces that she has been asked to be the maid of honor at her niece's wedding. As a birthday gift she wants the entire family to accompany her to the celebration, which is happening 1,000 kilometers northeast of Buenos Aires in the north-eastern province of Misiones. Although nobody seems particularly enthused by the idea, they all reluctantly agree to it. During the dinner scene the majority of the family members are introduced: Emilia's adult daughters Marta (Liliana Capuro) and Claudia (Ruth Dobel); Marta's husband Oscar (Bernardo Forteza) and their three children Paola (Laura Glave), Gustavo (Raul Viñoles), and Matías (Nicolas Lopez); and Claudia's daughter Yanina (Marianela Pedano). The others mention the absence of Claudia's husband Ernesto (Carlos Resta), and when he is introduced in the following scene the tension between him and his wife is palpable—he is entirely against the idea, while Claudia flatly states she is going and taking their daughter with her, whether he likes it or not. The next day the entire family, including a friend of Yanina's named Nadia (Leila Gomez) who has tagged along, meet at a service station, pack into Oscar's 1958 Chevy Viking campervan, and the journey north begins.

These opening scenes serve to introduce not only the characters themselves but also their very well-defined personalities. Emilia is shown to be quite aware of her position within the family and is willing to use emotional manipulation to get what she wants. Marta is incredibly stressed and feels guilty for supplying her mother with the pills she takes on a regular basis, while Claudia is visibly depressed. Marta's husband Oscar (referred to throughout the film as Gordo, an affectionate nickname for any fat man in Argentina) is the stereotypical father figure who mans the grill for the *asado* and assumes responsibility for the driving, while Ernesto (whom everyone refers to as Pelado, baldy) is as unhappy in his marriage as his wife, and makes his dislike of her family obvious. The eldest of the family's third generation, Paola is in her early twenties and has already had a baby, though she appears to have broken off the relationship with her child's father just before the family sets off. (Paola's boyfriend Claudio appears much later in the film and keen-eyed viewers will recognize the character—not only does he have the same name as Rulo's son from *Mundo grúa*, but he is played by the same actor, Fernando Esquerro.) The teenagers also fulfill certain stereotypes—Gustavo is going through the awkward phase of puberty, while his cousin Yanina, a year older than he, is boy-crazy and has her eyes set firmly on her cousin.

The Potent Symbolism of the Family

As with many of Trapero's early films, *Familia rodante*'s politics are only subtly hinted at throughout most of the narrative, and attempting to read the film through the same lens as might be used for any of the director's subsequent works would almost certainly lead one to discount the film's political statement. However, as Santiago Oyarzabal points out, the film's "politics of representation clearly work to unpack the myths constructed by conventional discourses of family and nation" (2017, p. 148). Rather than a broad, sweeping examination of Argentine society, what *Familia rodante* presents is a micro-level examination of what Urraca refers to as "micro-societies," which she defines as "restricted, stifling, almost claustrophobic locations," which contain "highly-regulated codes of behavior that are opaque to outsiders" (2011, p. 154). These micro-societies can, and often do, function as representative of society as a whole, and the conflicts and failings visible in them are often merely symptomatic of the same conflicts and failings seen in society generally. The family, in particular, serves as a good example of a micro-society because of the important role it plays in shaping broader societal norms and expectations. Using the family to meditate on society is something that is fairly common in Argentine cinema: Luis Puenzo's *La historia oficial*, perhaps the most internationally well-known film to come out of Argentina in the immediate post-dictatorship period, mediates the traumatic legacy of the dictatorship by focusing on one specific family. More recently, the 2002 film *Kamchatka* uses the family as a metaphor not only for the trauma of dictatorship but also the dictatorship's lasting effects on Argentine society. Gabriela Copertari compares the collapse of the family unit to the "generalized social orphanhood resulting from the absence of a protector or benefactor state" (2010, p. 119) and, in the postcrisis period, familial collapse is often used to symbolize the collapse of the nation's economy and subsequent social upheaval.

What is clear, then, is that the family has always been a highly symbolic site which allows Argentine filmmakers to reflect on whatever societal issues or pressures the country may be experiencing at any given time. Through its presentation of a large middle-class family that appears to be gradually ripping itself apart, *Familia rodante* can easily be understood as a metaphor for the experience of Argentine society, broadly, in the early postcrisis years. These "generational ruptures" (2009, p. 55), as Joanna Page refers to them, can be at least somewhat explained by the new paradigm in which Argentine society found itself in the aftermath of both the neoliberal and crisis years. Grimson and Kessler describe the devastating effect that period had on Argentine (especially middle-class) identity, stating,

> [the Argentine] historical-cultural model was reinforced by a generational model according to which each generation rose a rung or more above its predecessor on the social ladder. In the worst case it stayed in the same place; social descent was out of the question... the overriding tendency was always upward and onward to such a degree that "progress" and "future" were synonymous.... Impoverishment with no possibility of recovery has closed the book on this particular success story. (2012, pp. 89–90)

In broad strokes, therefore, the collapse of the family unit—which essentially comprises the bulk of *Familia rodante*'s narrative arc—can be understood as a larger metaphor for the collapse of Argentine society, the middle class (of which Trapero, growing up, was a part) in particular. However, the film also provides a much sharper criticism, one that goes beyond the immediate circumstance of the Argentine middle class. *Familia rodante* functions as Trapero's first pointed analysis of the violence inherent in the family structure. Indeed, the film suggests that the more time the family spends together, the weaker their bond becomes. With its focus on love triangles, betrayal, and the repetition of these things over the course of generations, the specific family around which *Familia rodante*'s narrative revolves is a particularly emblematic example of many of the criticisms of the family structure that both Foucault and Deleuze and Guattari offer in their respective analyses.

The Family as a Locus of Retention

As the family makes their way north away from the urban space of Buenos Aires they are confronted by a country that seems completely separate from their own reality—the landscape on either side of the highway is completely devoid of man-made structures, instead featuring feral horses grazing in flooded fields and the endless horizon of the pampa. When their truck breaks down and they are stuck beside the river, as the family passes the time swimming, locals wade through the water on horseback, the water rising to their horses' necks. Calling to mind Jorge Luis Borges's short story *El Sur*, the further away from the city they get, the less modern their surroundings become. This sense is reinforced when, to pass the time, Emilia begins reciting from memory the *Leyenda del Mojón*, a famous nineteenth-century *payada* (a type of lyric poem that is considered an integral part of gaucho culture). As if summoned by Emilia's recitation—Andermann describes them as being "like ghosts from a remote past" (2012, p. 65)—men on horseback wearing traditional gaucho attire appear on both sides of the road, blocking the route as they joyfully smash their machetes against the hood of the truck (Figure 3.1).

Figure 3.1 *Familia rodante* (2004). The gauchos seem to emerge from the ether, as if conjured by Emilia.

Shortly thereafter, Claudia wakes up with a terrible toothache and the family is forced to stop so she can visit the dentist. By chance the nearest town is Yapeyú, a village on the Argentina-Brazil border and the birthplace of Argentine liberator José de San Martín. When they arrive, the town is in the midst of celebrating a cultural festival, and as they drive along the town's dirt roads, Argentine flags draped overhead, their truck (the only vehicle in sight) is surrounded by a swarm of men on horseback and horse-drawn carriages (likely the same men who appeared on the road the previous night). The truck eventually disappears from view behind a mass of man and animal. While the family may find themselves in a population center, they are far from any sort of urban environment that they might recognize. In parallel to this increasingly unfamiliar setting, the family's interpersonal relationships become progressively more strained as they leave Buenos Aires further behind, as if the city itself were the only thing holding the family together. For Natália Pinazza, "[the] choice of Argentina's geographical limit as the final stage of their journey works as an effective metaphor for a family unit that is pushed to its limits" (2014, p. 110).

The strain of the journey begins pushing the family unit to its limits as they are camped on the banks of a river, their truck having broken down. As the agitation mounts as a result of the delay, two of the film's central story arcs begin to take shape. First, Yanina separates her cousin from the rest of the family and begins to kiss him, pulling his head to hers. Although Gustavo is certainly into it—the kiss lasts twenty seconds—he eventually draws away, laughing nervously and saying "si nos llegan a ver, nos cortan la cabeza" ("If they find us they'll cut our heads off"). Yanina, however, insists, declaring that she doesn't care. Gustavo, flustered to the point that he can only repeat the word "no," tries to back away from his cousin but is unable to, until finally she grabs him by the head and they kiss again. The segment ends with the two embracing each other, Yanina having yet again pulled Gustavo into a kiss (Figure 3.2). The film then immediately cuts to a shot of Ernesto (Yanina's father) and Marta (Gustavo's mother) sitting outside the campervan. The scene begins in medias res, with Marta asking "¿que me acuerde de qué?" ("what should I remember?") Ernesto, a note of incredulity in his voice, replies "vamos, Marta, ¿no te acordás?" ("come on, Marta, you don't remember?"), a question which appears to fluster its recipient. Marta's response lays bare the reasons behind the tension that exists between Ernesto and the rest of the family, as she answers "sí, la pasábamos bien, sí" ("sure, we had a good time, yeah"), before Ernesto says "por eso... acordate" ("exactly... remember")

Figure 3.2 *Familia rodante* (2004). Yanina rejects the norms imposed upon her by the arborescent family structure.

and walks away. These two interactions mirror each other—Ernesto's pursuit of Marta is reflected in his daughter's even more aggressive pursuit of Marta's son—and, in their awkwardness and tension, they set the tone for the majority of the interpersonal relationships to come in the film.

The two exchanges that occur by the riverbank are repeated, in a sort of inverse form, as the family is waiting for Claudia while she is at the dentist. The entire segment that is set in Yapeyú is perhaps the most important in the entire film, for it is in Yapeyú that the familial cracks that have been visible throughout the film begin to widen, threatening to break the family apart completely. As Marta and Ernesto accompany Claudia to the dentist and Gordo works on the truck's engine, Emilia and her grandchildren visit a local museum. At the museum Emilia begins to feel faint and complains that the family is not looking after her the way they should. She goes to sit down, leaving the teenagers to themselves, which allows Yanina the opportunity to confront Gustavo about their earlier tryst. Gustavo sheepishly admits that he is, in fact, more interested in Yanina's friend Nadia, and the idea that Yanina would be interested in him at all, considering they are cousins, strikes him as funny. This enrages Yanina, who storms out of the museum and locks herself in the campervan's bathroom. Gustavo and Nadia then proceed to isolate themselves from the rest of the group and share a kiss. As this is happening, Ernesto is shown confronting Marta outside the dentist's office, telling her "¿sabés lo que no puedo creer? Que todo el tiempo sea como no pasa nada. *Eso* no lo puedo creer." ("You know what I can't believe? That this whole time you've acted like nothing is going on. *That's* what I can't believe.") Despite Marta's insistence that nothing is, in fact, going on, Ernesto grabs her face and kisses her. This moment, and particularly Marta's reaction—pushing Ernesto off her as she calls him a "desubicado" (someone who acts completely out of line)—both parallels and contrasts with the budding love triangle that is emerging between the younger generation. Indeed, the kiss between Nadia and Gustavo immediately precedes Ernesto's move on Marta, a fact that emphasizes the difference between the two relationships—where the teenagers coyly lean in toward each other until finally meeting lips, Ernesto grabs Marta's face and pulls it toward his own. Although Marta at first stands up from her seat as if to storm away, she ultimately returns and asks Ernesto for a cigarette, while continuing to voice her displeasure toward him.

These four interactions, split between two concurrent scenes, bring to life some of the ideas expressed by Foucault when he discusses the deployment of sexuality. Foucault emphasizes that the deployment of sexuality was primarily centered around four "great strategic unities which . . . formed specific mechanisms of knowledge and power centering on sex" (1990, p. 103). These four unities, summarized as "the hysterical woman, the masturbating child, the Malthusian couple, and the perverse adult" (1990, p. 105), all play a role in both converting sexuality into an oppressive force and introducing that oppressive force into the family unit, thereby ensuring regulation over both sex and the family itself. The first unity which Foucault lists, and perhaps the most important, is the "hysterization of women's bodies," with the most visible example of this being variations of the hysterical woman: "the nervous woman, the frigid wife, the indifferent mother" (1990, p. 110). Both before and during the scene set in Yapeyú, Emilia, Marta, *and* Claudia are all presented, to a greater or lesser degree, as examples of hysterical women—Claudia, the apparently frigid woman in a loveless marriage; her sister Marta, high-strung and wracked with guilt, seemingly constantly on the verge of a nervous breakdown; and their mother Emilia, who despite being the family matriarch seems more concerned with her family looking after her than with her looking after her family. Foucault does not focus solely on hysterical women, either; as he lists various examples of other sexual unities manifested—"the impotent, sadistic, perverse husband, the hysterical or neurasthenic girl, [and] the precocious and already exhausted child" (1990, p. 110). All of these figures appear to correspond to characters found in *Familia rodante*'s narrative: Ernesto the perverse husband who seems to enjoy tormenting his wife and brazenly desires his sister-in-law; Paola the emotionally distressed young mother who begins the film in a fight with the father of her child; and all of the teenaged characters who seem sexually precocious far beyond their years. The family that serves as the center of *Familia rodante* is a sort of archetype of what Foucault describes in *The History of Sexuality*, Vol. 1, demonstrating the debilitating impact that the sexualized family structure, manipulated as a form of control, can have on individuals.

One of the primary concerns of Deleuze and Guattari's *Anti-Oedipus* is society's repression of desire, and the family is a particularly important element of that repression. For Deleuze and Guattari, the family is key in shaping and regulating the revolutionary concepts of desire and desiring-production:

> It must be borne in mind that the family relentlessly operates on desiring-production. Inscribing itself into the recording process of desire, clutching at everything, the family performs a vast appropriation of the productive forces; it displaces and reorganizes in its own fashion the entirety of the connections and the hiatuses that characterize the machines of desire. . . . Retention is the primary function of the family: it is a matter of learning what elements of desiring-production the family is going to reject, [and] what it is going to retain. (1983, pp. 124–5)

The family structure, therefore, reinforces itself through regulating desire and creating a sort of cycle into which generation after generation is entrapped. Perhaps the film's most obvious example of an individual combating against societal pressures (or, to use Deleuzean terminology, the possible repression of their desire) is seen in the case of Yanina, Claudia and Ernesto's boy-crazy daughter. Deleuze and Guattari's contention that the "family has become the locus of retention and resonance of all the social determinations" (1983, p. 269) is exemplified by Yanina's experiences over the course of the film, particularly the way in which she responds to the love triangle that emerges between herself, her friend Nadia, and Gustavo.

In desiring a family member, Yanina mirrors her father. However, where Ernesto is fully within the societal machinations of the family—he has conformed with and become a part of the structure—Yanina begins the film somewhat outside the repressive grasp of the societal expectations that should, in theory, be imposed upon her by the family structure. Yanina's actions are those of someone who is unencumbered by the repression of desiring-production; despite the obvious taboos involved with having a relationship with a first cousin, Yanina is determined in her pursuit of Gustavo. His eventual rejection of her (due in no small part to the fact that they are related), followed by his subsequent relationship with Nadia, affects Yanina significantly. Yanina's desiring of Gustavo is, of course, destined to fail, for it is precisely the sort of unchecked desire that Deleuze and Guattari refer to when they write "sexuality and love . . . cause strange flows to circulate that do not let themselves be stocked within an established order. Desire does not 'want' revolution, it is revolutionary in its own right, as though involuntarily, by wanting what it wants" (1983, p. 116). This revolutionary desire is precisely what established social orders are created to repress, and Yanina's response to her desire being repressed is noteworthy. At the wedding she meets a young man and, after a brief flirtation, has sex with him. They are then shown dancing together the next morning, a blissful look across Yanina's face as she embraces the boy. While it might be argued that this outcome is, in a sense, a victory for repression—Yanina's potentially revolutionary desire has been rechanneled away from her cousin and toward someone outwith the family— she nevertheless remains outside the family structure, rechanneling her desire without extinguishing it. By having sex with a complete stranger, and one who is of dark complexion—an important signifier in a country where skin color and class are still closely linked—Yanina can be understood to be rejecting the expectations of her middle-class family. Ernesto's socially unacceptable desiring of his sister-in-law is mirrored in Yanina's experience with her cousin. The difference between the two situations is found in the fact that Ernesto has long ago succumbed to the societal pressures which impact on Yanina. Precisely because of the socially taboo nature of both Ernesto's and Yanina's desires, the two characters function as the film's most crystallized examples of Deleuze and Guattari's contention that "no society can tolerate a position of real desire without its structures of exploitation, servitude, and hierarchy being compromised" (1983, p. 116). As it happens, Ernesto's revolutionary desire most likely causes the dissolution of his marriage and, possibly, that of Marta, as well; Yanina's desire, on the other hand, has resulted in both an explicit and more subtle rejection of society's expectations of her.

Discipline and Rebellion

The film uses the love triangle that exists between Gordo, his wife Marta, and her brother-in-law and former flame Ernesto to mediate the forces competing for dominance within the family structure. In particular, Gordo and Ernesto represent opposing desires: Gordo, the *pater familias* of the extended family, attempting to exert his control over everyone, Ernesto attempting to rebel against this control and the more general repression of the family structure. The film's primary setting—the interior of the campervan—forces these competing impulses into conflict. In the same way that *Carancho*'s cinematography heightens that film's tautness and sense of unease, the tight, claustrophobic framing of *Familia rodante*, especially in the case of scenes set inside the confines of the campervan, emphasizes the tense interpersonal relationships that exist between the various family members. As if to accentuate the restricted interior space of the campervan, characters are shot primarily in close-up, with the result that the camera lingers on the subtle facial expressions and unconscious tics of the different characters; just as each individual is unable to escape from the family's collective gaze, so they are incapable of hiding from the camera which watches over every character's actions, even hinting at their private thoughts. The entirety of a character's body is rarely shown, the edges of the frame often cutting out their hands or torso, and Trapero utilizes rapid cuts between different body parts, resulting in difficulty processing what is happening at any given moment.

This replicates the experience of the characters themselves—Gordo, for example, is stuck driving the truck and so is only able to catch snippets of what is going on behind him through his rear-view mirror. He sees his wife and Ernesto exiting the toilet simultaneously, but has no context for why they were there in the first place. While the explanation is simple enough—Marta's youngest son Matías had locked the bathroom door and Ernesto was curious to see why Marta was knocking on the door repeatedly—the sight of the two leaving the toilet together plants (or, perhaps more likely, reaffirms) suspicions in Gordo's mind that Ernesto may be chasing after Marta. The way in which the scenes inside the campervan are filmed and edited, then, can be understood as an attempt to reflect the tense and distrusting relationships that exist amongst the various family members. Emphasizing the concept of the family as a means of societal control, everyone is simultaneously watching and being watched at all times, with actions being judged and assumptions generated.

As if to heighten the inherent claustrophobia of the campervan (and the symbolic claustrophobia of the familial unit), the rural landscape through which the family is travelling is filmed in wide-open shots that accentuate the immensity of the Argentine countryside. Similarly, exterior shots of the truck, almost without exception, are filmed at a distance, with the vehicle occupying only a small portion of the frame and often being dwarfed by the commercial trucks that are speeding past. Where the cinematography inside the campervan implies anxiety and repression, the long shots of the truck travelling along the highway, first the seemingly endless pampa of Buenos Aires province and then the red dirt and green rolling hills of Misiones surrounding the relatively small vehicle on all sides, suggest a freedom that is constantly just out of reach, separated by the physical walls of the campervan and the symbolic walls of the family. Indeed, as the family makes its way further and further north, away from the Buenos Aires metropole, the campervan seems to become the only thing holding the family together, to such an extent that fights (of varying intensity) break out almost immediately every time the family exits the truck. Most significantly Gordo, who for much of the narrative is presented as a somewhat henpecked husband who is content to bend to the will of his family, begins to exert a sort of primal masculinity that both reflects and adds to the already increasing tension.

This masculinity verges on violent machismo in several scenes, and is first evident when Claudio, the father of Paola's child, appears on his motorbike, evidently attempting to make up for their previous fight. As Claudio gets off his motorbike and removes his helmet, the truck pulls up behind him and Gordo storms out. Screaming obscenities as he walks forward, Gordo punches Claudio flush in the face, a blow that sends the younger man sprawling to the ground. The rest of the family quickly arrive and separate the two, holding back Gordo as he repeatedly attempts to try and slough off his family in order to attack Claudio. Even after the threat of more physical violence has passed, Gordo continues to be enraged, threatening to burn Claudio's motorbike. Gordo is finally shown literally and figuratively cooling off as he sits on the front bumper of the truck along with his wife and youngest son, his shirt off and his wife handing him some sort of pill. While much of the action post punch is filmed in a handheld style that replicates the chaos and confusion of the moment, the initial shot, from the time Claudio catches up with and then pulls ahead of the family's truck to immediately after Gordo punches him, is a single long take shot from a considerable distance. The wide shot framing combined with the long take allow viewers to see that the road itself has become a sort of liminal space, still paved but covered with the red dirt of the surrounding country. Deliberate or not, the gradually receding pavement can be understood to symbolize the family's weakening ties. The family unit breaks down completely in the final stop before the group arrives at their destination. By this point in the film, whatever societal influences that might have held the family together have been well and truly left behind—indeed, society is so far away that even the roads on which the family travel are no longer paved, the vehicle instead cutting through thick jungle on a small dirt road.

It is in this wild setting that the seams of the family truly come apart, with particularly violent repercussions. As in the scene with Claudio, Gordo's latent machismo emerges in an explosive manner, albeit one that is less physically violent and more emotionally damaging. The critical moment involves the simmering feud between Gordo and his counterpart Ernesto. The relationship between the two men is characterized by an almost incessant bickering, beginning virtually the moment the family departs Buenos Aires. The two fathers' personalities are as different as their physical statures—Ernesto, thin and bald, represents a sort of particularly urban male identity that disdains physical labor and rejects the countryside, while Gordo, fat as his nickname implies, represents the more traditional macho identity of the man who makes his living with his hands. Where Ernesto is shown constantly toying around with his camera and camcorder, Gordo is responsible for maintaining the truck and repairing the engine when it breaks down. Ernesto is presented as exceedingly selfish, concerned only with his own needs and desires, while Gordo is willing to act as a father figure even to his niece—when Yanina returns to the campervan after being rejected by Gustavo, it is Gordo, rather than Ernesto, who attempts to console her—and his devotion to his own children borders on the obsessive, as demonstrated by his violent reaction when he finally comes face-to-face with Claudio. The confrontation between Ernesto and Gordo pits the two characteristics inherent to macho males—

aggressiveness and hypersexuality (Ingoldsby, 1991, pp. 57–8)—against each other. Although Ernesto is not nearly as stereotypically macho as his brother-in-law, he is almost entirely driven by his sexual desire for Marta, to the extent that his choices end up having violent repercussions for all involved. Gordo, on the other hand, possesses an aggressiveness that, although displayed only infrequently, is capable of frightening intensity. And, as might be expected with behavior driven by a force such as machismo, in the moment neither character seems aware of the long-term damage their actions will cause.

The conflict that leads to the ultimate breakdown of the family unit occurs as the group has stopped in a clearing in the middle of the jungle so that everyone can change into their wedding clothes. The consistent bickering between the two men reaches a boiling point in part because of their conflicting identities— using some ropes and a blanket Gordo jury-rigs an external shower and changing area, which enrages Ernesto, who wonders why they do not simply stop at a service station. This, in turn, infuriates Gordo, who asks Ernesto if he has seen anything of the sort in the previous two hours before telling him "no jodas más . . . si no, andá a sacar fotos que es lo único que hiciste hasta ahora" ("stop fucking around . . . otherwise, go take some photos, since it's the only thing you've done so far"). This dismissal is, perhaps, the catalyst for all that follows. Gordo has asserted his dominance over Ernesto by responding to his brother-in-law as if he were a child making unreasonable demands that must be rejected out of hand due to their impossibility. This causes Ernesto (who has already displayed his self-destructive streak when he kissed Marta in Yapeyú) to decide that he is willing to break apart not only his own family but also Gordo's, as well. Pacing outside the campervan's shower as Marta is using it, he finally musters the courage to open the door and make one last attempt to pursue his sister-in-law. Gordo, hearing the commotion, charges into the campervan just as Ernesto is attempting to exit and forces him backward, Gordo grabbing his counterpart by the shirt (Figure 3.3). The camera then shifts to images of the family as they go about getting dressed for the wedding; a muffled yet still audible argument can be heard coming from off-screen as the camera cuts from Matías rinsing soap from his head to Claudia craning her neck to see what is happening inside. Returning to the campervan, Gordo opens the shower door and forcibly removes the still-wet Marta, placing his finger on her lips in order to physically stifle her protestations while threateningly saying "mejor no digas nada, mejor no digas nada, ¿eh?" ("it's best if you keep quiet, it's best if you

The Violence of the Arborescent Family 123

Figure 3.3 *Familia rodante* (2004). In their confrontation, Gordo and Ernesto embody differing aspects of the same phenomenon: machismo.

keep quiet, alright?"). Again, the camera cuts away from the interior of the campervan, yet Gordo's muffled shouting can be heard in the background. The camera then cuts to a shot of the entire family standing outside of the campervan, an almost frantic Claudia demanding that Ernesto explain what is happening. As Ernesto tries to separate himself from his wife, his suitcase and shoulder bag are thrown out of the campervan onto the dusty road, followed in quick succession by Marta being shoved backward out of the van and then finally a shirtless Gordo stomping out, picking up Ernesto's luggage and shoving it at him. As he does so, Gordo tells everyone "no pasa nada, Ernesto decidió irse y se va. . . . YA" ("it's nothing, Ernesto has decided to go and he's leaving. . . . NOW"). As Ernesto says his goodbyes and his wife and daughter (and the rest of the extended family) react to this news, Gordo violently grabs Marta by the collar of her shirt and drags her back into the campervan. The stifled sounds of the continuing argument occurring inside the campervan can be heard off-screen as the family processes everything that has just happened.

The outcome of this scene is the ultimate breakdown of the family unit—by the end of the film Ernesto has been, essentially, expelled from the family, forced to return to Buenos Aires on his own while Emilia, run down by the family's constant bickering, decides she has no desire to return to the city, choosing instead to stay behind in Misiones. In particular, Gordo's actions, his machismo, precipitate this collapse, but the role of the family structure itself cannot be overlooked. Gordo's machismo emerges in the moments where he feels that his control over the family is most threatened—Claudio represents a challenge to his role as a father where Ernesto challenges his role as a husband—and his reaction to each challenge is a violent and decisive one. However, where Claudio is able to eventually earn Gordo's (grudging) respect (by going for petrol on his dirt bike when the truck unexpectedly runs out in the middle of nowhere), Ernesto is provided with no opportunity to redeem himself. This is due partly to the fact that he represents a more immediate threat to Gordo's overall dominance of the family, and partly because the father-daughter-boyfriend relationship (Oedipal triangle) is an accepted one in that it ensures the continuation of the family structure, whereas the husband-wife-brother-in-law relationship represents pure revolutionary desire. Gordo, who through violence establishes his position as the family's dominant male, has taken on the role of law, determining what is acceptable and what is not. Deleuze and Guattari state that "[under] the precocious action of social repression, the family slips into and interferes with the network of desiring-genealogy; it assumes the task of alienating the entire genealogy; it confiscates the Numen (but see here, God is daddy) . . . Social production delegates the family to psychic repression" (1983, p. 120). The family at the center of *Familia rodante* seems far removed from this concept—rather than function as agents of repression the individual family members seem intent on pursuing their desires. It is Gordo, then, who takes up the role of the subjugator, forcing the family into line, demanding that rules be followed, and ensuring that desire is repressed.

In its representation of the tensions that run rife through an archetypal Argentine family, *Familia rodante* speaks to a broader tension within Argentine society. The film's examination of the family mediates Foucault's belief, referenced earlier in this chapter, of the family as the critical component in the functioning of all societal disciplinary systems. In order to maintain the repressive, disciplinary agency of the family, Gordo must resort to violence, which only further drives the family apart. It is the very family structure itself—Ernesto's and Yanina's desire being considered taboo by the other members of their family; the patriarchal role of Gordo—that creates the physical and emotional violence by which the family ultimately comes to be defined. Even before the dissolution of the family toward the end of the work, the constant bickering and disagreements that characterize the family's interaction throughout the film suggest that the micro-aggressions of familial life wear away at individuals. Gordo's acts of violence, Ernesto's and Yanina's acts of rebellion, are simply the inevitable culmination of a cycle of violence. *Familia rodante* portrays the effects this cycle has on a representative Argentine family, while *El clan* extrapolates this idea into the larger social perspective.

El clan

Arquímedes Puccio (Guillermo Francella), the father figure at the center of *El clan* (2015), Trapero's most unique film, serves a similar function to Gordo. Rather than attempt to control the entire family, however, Arquímedes is primarily concerned with manipulating the actions and desires of one character, in particular—his son Alex (Peter Lanzani). Through a highly critical examination of the real-life Puccio family, the film exposes how the family unit is a site of violence in which power is manipulated and individuals are indoctrinated and controlled. In addition, the film functions as a condemnation of contemporary Argentine society and the passivity with which it approaches both subjective and objective violence. As a means of locating the viewer in time the film uses period-appropriate music—notably Serú Girán's 1980 hit *Encuentro con el diablo* and Virus' *Wadu wadu* from 1981—as well as clips from significant speeches from Argentina's recent past as signposts. This technique, which has become something of a trend in recent Latin American cinema, not only connects the narrative to the events taking place but also provides a sense of the rapidly shifting sociopolitical landscape of the early to mid-1980s. Furthermore, the interspersing of archival footage throughout the work lends the film a documentary feel, David Oubiña explaining that films that make use of this technique "tend to be documentarian (because they work from documentary material) or 'documentarized' (because they adopt an aesthetics that belongs to the documentary proper)" (2013, p. 33).

Finally, the use of archival material emphasizes the fact that the film is based on true events. Inspired by events that occurred in the early to mid-1980s, the film chronicles a series of murder-kidnappings committed by the upper-middle-class Puccio family between 1982 and 1985, focusing particularly on the experiences of family patriarch Arquímedes and his eldest son Alex. The Puccios resided in the highly affluent Buenos Aires suburb of San Isidro, and their victims were selected from amongst their neighbors and acquaintances. The revelation that the Puccio family were responsible for the kidnappings shocked not merely Buenos Aires but the entire nation—Alex Puccio was a star rugby player, going so far as to play for the Pumas, the country's national team, on several occasions, while Arquímedes Puccio was a well-respected business man (and a member of the SIDE, the Argentine state intelligence agency, although this was not widely known at the time).

The film begins by establishing Arquímedes's government connections and Alex's popularity in the community, both of which are manipulated in order to commit their first kidnapping. Despite receiving the ransom money they demand, Arquímedes and his men murder their victim, which deeply troubles Alex. As time passes Alex attempts to deal with his guilt while Arquímedes attempts to insulate himself as the military government collapses. In order to ensure his lifestyle, Arquímedes arranges another kidnapping and, through emotional and financial manipulation, convinces Alex to participate. The kidnapping goes as planned but Alex, who has recently begun a relationship and wants to begin a life with his partner, becomes increasingly distressed and begins drugging himself in an attempt to silence his conscience. The reintroduction of democracy to the country in 1983 results in Arquímedes becoming increasingly paranoid about his livelihood, a fear that is confirmed when a colleague is arrested for crimes committed during the dictatorship. In an attempt to secure more money another kidnapping is arranged but, unlike the previous two, this one does not go to plan and Arquímedes and his associates end up shooting the man in his car. Arquímedes blames the botch on Alex, who failed to appear when he said he would, and uses both emotional manipulation and the threat of physical violence to ensure that his son remains loyal to him. Although the group's fourth kidnapping goes as planned, the victim's family refuses to pay the ransom demanded. When the ransom is finally paid, the drop is a trap and Arquímedes and his crew are arrested. At the same time, the Puccio house is raided and Alex is arrested. In prison, Arquímedes continues his emotional manipulation of Alex, which finally sends the son over the edge. He begins savagely beating his father and is seemingly only prevented from killing him because the prison guards restrain him. The next day, as Alex and Arquímedes are being led to court, Alex breaks free of his handlers and attempts to commit suicide by throwing himself off the fifth-floor balcony. A series of epigraphs state what became of the various family members, including the fact that Alex's suicide attempt failed and he, along with his father, was sentenced to life in prison.

Adult Paranoiacs, Child Neurotics

Before the narrative begins, archival footage of President Raúl Alfonsín's statements upon receiving the "Nunca Más" (Never Again) report from the Comisión Nacional sobre la Desaparición de Personas (National Commission on the Disappearance of Persons) in 1984 is shown. The Puccio family's house is then shown being raided, with armed men forcing Alex into the basement at gunpoint. As the men descend the stairs an intertitle moves the film's timeline back three years, to 1982, and again we are presented with an official address, on this occasion the declaration of the loss of Stanley/Puerto Argentino, the act which signified Argentina's final defeat and (functionally) the end of the Falklands/Malvinas War. The speech, given by then-president Lt. General Leopoldo Galtieri, marked not only the Argentine nation's defeat in war but also served as the point of no return for the *Proceso* dictatorship. Arquímedes Puccio, watching the television from his couch, reacts with dismay, and the next day attends a meeting with several high-ranking government and armed forces officials. Shortly thereafter, the first of the Puccio family's kidnappings occurs. Alex waves down a car being driven by his friend Ricardo Manoukian, explaining that he has run out of petrol. Manoukian offers him a lift and Alex agrees; after the two travel a few blocks talking amicably their car is cut off and the two are carjacked by men wearing balaclavas and holding pistols. The masked men blindfold Manoukian and Alex and place Manoukian in the boot of their car; Alex gets in the passenger seat and removes his blindfold as the driver does the same, revealing Arquímedes, who asks "¿estás bién?" ("are you alright?")

In the wake of the kidnapping, the film shows how the Puccio family goes about their daily lives as if nothing has happened—Alex working in the family kiosk, talking rugby with the clientele, his mother and sister stocking the shelves; the family having dinner together, Arquímedes helping his daughter with her math homework—while also showing Arquímedes calling Manoukian's family, informing them that their son has been kidnapped and is being held for ransom by the "National Liberation Front." The film makes it quite clear that the entire Puccio family is shown to be at least somewhat aware of Arquímedes's actions, as Manoukian is held captive in the family's upstairs bathroom. Most significantly, Arquímedes's ability to emotionally manipulate his family is made exceedingly clear: at dinner one evening Alex explains that he might have the opportunity to travel to New Zealand and, while there, visit with the family's eldest son, Maguila. The mere mention of the name, however, causes Arquímedes to bitingly remark "sí, buenísimo. Y si lo ves, preguntale cómo hizo para olvidarse tan fácil de todos nosotros, y el esfuerzo que hicimos para que él pudiera viajar . . . capaz el pobrecito tuvo un ataque de amnesia y no fue con mal intención que nos dejó acá, solos con todo esto" ("yeah, great. And if you see him, ask him how he managed to forget all of us so easily, and the effort we put in so that he could travel . . . maybe the poor guy had an attack of amnesia and it wasn't with bad intentions that he left us all here, alone with all this").

These initial post-kidnapping scenes demonstrate Arquímedes's finely honed aptitude for controlling schizophrenia (in the Deleuzo-Guattarian understanding of the word) within his family structure. Deleuze and Guattari define schizophrenia as "the process of the production of desire and desiring-machines" (1983, p. 24). Desire is an inherently revolutionary idea, one that combats the rigidity imposed by structures like the nuclear (Oedipal) family. As such, it is something that must be combated if the family is to retain its repressive function. This is done, at least in part, by the introduction of Oedipus into the family unit, channeling the production of liberating desire, or schizophrenia, toward the reproduction of the family unit itself. Deleuze and Guattari believe that it is generally the father who introduces Oedipus into the family structure, stating "Oedipus is first the idea of an adult paranoiac, before it is the childhood feeling of a neurotic" (1983, p. 274). This is particularly demonstrated after the botched kidnapping attempt, in which Alex does not partake, results in the death of the target. Confronting Alex in his shop afterward, Arquímedes attacks his son, choking him against a wall and screaming at him "por tu culpa Naum fue asesinado. . . . ¡Ahora estamos en grave peligro! ¿Así es como te querías deshacer de tu padre?" ("because of you Naum was killed. . . . Now we are in serious danger! Is this how you wanted to rid yourself of your father, huh?") Throughout the film, Arquímedes's ability to manipulate the Oedipal urge is shown to be particularly effective on Alex.

This is first visible when it is revealed that, although Manoukian's ransom demands are eventually met, the hostage has nevertheless been killed; since Manoukian was a friend, Alex reacts particularly badly to the news. Sensing his son's internal conflict, Arquímedes assures him that Manoukian's death was necessary in order to ensure the safety of the entire family, including Alex himself—"las cosas se complicaron y no tuvimos otra opción, Alex, porque el pibe nunca se tragó tu interpretación en el auto" ("things got messy and we didn't have any other choice, Alex, because the kid never bought your act in the car"). By laying the blame for Manoukian's death on Alex's conscience, Arquímedes is contributing to his son's developing neurosis, a neurosis that will become more and more debilitating over the course of the narrative. This is precisely in keeping with what Deleuze and Guattari believe to be the central role of the family, as they explain that it is "the family's mission . . . to produce neurotics by means of [the family's] oedipalization, its system of impasses, its delegated psychic repression, without which social repression would never find docile and resigned subjects, and would not succeed in choking off the flows' lines of escape" (1983, p. 361). Throughout the film Arquímedes utilizes (perhaps abuses) his position as head of the family in order to consciously erode his son's self-esteem and independence: Arquímedes alternates between blaming Alex when things go wrong to praising him for the "feeling of security" he provides (while also handing over several thousand dollars in cash).

Alex is a highly conflicted character, possibly to the extent that he is bordering on schizophrenia (in the customary sense of the word). He certainly maintains at least two distinct identities—the sharp contrast that exists between the popular, talented, admired rugby player persona that defines his public life and the reserved, guilt-ridden, domineered figure he cuts within the confines of the Puccio household are striking in their difference. This duality is most clearly visible in the internal strife he experiences due to his involvement in his father's kidnapping schemes: he is quite visibly uneasy with partaking in the act itself, and the repercussions of his actions cause him to feel significant guilt, yet he is also quite happy to reap the benefits of those actions, using the ransom money to open a windsurfing shop and begin looking for a house of his own to move into with his girlfriend. Throughout the film Alex's torment is presented as a sort of unrelenting feeling of suffocation brought about by his father, both literally—such as when Arquímedes, in a rage, chokes Alex against a wall—and metaphorically. After the completion of the second kidnapping, Arquímedes gives Alex a large amount of money and thanks him for his involvement in the scheme. Throughout the scene Arquímedes dominates his son using subtle tools—the enormous piles of cash sitting on Arquímedes's desk dazzle Alex when he first enters his father's office, and after giving thanks he hands Alex a stack of bills that must be worth $100,000. Alex is left speechless, only able to ask for a bag to place the money into.

The next scene shows Alex sitting in his shop late at night taking stock of diving equipment, having trouble breathing as he sweats profusely. Eyeing one of the oxygen tanks next to him he removes the mouthpiece from its packaging, opens the tank's valve, places the mouthpiece into his mouth, and begins breathing deeply while staring directly into the camera (Figure 3.4). As he breathes the camera slowly crawls from a medium shot to a close-up of his face, heightening the claustrophobia and sense of entrapment Alex is feeling; after a few moments Alex raises his free hand to his throat and squeezes. As he chokes himself the image on the screen begins to wobble and blur, going in and out of focus in time with Alex's increasingly labored breathing. (This effect is repeated in a later scene, after his father has physically choked him.) By the end of the scene only Alex's face is visible, his eyes never moving from staring directly at the camera, as if pleading with the audience for help. This moment, in particular, manifests Alex's schizophrenia. Alex finds himself trapped in a situation that is quite similar to what Deleuze and Guattari describe in *Anti-Oedipus*. Rather than replace his father within the family structure, Alex desires to leave not merely his family but the entire country—despite his

Figure 3.4 *El clan* (2015). Alex is powerless in relation to his father, driving him to a kind of schizophrenic mania.

father's objections he does eventually travel to New Zealand, bringing back his brother Maguila (perhaps in the hopes that Maguila will assume his role in the kidnapping scheme), and upon meeting his girlfriend Mónica they decide to travel to Sweden together. As examined earlier, however, Arquímedes continually projects his neuroses and paranoia onto his son, so that by the end of the film Alex has not merely attempted to kill his father, he has been driven to attempt suicide, preferring death to remaining within the family structure that has been imposed upon him.

The film's climactic final moments bring Alex, the Deleuzean schizophrenic, into a long-awaited confrontation with his father, "the simulacrum of the despotic Law" (Deleuze and Guattari, 1983, p. 269). The confrontation between father and son in the prison begins when Arquímedes berates Alex, claiming that all of Alex's success has been predicated on his father's careful planning, pointing out the fact that Alex has benefitted as much as anyone from Arquímedes's schemes. This enrages Alex to such an extent that he finally lashes out, the rage that has been building throughout the film released in one violent burst of aggression. It is only after he has been separated from his father that he realizes he has, yet again, done exactly what his father wanted him to do (Arquímedes intends to use his bruised face as proof that he was forced to produce a confession under torture). This realization proves one step too far for Alex and the next day he attempts suicide (Figure 3.5). Essentially, Alex is finally driven mad enough to attempt suicide because Arquímedes, well aware of the repressive potential that is inherent to father-son relationships, manipulates his son in a way he is incapable

Figure 3.5 *El clan* (2015). *El clan* presents a hierarchical structure so repressive that Alex's only means of escape is to attempt suicide.

of resisting. Throughout the film Arquímedes has been trying to break the flow of his son's desire and convert him into a subject. While the beating Alex dishes out may appear to be an act of rebellion, in fact he only succeeds in doing exactly what his father wants him to do, a father's final act of domination over his son. The realization that he has virtually no freedom whatsoever drives Alex insane and he attempts to kill himself. And yet, it is with this act that he truly becomes the ultimate schizophrenic, refusing to become a "docile and resigned subject," rejecting the control that his father so desperately attempts to impose on him.

The Violence of the Family

Arquímedes's manipulation of Alex, indeed his manipulation of the family unit generally, reflects the tactics employed by the *Proceso* government to justify their actions after their atrocities were made public. At every turn, Arquímedes is able to explain why he is committing the crimes he does, his justifications ranging from being in a "delicate financial position" to claims of being forcefully coerced by the Argentine government. These sorts of rationalizations and manipulations call to mind statements made by the military junta in its infamous "*Documento final de la junta militar sobre la guerra contra la subversión y el terrorismo*" ("Final document of the military junta concerning the war against subversion and terrorism"), a report released by the armed forces in April 1983 in which the military attempted to justify its actions during the Dirty War. Echoing Arquímedes's own highly cynical language, the document claims that pre-dictatorship domestic terror "se proponía llegar a la desaparición de la República como estado democrático" ("intended to result in the disappearance of the Republic as a democratic state"). This hypocrisy—the fact that by eliminating democracy the military junta achieved the very thing they claimed to be fighting against—resonates in Arquímedes's explanation to Alex that he is protecting the family, despite his own actions placing the family in the gravest of danger. Furthermore, the way Arquímedes justifies Manoukian's murder seems taken directly from the *Documento*, which claims that any crimes committed by the armed forces were merely the result of a desire to protect the nation and its people—

> Las acciones así desarrolladas fueron la consecuencia de apreciaciones que debieron efectuarse en plena lucha, con la cuota de pasión que el combate

y la defensa de la propia vida genera, en un ambiente teñido diariamente de sangre inocente, de destrucción y ante una sociedad en la que el pánico reinaba. En este marco, casi apocalíptico, se cometieron errores que, como sucede en todo conflicto bélico, pudieron traspasar, a veces, los límites del respeto a los derechos humanos fundamentales. (Documento, 1983, pp. 8–9)

[The actions committed were the consequence of the type of decisions that must be made in full-scale war, with an appreciation for the passion that combat and defense of one's life generate, in an environment stained daily by innocent blood and destruction and in a society in which panic reigned. As occurs in every armed conflict, in this almost apocalyptic reality errors were committed that may have, at times, crossed the line of respect for fundamental human rights.]

Arquímedes's highly studied rhetoric, the ease and comfort with which he is able to manipulate those around him, and the fact that, as an agent of the SIDE, he serves as a representative of the government all combine to create a character who is both an easily identifiable villain within the context of the family while also representing a much broader narrative in relation to the Argentine government's crimes against the nation.

Although the film presents Arquímedes as the unquestionable villain of the piece, Trapero makes it clear that every member of the Puccio family shares in his culpability. This is most visible in the way the various members of the Puccio family are presented while living in a house in which kidnapped victims are being actively held. Reflecting the sentiments of Judge María Servini de Cubría, who presided over the court cases against the Puccio family, Trapero's presentation of the family makes clear that the entire family, from youngest daughter Adriana to Arquímedes's wife Epifanía, were, if not active participants in the sequestering of the kidnapped individuals, at the very least well aware of what was happening. Despite this, not one member of the family ever did anything to stop the crimes from occurring. (Youngest son Guillermo did escape from the family, but running from a crime is not the same as attempting to stop it.) Perhaps the most significant example of this in the film is the scene when the hostage arrangement is first shown on-screen. Shot in a single two-minute-long take (highly reminiscent of the famous through-the-kitchen shot from Scorsese's *Goodfellas*), the scene begins with the camera focused on Arquímedes and Epifanía standing in the kitchen, Epifanía talking to her husband about the stress her job is causing her while she cuts pieces off a roast chicken and places them on a plate next to her. In response to Epifanía's complaint of a painful knot Arquímedes begins to rub her neck, locating the knot and massaging it out. When he finally works the knot out Epifanía tells him "tenés unas manos especiales. Que suerte que tengo" ("you have special hands. I'm so lucky"). After another piece of chicken is added to the plate on Arquímedes's suggestion—telling his wife "y se nos va a morir de hambre este hombre" ("this guy might die of hunger on us")—he picks up the tray of food and begins walking through the house. The camera circles around Arquímedes as he exits the kitchen and enters the living room, where Alex is watching television. Guillermo can be seen in the background setting the dinner table. Arquímedes continues through the living room and up the stairs, where he first knocks on Adriana's door, telling her that dinner will be ready soon. He continues down the hall, closing an open door as he passes by it, before finally arriving at a locked door that he unlocks and opens. Finally the camera, which has been circling him as he walks through the house, settles behind Arquímedes as he enters the bathroom, a position which allows for a view of the shrouded hostage chained to the pipes inside the bathroom wall, the chain emerging from a hole that has been smashed through the tiles. During the majority of the scene the only hint that something is amiss is a persistent banging that can be heard as the family goes about its nightly routine. The banging, which echoes through the house, is certainly noticeable; however, it is faint enough and there is enough noise going on throughout the scene that it is easily dismissed, as if it were coming from the house next door. As Arquímedes approaches the bathroom door, however, the banging becomes louder, the shot finally revealing the source to be the prisoner's chains banging against the plumbing.

The scene's final moment, when the hostage reacts with terror and panic to the opening of the bathroom door, functions as a counterpoint to the banality of the scene up to that point (Figure 3.6). A husband and wife chat to each other while preparing dinner, the husband rubbing his wife's neck to help relieve the stress of a full day; as the man walks through his house he performs the typical duties expected of a father, telling one child to take his feet off the coffee table and go help his mother with dinner while having to call another twice because she has her headphones on while doing homework. The scene makes it clear that the entire family must be held responsible for the crimes committed by Arquímedes because they are in no position to

The Violence of the Arborescent Family 135

Figure 3.6 *El clan* (2015). The victim being held hostage in the family's bathroom functions as both a broad and specific metaphor.

claim innocence. By never cutting away from Arquímedes as he deals with his family, the camera implies that the hostage being held in the bathroom is merely one more member of the family—the hostage is simply another thing Arquímedes must deal with before the family can sit down to eat, no different than knocking on his daughter's door and telling her to head down to the table. We are even shown how the various family members deal with the constant noises emerging from the bathroom—Epifanía, in the kitchen, is least affected by it; Alex, in the living room, watches the TV with the volume higher than it needs to be; while Adriana, in her room upstairs and nearest to the bathroom, drowns out the banging by listening to her Walkman so loud that she doesn't even notice her father standing at her door. (It is, perhaps, significant that Guillermo, the only member of the family without a way to drown out the sound, is the one who escapes from the family.)

This scene, of course, can be understood as a metaphor for the actions of the *Proceso* dictatorship, but it also functions as a commentary on the repressive nature of the family. Indeed, the national allegory that dominates the film's narrative is played out both in a broad metaphor—the parallels between the *desaparecidos* and the Puccio family's victims—and in a more specific circumstance, with Arquímedes's cowing of his family (and Alex in particular) reflecting the government's repression of the country during the dictatorship and the lasting effect violence continues to have on Argentine society. It is important to recall that the film opens with President Alfonsín's statement upon receiving the Nunca Más report, for it provides an insight not only to the film's central message but also to Trapero's personal thoughts on the current state of Argentina. The film that follows this declaration suggests that culpability for the crimes of the dictatorship lies not only with the Argentine government but also with the Argentine populace generally. Alfonsín's statement bears quoting in full here:

> Lo que ustedes han hecho, que ha entrado en la historia de nuestro país, constituye un aporte fundamental para que, de aquí en adelante, los argentinos sepamos cabalmente, por lo menos cual es el camino que jamás deberemos transitar en el futuro. Para que nunca más el odio, para que nunca más la violencia perturbe, conmueva, y degrade a la sociedad argentina.
>
> [What you have done constitutes a fundamental contribution, which has entered into the history of our country, so that, henceforth, Argentines will at the very least know exactly the path that we should never follow in the future. So that hate will never again . . . so that violence will never again disrupt, unsettle, and degrade Argentine society.]

By placing this statement at the start of a film about crimes that, while similar to those committed by the government, were perpetrated by private citizens (and who continued to perpetrate those crimes even after the fall of the dictatorship itself), Trapero forces the viewer to examine what role Argentine society, the Argentine people, have played in allowing violence to occur throughout their history. In making it clear that every member of the Puccio family was guilty of, at the very least, willful ignorance, the film implies not only that the Argentine people must bear a certain amount of guilt for the collective blind eye large segments of the population turned to the atrocities occurring around them but also that the very structure of Argentine society, from the basic family unit up, allowed, perhaps even encouraged these things to occur.

The date of the film's release in Argentina—August 13, 2015, almost thirty years to the day of the August 23, 1985, police raid that resulted in the Puccio family's detention—cannot be dismissed as pure coincidence. Indeed, a month after Trapero's film debuted, Argentines were also able to view the miniseries *Historia de un clan/History of a Clan* (Luis Ortega, 2015), which aired for eleven weeks from September to November on Telefe, one of Argentina's free-to-air channels. Despite taking different approaches to the source material—*El clan*'s verisimilitude contrasts with *Historia de un clan*'s more artistic license—both Trapero's film and Ortega's miniseries were exceptionally well received by critics and the public. That these works were so highly acclaimed speaks not only to their individual quality (of which there is no denying, in either case) but also, it can be argued, to something more pernicious within contemporary Argentine society. Viewed through the prism of contemporary Argentina, a nation plagued by "*inseguridad*," it becomes clear that *El clan* (and, indeed, *Historia de un clan*) is not merely a critique of Argentine culture in the 1980s, but in fact of contemporary Argentine society, as well.

Inseguridad, insecurity, has been an increasingly hot-button issue in Argentina in recent years—organized marches and protests with hundreds of people carrying signs with the slogan "basta de inseguridad" ("no more insecurity") occurred throughout 2015, and even government figures have acknowledged the problem, with Jorge Henn, the then-vice-governor of Santa Fe province, admitting in August 2015 that "la inseguridad en la Argentina se ha vuelto intolerable" ("insecurity in Argentina has become intolerable"). In an interview conducted with Trapero in April 2015, shortly before *El clan*'s domestic release, the director recalled,

> I remember my father, thirty years ago, saying "we've never been worse off." I think today my father would say the same thing. He said, "Where are we going to end up? It can't be any worse, the world is more violent than ever, things are getting out of control." . . . I remember that moment very clearly, right in the middle of the 1970s, the most violent years in Argentina's history, like, there will never be worse years than those. And yet today, thirty-some years later, I think there might even be *more* violence than before! (Interview with Pablo Trapero)

This comment requires a rethinking of *El clan*, and provides a different subtext to President Alfonsín's statement at the beginning of the film. Those words, urging the nation to leave its violence in the past and focus on a peaceful future, now resonate as a moment of lost opportunity. The actions of the Puccio family three decades ago can perhaps be, if not justified, at least contextualized: although the dictatorship had ended, the Argentine nation had yet to fully emerge from perhaps the most violent moment in its history, and the insidious nature of the *Proceso* dictatorship meant that a man like Arquímedes Puccio would feel emboldened enough to believe that he could commit his atrocities with impunity. But by emphasizing Alfonsín's plea to move forward into peace, Trapero's film demands that the contemporary viewer ask a series of questions: Why has Argentine society not embraced Alfonsín's message? How can we contextualize the violence that plagues contemporary Argentine society? Why do people believe there is more violence now than there was thirty years ago? While a critique of dictatorship- and transition-era Argentine society is certainly present in the film's narrative, in fact the film functions as a damning condemnation of contemporary Argentine society and the violence that characterizes life in the country's urban centers in the postcrisis age. Far from being a mere commentary on the violence of Argentina's past, *El clan* is a pointed critique of Argentina's troubled present.

La quietud

Trapero continues this thread in his most recent film, *La quietud*, in which the characters are haunted: by the past and the present, by the dead and the living, by choices made and not made. *La quietud* carries on a trend within Trapero's oeuvre that began with *Elefante blanco*; although it might not have been immediately clear when that film was first released a decade ago, it must now be understood as the first in a trio of films (so far) in which Trapero examines the lingering effects of the *Proceso* dictatorship on Argentine society. This trio is completed by *El clan* and *La quietud*. While it is certainly the case that many of Trapero's films hint at the dictatorship in various ways—*Nacido y criado*, for example, serves as a powerful metaphor for the *desaparecidos*—*Elefante blanco*, *El clan*, and *La quietud* speak directly to the dictatorship's legacy and the damage it has done to Argentine society. In much the same way that *Leonera* seems to be in dialog with *Nacido y criado*, *La quietud*, Trapero's ninth feature film, can be understood as a companion piece to *El clan*, the film that immediately precedes it in the director's oeuvre. Where *El clan* is a period piece that examines the relationship between a father and son, however, *La quietud* is set in the present day and focuses primarily on the complex web of relationships connecting a mother and her two daughters. Just as *El clan*'s combative familial relationships function as both a commentary on, and metaphor for, the violence of the *Proceso* dictatorship, so too the long-held anger that defines the relationships of *La quietud* speaks to the lasting damage done to Argentine society during the dictatorship. Indeed, although the film most obviously connects with *El clan*, it expands its focus and subject matter by examining the effects of haunting as the concept is defined by Avery F. Gordon—that is, the way in which "abusive systems of power make themselves known and their impacts felt in everyday life, especially when they are supposedly over and done with . . . or when their oppressive nature is denied" (2008, p. xvi). In this way, the film also echoes some of the same concerns as those found in *Elefante blanco*, another film set in the present which nevertheless engages, in ways both subtle and overt, with the unreconciled past. Finally, through its intimate, almost claustrophobic examination of the convoluted psychological and emotional dynamics of a family unit that is characterized equally by devotion and resentment, the film references not only Trapero's earlier *Familia rodante* but also Lucrecia Martel's masterwork, *La ciénaga*. As such, *La quietud* very much stands as a testament to the entirety of Trapero's twenty-year career, both standing on its own merits while also functioning as a sort of medley of everything that has, to this point, defined his cinema.

The film begins with Mia Montemayor (Martina Gusmán) arriving at La Quietud—the Montemayor family's *estancia* which, with its pink and white color scheme, calls to mind the Casa Rosada—and finding her parents Augusto (Isidoro Tolcachir) and Esmeralda (Graciela Borges) engaged in a ferocious argument. Mia chauffeurs her father into Buenos Aires for a meeting with a *fiscal*—a public prosecutor—but before entering the lawyer's office Augusto gives his daughter his briefcase, telling her that if he needs it he will ask her for it. During this meeting the *fiscal* lists a number of properties including La Quietud and asks Augusto if he knew the people that he represented and whether he saw them sign over power of attorney. Throughout the meeting Augusto seems to be experiencing a kind of panic attack, until finally he collapses, suffering what is later revealed to be a stroke. This leads Mia's sister Eugenia (Bérénice Bejo) to return to Argentina from France, the two passports she carries with her making it clear that she lives in Europe full time. As the days pass the conflicting nature of the various relationships within the family is laid bare—Eugenia and Mia share an incredibly close bond (one that will be analyzed in further detail later in this chapter), despite the fact that their individual relationships with their parents could not be more different. Esmeralda makes no attempt to hide her affection for her elder daughter, while the interactions with her younger daughter seem to be limited to either disregard or contemptuous confrontation. The contrast between how each daughter interacts with their parents is further highlighted the next day when, at breakfast, Eugenia announces she is pregnant, much to Esmeralda's delight. This is followed by the sisters visiting their father in hospital; although he is in a coma, Mia's warm reaction to being near him stands in stark contrast to Eugenia's reserved demeanor, demonstrating that the close bond that Eugenia shares with Esmeralda is mirrored in Mia's relationship with Augusto. Similarly, just as Mia lacks a connection with her mother, so Eugenia struggles to make a connection with the comatose man lying before her.

The film gradually reveals the many complexities, hypocrisies, and sexual tensions that characterize the Montemayor family. Most significantly, Mia and Eugenia's relationship is portrayed as borderline incestuous, with the two women bringing themselves to climax during a mutual masturbation session the night Eugenia arrives. Away from her sibling, Eugenia has been having a long-term affair with Esteban (Joaquín Furriel), the family's lawyer and son of Augusto's business partner; Eugenia attempts to break off the affair after sleeping with him one last time, but upon learning that she is pregnant Esteban claims that the child might be his and so demands she take a paternity test. Mia, although ostensibly single, is having an affair with Eugenia's husband Vincent (Edgar Ramírez), who arrives in Buenos Aires a few days after his wife. The extent of the animosity between Mia and her mother is made clear in several scenes during which the two engage in violent arguments, the catalysts for which are as seemingly trivial as the year a home video was recorded or a choice of words. Finally, the confrontation between Esmeralda and Augusto that introduces the couple proves to be much more than a mere disagreement. Although Augusto remains in a vegetative state, sometime after his stroke he is returned to La Quietud along with the life support mechanism keeping him alive. Esmeralda is unable to spend even one night in the same room as her comatose husband, and she generally leaves his care to Mia or the family's live-in maid. One day the police arrive and notify Esmeralda that she must testify as a witness in her husband's ongoing court case; that evening she enters the bedroom and, after gently kissing him and whispering "moríte, hijo de puta" ("die, son of a bitch"), detaches Augusto's breathing apparatus, killing him. This attempt at ridding herself of the ghost of the past, however, only ensures that not merely Esmeralda but her entire family will continue to be haunted by it.

The Past Made Present

In *Specters of Marx*, Jacques Derrida writes that "[h]egemony still organizes the repression and thus the confirmation of a haunting. Haunting belongs to the structure of every hegemony" (1994, p. 46). A haunting is carried out by a specter, a "becoming-body, a certain phenomenal and carnal form of the spirit" (1994, p. 5). Estela Schindel expands on this, stating that "the specter as conceived by Derrida... is the conveyor of legacies and demands from the dead" (2014, p. 257). Through its examination of an upper-class family with close ties to the *Proceso* dictatorship, *La quietud* both engages with and mediates these concepts, with the different interfamilial relationships portraying many of the ideas that Derrida introduces in his work. The nature of these relationships is gradually revealed over the course of the film's narrative, such that *La quietud* is dominated by these types of specters and they influence, in one way or another, virtually every major character in the film. While the film is something of an ensemble piece, the two primary axes around whom the narrative rotates are Mia and her mother Esmeralda, and it is this latter character, in particular, who functions as the center of gravity for the haunting that permeates the film. This has much to do with the actions taken by her and her husband in a past that is constantly referenced but never fully explained. By the time the film begins this unspoken past has come to dominate the lives of Esmeralda and Augusto, and the fundamentally intertwined nature of the Montemayors's relationships means that shortly thereafter it subsumes the entire family. Even Augusto, who suffers a stroke within the film's first ten minutes and remains comatose until his death, plays a pivotal role in this process, for it is his stroke that serves as the catalyst to bring the characters together at La Quietud, and his (and, as we will come to see, Esmeralda's) actions in life that continue to haunt the family even after his death. Avery Gordon explains that through haunting "we are notified that what's been concealed is very much alive and present" (2008, p. xvi).

La quietud gradually reveals to just what extent the ghost of the past still very much haunts the remaining members of the Montemayor family. Trapero has acknowledged this aspect of the film in interviews, stating "[e]l pasado en esta familia es muy importante. El pasado es presente, como ocurre en otras de mis películas" ("the past is very important for this family. The past is present, like what happens in my other films") (Beauregard, 2018). The tensions of the past are made manifest in various ways throughout the film, and they boil over both between members of the same generation—most noticeably, because of their past liaisons Eugenia and Esteban clash over the paternity of Eugenia's unborn child—and between members of different generations. The most significantly conflicted relationship in the film is that between Mia and her mother, and the enmity between the two characters drives much of the film's narrative. As this chapter demonstrates in its analysis of both *Familia rodante* and *El clan* (to say nothing of films like *Mundo grúa* and *Leonera*), clashes between parents and their children are a rather common theme in Trapero's work. It is the particular nature of Mia's arguments with Esmeralda, however, that is unique, for those arguments are almost entirely centered on contestations of the past.

The first inkling of the contentious nature of their relationship is shown when, toward the end of the celebration held to mark Eugenia's return to the country, the family and friends gather to watch a series of home movies. Mia mentions her friends, to which Esmeralda responds "pero si vos no tenés amigas" ("but you don't have friends"). Immediately after this Mia contradicts her mother when Esmeralda states that the video they are watching was filmed in 1996; Mia insists that the video was from 1997 and refuses to let the issue die, despite repeated pleas by Eugenia and other people in the room. Esmeralda's repetition of the word "noventa y seis" enrages Mia to the extent that she stands up and begins screaming at her mother, asking her how she could possibly think that the video was filmed in 1996. Esmeralda dismisses everything Mia says and remains focused on the video, hardly glancing at her daughter, which only enrages Mia further, finally bringing her to tears. Approaching hysterics, Mia asks why her mother never agrees with her, to which Esmeralda replies, "cuando tengas razón te voy a dar la razón" ("when you are right I'll agree with you"). Mia's response is quite significant in providing context to the nature of their relationship, as she replies, "no quiero que me des la razón porque sí, quiero que pienses, que reflexiones, que tal vez existe la remota posibilidad de que haya una sola vez en la vida que yo tenga razón" ("I don't want you to agree with me just because, I want you to think, to reflect, that perhaps there exists the remote possibility that, just once in my life, I am right"). Finally Esmeralda decides she has had enough and she and everyone else depart, leaving Mia alone in the room, distraught as she watches the images being projected onto the wall (Figure 3.7).

The Violence of the Arborescent Family 143

Figure 3.7 *La quietud* (2018). The implied tension between Mia and her mother erupts into the open.

This situation is reversed later in the film when, while explaining why the Montemayors are implicated in the court case involving Augusto's business partner, Esmeralda makes reference to "el gobierno militar" ("the military government"), a phrase Mia immediately challenges by stating, simply, "la dictadura, mama" ("the dictatorship, mom"). Esmeralda reacts to this with exasperation, but Mia insists, "¿[n]o te parece un detalle importante? Supongo que no es gratis que te vayas a vivir todo pago a Paris por un gobierno al menos dudoso, ¿o no?" ("That doesn't strike you as an important detail? I suppose it wasn't for free that you got to go live in Paris all expenses covered by a government that was, at the least, questionable, was it?") When Esmeralda retorts that there is nothing revelatory about bringing something up over and over again, Mia states, "hablar las cosas siempre es revelador" ("speaking about things is always revelatory").

This interaction is particularly illuminating for two reasons. First, the way in which Esmeralda and Mia engage with this knowledge speaks to the way in which each woman engages with the past. Second, in just a few lines of dialog the inescapable specter haunting Esmeralda is given a sort of shape—the family was complicit with the *Proceso* dictatorship. The true extent of the family's connection with the crimes of the past is made clear when, after receiving a summons to appear in court, Esmeralda gives her deposition concerning Augusto's actions during the dictatorship. She states that her husband and his business partner had illegally sold deeds of property by forcing detainees at perhaps the *Proceso* dictatorship's most infamous torture center—the *Escuela Superior de Mecánica de la Armada* (more generally known in both Spanish and English as the ESMA)—to sign over power of attorney to Augusto, with the assurance that by doing so they or their families would be spared. Most damningly, Esmeralda states that Augusto attained these signatures himself, personally visiting the basements of the ESMA where so many *desaparecidos* were tortured. Although this would seem to end the matter, since Augusto is dead and so can no longer be prosecuted, the evening following her deposition Esmeralda is confronted by an enraged Mia, who refuses to believe that her father was capable of what has been claimed and demands to know "the truth." Although hesitant at first, Esmeralda finally opens up, explaining that following the dictatorship her marriage had deteriorated to such an extent that she felt like a "hostage in [her] own house," that she was the victim of marital rape, and that Mia was the product of one of those violations. For this reason, she claims, she has never, "not even an instant," been able to love Mia. This admission motivates Mia to meet with Esteban and finally reveal the contents of the briefcase her father had given her immediately before his stroke. It proves to be the ESMA's sign-in register, listing the names and dates of everyone who visited the site during the dictatorship. It is not Augusto's name that appears throughout the register but, rather, Esmeralda's.

Once this information is revealed the motivations that differentiate Mia and Esmeralda become clear: Mia revels in questioning the past and confronting its failures, even at the expense of opening old wounds (or, perhaps, preventing old wounds from healing) because, as is made clear later in the film, she is not entirely aware of the true extent of the family's complicity with the dictatorship. Esmeralda, on the other hand, is burdened by her and her family's history and, although she spends much of the film denying it, it weighs on her almost literally. In her examination of haunting within the context of Argentine society and the legacy of the terror inflicted by the *Proceso* dictatorship, Gordon explains that

> [t]o look for lessons about haunting ... when the whole purpose of the verbal denial is to ensure that everyone knows just enough to scare normalization into a state of nervous exhaustion ... when the whole of life has become so enmeshed in the traffic of the dead and the living dead.... To broach, much less settle on, a firm understanding of this social reality can make you feel like you are carrying the weight of the world on your shoulders. (2008, p. 64)

With Esmeralda, this weight, this guilt, is particularly noticeable. It emerges whenever she is forced to confront a past that she has attempted to conceal, and is manifested as a kind of labored, heavy breathing that is distinctly audible and which seems to require all of her strength, as if she were quite literally "carrying the weight of the world on [her] shoulders." The breathing is particularly noticeable in three specific scenes—immediately before Esmeralda effectively kills her husband by unplugging him from his life support machine; during her deposition in court; and in the subsequent scene, when she attempts to justify her harsh treatment of Mia throughout her life. All three of these scenes are moments in which the past is made present. In her examination of the ghost stories that surround former torture sites in Argentina, Estela Schindel explains that "[l]iving with the disappeared can . . . mean assuming their inheritance as a constitutive part of Argentinean identity. But it can also mean a very literal coexistence with their effect as both specters *and* ghosts" (2014, pp. 258–9). In contrast to the gothic ghost-story-as-metaphor that forms the basis of many studies on haunting (Gordon, 2008; González, 2012), *La quietud* features no apparitions or ethereal beings who haunt the protagonists. Rather, the specter that haunts Esmeralda is one of knowledge and of withholding. With Augusto dead, only she and his former business partner know the true extent of their collaboration with the dictatorship. When that specter, that "conveyor of legacies and demands from the dead," impresses itself upon her, that labored breathing functions as a kind of outward sign of inward struggle. Furthermore, it is significant that each of these scenes can be understood as an attempt by Esmeralda to unburden herself of the hauntings of her past, a past that is fundamentally tied to the very estate that serves as her home. Esmeralda's inability to escape her past is symbolized by her connection to La Quietud, a connection that exemplifies Fisher's contention that "[h]aunting can be seen as intrinsically resistant to the contraction and homogenization of time and space. It happens when a place is stained by time, or when a particular place becomes the site for an encounter with broken time" (2012, p. 19).

La Quietud and De-Oedipalization

Where the elder generation of the Montemayor family is haunted by their past, the younger generation is struggling against a different kind of specter— the traditional, arborescent family structure itself. In this regard, La Quietud serves as an axis around which these two concepts are balanced. The revelation that Esmeralda partook in the atrocities of the dictatorship overwhelms the remaining members of the Montemayor family, with the result that the arborescent family that once existed is rent apart entirely. Esmeralda is arrested and the sisters silently pack up La Quietud and leave together, ostensibly for good. The symbolism of this decision should not be minimized—throughout the narrative the only thing that seems to hold the family together throughout their many conflicts is La Quietud itself. Indeed, in a manner reminiscent of La Mandrágora in Martel's *La ciénaga* or the camper in *Familia rodante*, the estate functions not merely as a site in which action takes place but also as a kind of secondary character. This continues a trend, identified by Inela Selimović, that runs across many of Trapero's films of "the fragmentation of ... relatively typical family homes" (2019, p. 34). Many of the director's films feature homes and living spaces that are characterized by what Selimović describes as a "palpable, even if not always directly visible, uneasiness" (2019, p. 39), and while *La quietud* hints at this—it is most noticeable on the occasions when the power shuts off momentarily and the inhabitants are plunged into darkness before the generator kicks in—the estate is generally not portrayed as a suffocating presence that constricts the characters and, by extension, viewers.

Rather, La Quietud is shown in wide, sweeping shots framed by the long shadows and warm hues of sunrise and sunset, emphasizing the beauty of both the built environment and the nature that surrounds it. In a sort of mirror image of *La ciénaga*'s highly symbolic naming of the estate in that film—La Mandrágora, the sedative mandrake plant—the name of the estate in *La quietud* speaks to the one thing the Montemayor family fundamentally lacks: quietude. In fact, far from serving as a place of respite, by the end of the film La Quietud functions as an immutable reminder of the specters that haunt the film's protagonists. Aline Fischer and Sandra Vaz find that Argentine cinema is full of examples of the nuclear family functioning as a site of contention:

> No cinema argentino, instância significativamente reveladora de memória pós-ditatorial ... a instituição familiar estrutura-se ... alicerçada por meio de sistemas que articulam reiterados processos de dominação que referenciam, justamente, imobilidades que tiveram lugar em uma Argentina subjugada a governos repressores. (2018, p. 228)

[In Argentine cinema, a significantly revelatory instance of post-dictatorial memory . . . the family institution structures itself . . . based on systems that articulate repeated processes of domination that reference, precisely, occurrences that took place in an Argentina subjugated by repressive governments.]

With La Quietud—a property that was acquired using means both illegal and immoral—the film presents the physical structure as a manifestation of the oppressive family structure Trapero's films consistently scrutinize and rebel against. The collapse of the nuclear family and the abandonment of the estate necessarily go hand in hand with one another, for the connection between the family and the *estancia* cannot be broken until the arborescent family itself no longer exists as such.

If the most significant event in the breakdown of the arborescent family is Esmeralda's confession that she has never loved Mia, the moment in which the seeds of that breakdown are planted occurs halfway through the film, at Augusto's funeral (Figure 3.8). This sequence of events serves as the start of what Deleuze and Guattari refer to as de-oedipalization, a process that results in "undoing the daddy-mommy spider web, undoing the beliefs so as to attain the production of desiring-machines" (1983, p. 112). The scene is shot in one single four-minute-long continuous take that tracks all four of the younger generation of characters. Where Trapero used this technique to highlight the mundanity of the Puccio family's evil in *El clan*, the long take in *La quietud* serves to emphasize the chaos that defines the Montemayor

Figure 3.8 *La quietud* (2018). Augusto's funeral marks the point at which the arborescent family structure begins to collapse.

family in general and the lives of Mia and Eugenia in particular. The camera floats around the funeral, tracking from one sister to the other and back again; outside the chapel a drunken Mia confronts Vincent about his decision not to tell her about Eugenia's pregnancy while inside, as she contemplates her father's corpse, Eugenia is threatened by Esteban that if she does not submit to a paternity test he will tell her husband about their affair. Finally Eugenia, on Vincent's advice, decides to take Mia home. In the car Mia suffers an emotional breakdown before demanding that Eugenia turn the car around and take her back to the funeral so she can see her father one last time. When Eugenia refuses Mia grabs the steering wheel causing the car to lose control and swerve into oncoming traffic, where, in a scene reminiscent of *Nacido y criado* and *Carancho*, it is slammed into by an oncoming truck. While both sisters are in hospital Esmeralda enquires into the status of Eugenia's child. She is informed that Eugenia was not, in fact, pregnant, that in fact she had been experiencing a false pregnancy.

Several key interventions occur in the wake of the accident. Mia returns from the hospital first, and the night she returns home she and Vincent make love in the house, with Esmeralda able to hear everything that is going on. To this point Mia and Vincent have attempted to hide their affair—the only other time they are shown having sex is in Mia's car after she picks him up from the airport—but the knowledge that Eugenia was not actually pregnant seems to remove the social repressions that surrounded them. This break is further emphasized when, after Eugenia returns from the hospital, she and Vincent split up. This moment is significant because it marks the first in a series of points of rupture between the past and the future. That past is one defined by the arborescent family and the traditional, repressive expectations that accompany that structure. Throughout *La quietud* Mia and Eugenia are shown to be in constant tension with this repression, which manifests as the demands placed upon them by the expectations of (and for) a traditional family.

This tension is exemplified by the exceptionally, perhaps even peculiarly, close relationship the sisters share. Beyond the typical finishing of each other's sentences and knowledge of inside jokes, the sisters appear to share a sexual attraction for one another that flirts with the incestuous. After dinner the night that Eugenia arrives they reminisce over old photographs and mementos, with one particular photograph causing Eugenia to ask "do you remember how we used to masturbate thinking about him?" Their memories of childhood lead to them rekindling a kind of game they used to play, in which Eugenia narrates the scenario of the sisters spying on the man in the photograph, describing him undressing and then seducing the two of them. As she does this Eugenia mounts Mia, whispering into her sister's ear as she continues the narration. Eventually Eugenia rolls off her sister and, as she continues to describe the erotic scene of her imagination, both women begin to touch themselves as they lie next to each other in bed (Figure 3.9). Mia picks up the narration as well, the camera showing both sisters now masturbating and caressing themselves. As they bring themselves closer to climax the narration devolves into a series of moans, and the sisters begin to caress one another, eventually climaxing at the same time before finally bursting out into riotous laughter and falling asleep in the same bed. Deleuze and Guattari contend that "[r]epression cannot act without displacing desire, without giving rise to a *consequent desire* . . . and without putting this desire in the place of the *antecedent desire* on which repression comes to bear in principle or in reality" (1983, p. 115, emphasis in original). If the quasi-incestuous attraction between the two sisters is understood as an "antecedent desire," the events of the next morning—Eugenia informing her mother and sister that she is pregnant—demonstrate the manner in which repression acts to displace that desire with the "consequent desire" of creating a traditional, arborescent family. Eugenia's split from Vincent marks the initial stage in the process of rejecting repression. That process is completed by the discovery that Esmeralda was central to the crimes committed by the family during the dictatorship.

Figure 3.9 *La quietud* (2018). The sisters' quasi-incestual sex play signifies the rejection, however temporarily, of the repressive traditional family structure.

It is only once the connection to La Quietud is broken that the sisters are able to acknowledge the specter that has been haunting their relationship—the long-term love triangle with Vincent in which the two women have been involved. The confrontation, such as it is, is fairly subdued; Mia asks her sister why she would choose to marry the same man that Mia had admitted to being in love with, and though at first Eugenia attempts to justify her actions she eventually admits that she has known about the affair for "fifteen years," and that she simply tolerated it. She did this, she says, because "knowing that I share him with you gives me relief. Knowing that I can give you what you need makes me happy." Mia responds to this by telling her she never asked Vincent to leave Eugenia, and that the affair "is a way for me to be close to you, as well." The two sisters then hug and Mia, in tears, tells Eugenia "it doesn't matter that we talk every day, I miss you the same. I think about you all the time." The sisters hold each other for a few moments until the scene cuts to them leaving La Quietud behind, closing and locking the gate to the estate before driving away. The scene then cuts to a monitor displaying the microscopic image of an ovum being artificially inseminated, before panning to reveal Mia laying on a consultation table, Eugenia sitting next to her holding her hand. A nurse explains in French that Eugenia's fertilized egg has been successfully implanted in Mia's uterus and that the embryo is now eight weeks old. The nurse congratulates "the mothers" as she leaves, and the camera then lingers on the two women as they embrace, Eugenia leaning in as if to kiss Mia on the lips. As the focus slowly fades to a blur, the space between two women's mouths disappears, and though it is obscured, it is understood that they are kissing. This final, blurry kiss is both a nod to and a subversion of a traditional happy ending. Eugenia and Mia have rejected the arborescent family and by the end have created a rhizome of sorts—they will be joint parents to a child that comes from Eugenia's egg but given birth by Mia, and they will do so in France, away from an Argentina defined by the past. In doing so they have embraced the "antecedent desire" that the repressive arborescent structure acted against and have created a desiring-machine in the shape of a rhizomatic family structure.

Taken as a trio, *Familia rodante* and *El clan* present a society in which violence is generated within the family, perpetuated by the family, and then recycled back into the family unit by external factors. Within the family structure, there appears to be no escaping this cycle of violence—even Alex's attempts to escape by committing suicide ultimately fail. As with many of the protagonists from Trapero's other films, any resistance against repressive forces is doomed to futility. This would, in general, suggest that Trapero holds a highly negative view of the family unit. *La quietud*, however, presents an alternative to the traditional family structure. The films analyzed in Chapter 4—*Nacido y criado* (2006) and *Leonera* (2008)—suggest that some sort of family is vitally important to human interaction and provide a notable counterbalance to the pessimism seen in *Familia rodante*, *El clan*, and *La quietud*.

4

The Rhizome as an Alternative Family Model

Nacido y criado and *Leonera* serve as a sort of turning point in Pablo Trapero's career, demonstrating a director whose work is changing significantly in terms of content. With *Nacido y criado* Trapero's films begin to embrace a darker, more explicitly violent tone. Moving away from the examinations of inherent, structural violence that characterized Trapero's first three films, *Nacido y criado* considers the effects of direct physical violence on an individual's psyche and the lasting scarring (both literally and figuratively) that sort of violence can cause, while *Leonera* begins in the immediate aftermath of a murder and chronicles the experiences of both mother and child in the maternity ward of a female penitentiary. The two films are connected in that they both focus on protagonists who have suffered through a particularly violent event and, as with the films analyzed in Chapter 3, both *Nacido y criado* and *Leonera* focus on family dynamics. However, the simmering tension of *Familia rodante* has been left behind in favor of the sort of explicit violence that would reach its most prominent display in *El clan*. Additionally, the broadly negative depiction of the family found in those films, and particularly so in *La quietud*, is contrasted here with a more nuanced approach—both *Nacido y criado* and *Leonera* provide examples of alternative family structures, ones based less on bloodlines and marriage than on mutual understanding, shared experienced, and communal solidarity. Where the family structure is shown to be an inherently negative construct in the films analyzed in the previous chapter, *Nacido y criado* and *Leonera* present more ambiguous understandings of the family. Both films feature, to some extent, an alternative form of family that is in fact rather positive and serves as a means for the films' protagonists to persevere in the face of violence. However, in both films the protagonists eventually return to (a variation of) the more traditional family structure, with the end result being that rather than a clear favoritism being defined between traditional and alternative family structures, the films function as examinations of the broad concept of family, in all its guises.

It is through their consideration of the family that both films fit into Trapero's broader corpus of political films. Where *Leonera* is explicit with its political commentary—the majority of the film takes place in a prison, perhaps the most concentrated and refined expression of the Repressive State Apparatus possible—*Nacido y criado* takes a more personal approach and expresses its politics much more subtly. Indeed, the politics of *Nacido y criado* are based significantly more on Trapero's own personal understanding of the world as a place in which violence is fundamental—

> In my view violence, what it does, it's a catalyst, it's something that accelerates a reaction. . . . I feel that, especially in our societies but also within nature because I'd say that it's innate in the necessity to survive, to overcome violence. If a punch is thrown what does one do? Defend oneself? Punch back harder? Run away? (Interview with Pablo Trapero)

Rather than examining the immediately obvious physical effects that violence has on society, *Nacido y criado*'s focus is much more on how one reacts to the world and attempts to overcome once violence has entered into an individual's life. Perhaps surprisingly, given the way it is presented in films both before and after *Nacido y criado*, the family plays a subtle, yet critical role in this process.

Rhizomes and the Becoming-Family

The traditional nuclear family unit dominates the narratives of both *Familia rodante* and *El clan*, the works examined in the previous chapter. Generally, the two films analyzed in this chapter, *Nacido y criado* and *Leonera*, examine a different form of family, one that is based less on blood relations and more on the familial bonds created through friendship, proximity, and autonomy. While it is not entirely accurate to state that the families (such as they are) featured in the two films are based solely on free will—in both works the protagonists are isolated from the majority of the population, whether through incarceration or geographical distance, thereby limiting the possible relationships available to them—the relations portrayed in both films (especially when compared to the films discussed in Chapter 3) call to mind the Deleuzo-Guattarian dichotomy of filiation versus alliance. These relations are both forged and tested as a result of the circumstances in which the protagonists of the two films find themselves.

Throughout both volumes of *Capitalism and Schizophrenia* Deleuze and Guattari contrast relations of filiation with relations of alliance. Ian Buchanan explains "[t]here are two kinds of relationships between people in groups ... affiliations and alliances, the former is linear in composition (uniting father and son to form a lineage) while the latter is lateral (uniting brothers and cousins to form a tribe)" (2008, p. 99). Where relations of filiation are "inalienable" and based on traditional Oedipal structures—the "daddy-mommy-me" referred to throughout *Anti-Oedipus*—relations of alliance are "mobile" and based on desire, rejecting any sort of structural rigidity (Deleuze and Guattari, 1983, p. 152). Explaining the difference between the two concepts, Deleuze and Guattari propose the metaphor of a tribe, describing "genealogical filiative units of major, minor, and minimal lineages, with their hierarchy, their respective chiefs, their elders who guard the stocks and organize marriages" on the one hand, and "territorial tribal units of primary, secondary, and tertiary sections, also having their dominant roles and their alliances" on the other (1983, p. 152). We can see, therefore, two contrasting ways of creating community: one based on familial relationships that are immutable and binding, the other based on relationships that are able to change and evolve, flowing from one person to the next. Not only is the filiation-alliance dichotomy considered "absolutely central to any understanding of the political dimension of [Deleuze and Guattari's] work" (Buchanan, 2008, p. 99), it is also crucial to understanding the Deleuzo-Guattarian concept of the rhizome.

Taking inspiration from the root structure found in plants such as potatoes and garlic, rhizomes as a societal construct are presented in the introductory chapter of *A Thousand Plateaus*, *Capitalism and Schizophrenia*'s second volume. Beginning with examples from nature, Deleuze and Guattari then expand the concept into the broader world, providing numerous instances of systems they consider rhizomatic—"[b]ulbs and tubers are rhizomes.... Rats are rhizomes. Burrows are too, in all of their functions of shelter, supply, movement, evasion, and breakout. The rhizome itself assumes very diverse forms, from ramified surface extension in all directions to concretion into bulbs and tubers" (2013, p. 5). Deleuze and Guattari contrast the rhizome, with its free-flowing, multidirectional structure, to the arborescent, binary structure of the tree, which for so long has been used as a metaphor for organization and hierarchy (2013, pp. 3-4). Rhizomatic systems lack a center, instead spreading in every direction and with every point potentially functioning as the start of a new system: "[u]nlike a structure, which is defined by a set of points and positions, with binary relations between the points and biunivocal relationships between the positions, the rhizome is made only of lines" (2013, p. 22). Conversely, tree-like structures are focused entirely on the center—"[a]rborescent systems are hierarchical systems with centers of significance and subjectification, central automata like organized memories. In the corresponding models, an element only receives information from a higher unit, and only receives a subjective affection along pre-established paths" (2013, p. 16).

This contrast between rhizomatic and arborescent systems offers a more in-depth understanding of the difference between relations of filiation and relations of alliance. With their basis in hierarchy and ancestors and descendants, a similarity can be clearly established between trees (to summarize the concept into a word) and filiation; indeed, this is inherently acknowledged in terms such as "family tree." Because of their binary nature, relations of filiation, like arborescent systems, are limited in their potential. Relations of alliance, on the other hand, are free from the constraints of hierarchy and binarism, and as such are capable of developing in innumerable different ways and forms, mimicking the spread of roots and stems and branches that characterize the growths emerging from a rhizome. Indeed, one of the primary benefits of the rhizome is that it allows for constant creation, it produces what Deleuze and Guattari refer to as "becomings"—"the pure movement evident in changes *between* particular events" (Stagoll, 2005, p. 26). Modelling relationships on the rhizome, then, provides the opportunity to create a new type of familial relationship, one that is founded on alliance rather than filiation, one that flows and pursues desire in the style of the rhizome, one that is constantly *becoming*. In stark contrast to the rigid, arborescent, filiation-based Oedipal family, relations of alliance create something new: the becoming-family. Because the becoming-family does not adhere to the confines of filiation and arborescence, it functions outside the traditional confines of the State Apparatus, and so does not produce the same always-already subjects as the traditional family.

Indeed, through its constant evolution and changing nature the becoming-family actively pushes against the State Apparatus. The becoming-family is the family ISA in negative, rejecting the State Apparatus, taking in always-already subjects and producing flows and desire-machines.

Prison: Arborescent or Rhizomatic?

While the two films analyzed in this chapter are connected through their examination of the (becoming-) family, they differ in regard to the environment in which that particular form of solidarity is developed. In order to appreciate why the rhizomatic family structure is so significant to each film's message of resistance, it is important to understand the settings in which they occur. Where the films analyzed in the previous chapter focus on the debilitating effects of the traditional, arborescent family, *Nacido y criado* and *Leonera* use the (objective and subjective) violence of the state of exception and the prison, respectively, as a domineering force against which the rhizomatic family functions as a form of resistance.

Leonera, set primarily in a prison, examines the process through which the state attempts to create subjects using the means of the Foucauldean "disciplinary society." Where the traditional Oedipal family is an ISA, the prison is one of the most obvious cogs in what Althusser defines as the (repressive) State Apparatus. Althusser appends the term "repressive" to the State Apparatus because, he contends, it "suggests that the State Apparatus in question 'functions by violence'—at least ultimately (since repression, e.g., administrative repression, may take nonphysical forms)" (1971, p. 96). Rather than create subjects through ideology, the repressive apparatus of the State "secures by repression (from the most brutal physical force, via mere administrative commands and interdictions, to open and tacit censorship) the political conditions for the action of the Ideological State Apparatuses" (1971, p. 101). The RSA, then, is the instrument that creates the environment necessary for the ISAs to be able to function properly. Althusser, however, finds that reverting to repression is, to a certain extent, a final recourse for the State, as it would prefer to rely more heavily on the ISAs to create willing subjects. It is the threat of the RSA, the threat of police action or imprisonment, which ensures the efficacy of the family, Church, and other ISAs.

Foucault, on the other hand, argues that rather than ideology being the dominant force in society, it is the Repressive State Apparatus itself that subjugates society. (It must be noted here that, while he may be writing about similar ideas, Foucault does not use Althusser's terms in his work.) Foucault examines the fundamental role that one aspect of the RSA—the prison (and in particular Bentham's panopticon design)—played in creating what he terms the disciplinary society. The panopticon allows for a concentration of power and control, and results in a society in which "[t]he crowd, a compact mass, a locus of multiple exchanges, individualities merging together, a collective effect, is abolished and replaced by a collection of separated individualities" (Foucault, 1991, p. 201). Foucault labels this societal model "panopticism," describing it as "the general principle of a new 'political anatomy' whose object and end are not the relations of sovereignty but the relations of discipline" (1991, p. 208). Discipline, in turn, is a type of power that emphasizes panopticism's individualizing nature—"instead of bending all its subjects into a single uniform mass, it separates, analyzes, differentiates, carries its procedures of decomposition to the point of necessary and sufficient single units" (1991, p. 170).

The lasting impact of all of this, Foucault believes, is that society is increasingly fragmented and constituted of isolated individuals who have no conception of social unity. Furthermore, Foucault's description of panopticism proposes a society in which ideology is secondary to repression, a society where the Repressive State Apparatus has become so dominant and pervasive as to be invisible. Where Althusser believes that ideology brings in individuals and subjugates them, Foucault believes that discipline, through the model of the panopticon, creates subjects by individualizing them, avoiding the hard-to-govern mass in favor of the more easily manageable individual. These are two widely divergent understandings of what role the prison plays in society. In the first view, which sees society dominated by ideology, the prison (and institutions affiliated with it, such as the police) serves a proscriptive role for those upon whom ideology does not take hold. In the second view prison is, perhaps, the disciplinary society's defining institution.

In his article "Postscript on the Societies of Control," Deleuze offers an alternative to (or, perhaps, evolution of) Foucault's disciplinary society. While acknowledging the importance of Foucault's examination of discipline, Deleuze believes that even at the point Foucault was writing about its influence, we had already moved beyond the disciplinary society. Deleuze states that we are living in a society dominated not by disciplinary mechanisms but, rather, by mechanisms of control. The difference, Deleuze states, is that "[c]ontrol is short-term and of rapid rates of turnover, but also continuous and without limit, while discipline was of long duration, infinite and discontinuous" (1992, p. 6). To further explicate this difference, Deleuze compares the (outdated) factory, an example of a disciplinary mechanism Foucault uses throughout *Discipline and Punish*, with the (contemporary) corporation. Emphasizing the all-encompassing nature of the society of control, Deleuze writes,

> In the disciplinary societies one was always starting again (from the school to the barracks, from the barracks to the factory), while in the societies of control one is never finished with anything—the corporation, the educational system, the armed services being metastable states coexisting in one and the same modulation. (1992, p. 5)

The control society, Deleuze contends, places less importance on the primacy of the individual and favors, in its place, a concept Deleuze calls the "dividual." Where the disciplinary society attempts to reduce everything to the individual, control societies go further, fragmenting individuals even more than was previously thought possible. Deleuze writes of the "apparent acquittal," the starting over, that occurs in a disciplinary society when an individual moves from one enclosure to another—from the school to the factory, for example—contrasting that with the "limitless postponement" that is found in control societies (1992, p. 5). This obligates members of a society to be constantly engaged in that society, unable to retreat, unable to form a unique identity. The result, John Marks explains, is a society in which the individual has been turned "into an object that has no resistance, no capacity to 'fold' the line of [control]" (2005, p. 56).

The State of Exception

Deleuze's society of control brings to mind the work of Giorgio Agamben, particularly his concept of the "state of exception." Both Santi and Julia, the respective protagonists of *Nacido y criado* and *Leonera*, can be understood as existing within variations of the discipline and control societies, and the result is that they have become precisely the sort of "dividual" that Deleuze describes in his work. The characters have become so fragmented, their sense of identity so distorted, that they find themselves in a state of exception.

Closely (if not inexorably) linked with the power of the sovereign, the state of exception, as posited by Carl Schmitt, is that period where the sovereign wields absolute control over a society. Agamben expands upon this definition by describing the state of exception as "the technical term for [a] consistent set of legal phenomena ... not a special kind of law (like the law of war); rather, insofar as it is a suspension of the juridical order itself, [the state of exception] defines law's threshold or limit concept" (2005, p. 4). Previously reserved for times of crisis such as periods of war or dictatorship, Agamben contends that, in the face of the multitude of military and terrorist actions which have defined the first two decades of this century, the state of exception has become much more prevalent in contemporary society. This is especially problematic because the state of exception is so closely linked with despotism:

> Modern totalitarianism can be defined as the establishment, by means of the state of exception, of a legal civil war that allows for the physical elimination not only of political adversaries but of entire categories of citizens who for some reason cannot be integrated into the political system. Since then, the voluntary creation of a permanent state of emergency (though perhaps not declared in the technical sense) has become one of the essential practices of contemporary states, including so-called democratic ones. (2005, p. 2)

Although Agamben never mentions Argentina specifically, the parallels between this statement and Argentina's (relatively) recent history are clear. In the late 1970s and early 1980s, the *Proceso* dictatorship entered an acknowledged state of exception, committing exactly the crimes that Agamben describes while using the very concept of civil war (or the potential threat of it) to justify their actions. Conversely, since the economic collapse of 2001 the country has in many ways existed in a sort of perpetual but unacknowledged state of exception, most notably in relation to the police force, as exemplified in *El bonaerense*.

Another of Agamben's concepts that is closely related to the state of exception is that of the *homo sacer*, literally "sacred man." Agamben takes the idea of *homo sacer* from "an obscure figure from archaic Roman law" who "may be killed and yet not sacrificed," and whose life is "included in the juridical order solely in the form of its exclusion" (1998, p. 12). Essentially, *homo sacer* refers to an individual who has been cast out of society and who may be killed without the perpetrator fearing any sort of repercussion; the *homo sacer* is an individual who has lost all political rights (what Agamben calls *bios*) and who therefore represents a specific type of what Agamben refers to as "*zoē*" or "bare life." (The differentiation between *zoē* and *homo sacer* arises from the fact that while *zoē* represents all life that is excluded from the sociopolitical, *homo sacer* refers specifically to an individual who has been stripped of his *bios*, expelled from the political.) Despite being officially excluded from political life, *homo sacer* is nevertheless an incredibly political figure since, like a bandit or thief, "he is in a continuous relationship with the power that banished him precisely insofar as he is at every instant exposed to an unconditional threat of death ... and must reckon with it at every moment" (1998, p. 103). *Homo sacer* exists, then, in a perpetual state of exception—since he may be killed by anyone at any moment the laws concerning the protection of his life, laws that are applied to those within society, have been suspended in his case, in the same way that the state of exception represents the time when laws in society, generally, have been suspended. Critically, Agamben finds that the state of exception has become no longer exceptional but rather the norm, and therefore all members of society have become *homo sacer*— "[w]hen life and politics—originally divided, and linked together by means of the no-man's-land of the state of exception that is inhabited by bare life—begin to become one, all life becomes sacred and all politics becomes the exception" (1998, p. 86). It is in this specific context—this "no-man's-land" in which "all life becomes sacred"—that much of *Nacido y criado*'s narrative occurs, and the challenges posed by the *homines sacri* who populate the film propel the majority of the film's drama.

Nacido y criado

Trapero's fourth film shares some marked similarities with his earlier work—as with *Mundo grúa* and *Familia rodante* much of the action occurs in rural locations far from the *conurbano*, and, while the production values have improved noticeably, the film's cinematography nevertheless maintains a certain grittiness to its images (especially once the narrative shifts to Patagonia) that is consistent with the other films from Trapero's early career. Most significantly, the narrative centers on the experience of a group of disaffected men who have been exiled (albeit by choice, for the most part) from mainstream Argentine society and who now exist on the country's literal and figurative margins. The film's primary narrative arc concerns Santi (Guillermo Pfening), a character who, at the start of the film, could not be more different from the sad-sack Rulo or the inept Zapa of Trapero's earlier films. Blonde and handsome, Santi lives an idyllic upper-class existence; he and his wife Milli (Martina Gusmán) run a boutique interior design studio catering to Buenos Aires' wealthy, while their young daughter Jose (short for Josefina) (Victoria Vescio) is dressed and walked to school every day by the family's maid. Santi's seemingly perfect life, however, changes dramatically and irrevocably when, on holiday with his wife and daughter, he becomes distracted while driving and drifts into oncoming traffic before swerving wildly off the road, resulting in a terrible accident. While the fates of Milli and Jose are left unclear, in the aftermath of the accident Santi moves to the tiny Patagonian settlement of Veintiocho de Noviembre, located on the Argentine-Chilean border in the far-southern province of Santa Cruz. At the literal edge of Argentina's contiguous territory (the country's most southerly province, Tierra del Fuego, is separated from the rest of the country by Chile), the town exists almost solely to service the airstrip which, when the weather permits, allows small propeller planes to shuttle in workers from northern Patagonian cities.

Taking up a menial laborer's position at the airport, Santi spends his days with Robert (Federico Esquerro), an unmotivated thirty-year-old *porteño* who has abandoned his recently pregnant girlfriend and lives with Santi in the airport's dormitory-style accommodation, and Cacique (Tomás Lipan), an indigenous Argentine who lives in the town with his wife (who is suffering from an unspecified but terminal illness) and children. Ostensibly working as the airport's ground staff, the terrible weather means that the men do very little actual work, instead passing most of their time getting drunk or hunting for rabbits, which they sell to the local canteen in exchange for alcohol. Much of the film chronicles the mundane quotidian existence of the men—they fulfill their duties at the landing strip, well aware that the flights for which they are setting up will most likely be canceled; they drink wine in the canteen while chatting up Betty (Fernanda de Almeida), seemingly the only single woman in the town; they trudge through the snow-covered countryside, Cacique finding hunting spots as Robert attempts to teach Santi how to shoot. A modicum of excitement enters their life when they discover an escaped sheep on the side of the road; instead of returning the animal they load it into the back of their truck, slaughter it, and have an *asado*.

While Santi remains obviously tortured by his experience—he often wakes up in the middle of the night to vomit and suffers repeated panic attacks—it is unclear exactly how much he knows about what has happened to his wife and daughter. At several points he is shown calling someone and asking for Milli or Jose, yet each time the response he receives is confused and ambiguous. Although Robert and Cacique open themselves to Santi he nevertheless remains withdrawn, never giving any indication of his past or what has caused him to come to Veintiocho de Noviembre. This changes, however, after a night of heavy drinking in the neighboring village, when the three men return home and learn that Cacique's wife has died. The funeral triggers something in Santi and, after suffering a psychological meltdown while out hunting, he finally tells Robert everything that has happened. Removing this metaphorical weight from his shoulders seems to free Santi from his self-constructed prison and he decides to return to Buenos Aires. The film's final scene, which includes almost no audible dialog, shows Santi and Milli reuniting. Milli, now badly scarred on her face, is visibly conflicted by Santi's reappearance, alternating between crying on his shoulder and pushing him away in anger. The film ends with the two walking down the street together, the question of whether they will be able to reconcile left unanswered.

Nacido y criado is not a narrative that is dominated by an obviously political message in the manner of *El bonaerense* or *El clan*. This is not to suggest that the work is devoid of any sort of politics; rather, similar to *Mundo grúa*, the film's politics are fairly subtle, focused more on the individual experience than on broad social themes. Santi is a particularly interesting character for he suffers perhaps the most violent reversal of fortune of anyone in the director's entire oeuvre. At the start of *Nacido y criado* Santi could not be more different from the typical Trapero protagonist: where the director's first three films feature middle- and working-class people who are struggling to make ends meet, Santi lives an idyllic upper-class life. He and his family live in an apartment that seems straight from the glossy pages of an architecture magazine, the white

Figure 4.1 *Nacido y criado* (2006). The almost pure white of Santi's house gives his life pre-accident an ethereal quality.

walls and white leather couches matching the family's linen pajamas and the soft white sunlight that fills every room, giving the space an ethereal quality.

Santi's life pre-accident seems incongruous with postcrisis Argentina, as if he and his family are entirely removed from the country that experienced such massive social and economic upheaval (Figure 4.1). Indeed, Santi has even managed to use that upheaval for his own personal gain—his business relies on Buenos Aires' many flea markets, where he is able to exploit the misfortune of others by purchasing used appliances at a reduced rate. He then makes a substantial profit by selling those goods to Europe (Milan is mentioned specifically), re-packaged as authentic vintage pieces. Where in most of Trapero's films, both before and after *Nacido y criado*, daily life is a constant struggle, Santiago spends his days leisurely browsing antique and secondhand shops looking for just the right vintage fan to complement whatever project he is working on. This all changes dramatically, however, in the aftermath of the devastating car accident that Santi unwittingly causes. The crash—a sudden, highly traumatic, highly violent event which causes irreparable damage both physically and mentally—serves as both a literal and symbolic introduction of violence into Santi's life. Where before the accident Santi seems unaffected by the socioeconomic realities of postcrisis Argentina, in its wake, violence is inescapable. Santi attempts to distance himself from the (physical) site of violence by moving to a place that is, figuratively, an entirely different world when compared to Buenos Aires; his experiences in Patagonia show, however, that he has interiorized that violence and, as a result, he is unable to escape the pain that the accident has caused.

Desaparecidos

Concerning the loss of family that Santi experiences in the film, Trapero has stated that the film is, at least partially, a metaphor for the experiences of the *desaparecidos* and their families, saying, "[t]he main story ... is a drama about this dreamy family that descends into hell. But underneath that is a story about the *desaparecidos*, which is a part of our shared history in Argentina. The process of accepting that a loved one has disappeared, for those who survived, was a nightmare" (Matheou, 2010, pp. 282-3). This is visible by the fact that the film's first act appears to be inspired by the typical manner in which family members of *desaparecidos* recall the moment their loved ones were taken. Ludmila da Silva Catela, who interviewed more than thirty family members of *desaparecidos*, describes the pattern:

> La experiencia del secuestro es contada resaltando el momento previo, donde generalmente se detallan las actividades más cotidianas, más intimas, como mirar televisión, estar en la cama, escuchar un cuento. Ello marca la dimensión íntima de la casa como lugar "sagrado." La descripción de los movimientos en el interior de la casa destacan la tranquilidad, la comprensión, el cariño recibido por los compañeros o los padres que luego serán el centro de la violencia. ... Las narrativas de los familiares enuncian así cómo se quebró la vida cotidiana. Describiendo primero la tranquilidad del hogar, luego la invasión y por último el calvario, producto de esa intervención en la vida cotidiana. (1998, p. 93)

> [The experience of the kidnapping is told by emphasizing the moments just beforehand, generally detailing the most quotidian, most intimate activities, such as watching television, lying in bed, listening to a story. This marks the personal dimension of the home as a "sacred" space. The description of the movements in the interior of the house emphasize calmness, understanding, the warmth received from companions or parents who will later become the center of the violence. ... The narratives of family members explain how that daily life was broken, describing first the tranquility of the home, then

the invasion and finally the torment, which is a product of this intervention in their daily life.]

The film's opening fifteen minutes follow the pattern described in Catela's interviews. Everything is included—the soft white light of the house makes the space feel ethereal, like a sanctuary; Santi and Milli go about their daily activities, fundamentally content; at the end of the day they spend time with their daughter before she goes to bed, and then make love. The accident, then, functions as a stand-in for kidnapping; though the process is different, the result is the same.

This is particularly interesting because there is a sort of double narrative occurring throughout the film, yet only one of them is presented on-screen. Although it is never made explicitly clear whether Santi's daughter dies as a result of the accident, over the course of the film Santi makes three calls to his mother-in-law Victoria's house, each time asking to speak with Jose. He never identifies himself, and the first time he calls the woman on the other line (the voice is Milli's, although she also does not identify herself), she reacts with confusion when the name Jose is mentioned. The next time Santi calls (using Robert's mobile phone) Victoria answers; again he asks to speak with Jose but this causes Victoria to realize that she is speaking with Santi and she begins crying, frantically asking him where he is. Because the call was made from a mobile phone rather than the airport's pay phone, Robert begins receiving calls asking for Santi. When Robert confronts Santi about the numerous calls he is receiving, Santi first tells him the people calling must be mistaken. When Robert refuses to accept this and asks what he should say to the people, Santi simply tells him "decíles que no estoy" ("tell them I'm not here"). The final call Santi makes is after the funeral of Cacique's wife, and this time he speaks with Milli directly. As with his earlier conversation with Victoria, Santi asks to speak with Jose, and Milli begins crying, asking Santi where he is and begging him to speak with her. Again, he is unable to respond.

What this series of phone calls and aborted conversations makes clear is that Santi is suffering severe and lasting psychological damage. It can be assumed that Jose has died in the accident and the loss of his daughter is, to a certain extent, driving Santi crazy. The (presumed) death of his daughter, then, is an obvious example of Trapero's "story about the *desaparecidos*"—like those mothers and fathers whose children had disappeared during the Dirty

War, Santi is forced to confront the disappearance of his child and is practically unable to cope. The reactions we hear from Milli and Victoria to Santi's phone calls, however, hint at an unseen trauma, one that Santi himself seems entirely unaware of for most of the film. Indeed, when Santi finally recounts the series of events that drove his decision to move to Patagonia, he makes it clear that his actions were based primarily on the assumption, rather than the explicit knowledge, that his entire family had been killed. He tells Robert,

> Estuve mucho tiempo en el hospital, muchos meses. Mi familia eran Jose y Milli y yo preguntaba todo el tiempo por ellas y nadie sabía que decirme, no me querían decir nada. Y yo me empezaba a dar cuenta de lo que había pasado y ¿qué... qué iba a hacer? ¿Que me quedara allí a esperar que me digan... qué? Así que me arranqué todos los cables y me fui.
>
> [I was in the hospital a long time, several months. My family was Jose and Milli and I asked about them all the time and nobody knew what to tell me, they didn't want to tell me anything. And I began to realize what had happened and what... what was I supposed to do? Stay there waiting for them to tell me... what? So I ripped out all the tubes in me and left.]

The combination of confusion, surprise, and shock audible in the voices of Milli and Victoria when they realize Santi is attempting to contact them begins to take on further meaning when we understand that, by completely abandoning his former life, Santi himself has become a *desaparecido*. Milli's experience, perhaps even more than Santi's, echoes the experiences of thousands of people whose partners were taken from them during the Dirty War without any hint as to where they had gone or what had happened to them. The film's narrative focuses primarily on Santi as he attempts to deal with the pain and guilt caused by the car accident and what he believes to be the death of his wife and daughter. It merely hints at the pain Milli is forced to endure, but it does suggest, by means of brief telephone conversations, that the pain she experiences due to the death of her daughter is amplified by the concurrent disappearance of her husband.

Homo Sacer and the State of Exception

While all of Trapero's films deal with the concept of objective violence, each film manifests that violence in a different way. *El bonaerense* focuses on corruption within the police force; *Mundo grúa* examines the effects of Menemist neoliberalism on the Argentine working class; *Familia rodante*, *El clan*, and *La quietud*, in their own ways, chronicle the stresses placed on and created by the family. *Nacido y criado* differs from Trapero's other films in that it is far-less concerned with the systemic violence that permeates Argentina's economic systems and social institutions. Instead, the film focuses on characters who face their own unique challenges. The characters do not necessarily represent a group of people or social class; they are simply a group of individuals who are each dealing with their personal demons.

When asked about why violence is such a fundamental aspect of his films, Trapero has made it clear that his work is a direct reflection of his personally held beliefs:

> Reality is pure violence, from the violence within nature to survive to the violence within society to encounter a space within that society that is, let's say, more modern than the primitive, to state it briefly. In the individual, in group dynamics, in the social, violence is like a silent war that is lived every day. Your social class matters, because you want to change class and you have nothing and you want something, or you have a little and you want a lot, or you have a lot and you want *more*. It's a permanent tension between what you are and what you want to be. And that violence manifests itself in many forms—in physical violence, in emotional violence, in moral violence, in ethical violence. (Interview with Pablo Trapero)

The different forms of violence to which Trapero refers are visible in numerous ways within the context of *Nacido y criado*—the scarring on Santi's body, his inability to sleep without suffering panic attacks, and the torture he puts his wife and mother-in-law through with his phone calls are all examples of the physical and emotional violence that Trapero believes defines reality.

In a sense, however, the true violence that permeates *Nacido y criado* is the violence of fear. Both Santi and Robert, to varying degrees, have allowed fear to imprison them. For Robert, this fear is based essentially on immaturity: he believes himself too young to take on the responsibility of becoming a father, despite being thirty years old. For viewers familiar with Trapero's previous work this immaturity is signaled from the moment he appears on-screen by the fact that the character is played by Federico Esquerro, the same actor who had previously played "Claudio," a character defined by his irresponsibility, in *Mundo grúa* and *Familia rodante*. Even if they are supposed to be different

Figure 4.2 *Nacido y criado* (2006). Santi's scars mediate Trapero's belief that "reality is pure violence."

characters Robert seems like the natural progression of the Claudio character, almost as if Robert had assumed Claudio's mantle (as it were) and followed in Rulo's footsteps by looking for work in Patagonia. While a particularly unsympathetic type of fear may motivate Robert's actions, Santi is tortured by something else entirely. Prior to the car crash Santi seems entirely devoid of any sense of the catastrophic possibilities of violence; however, it is manifested. The upheaval that has characterized the Argentine economy for most of the twenty-first century is only demonstrated in the prevalence of used goods that Santi purchases secondhand; if anything, the collapse has helped his business. Of the many ways that Santi's life changes postaccident, the most significant must surely be the forced introduction of violence into it. And while Santi is confronted by that violence on a daily basis, the confrontation reveals itself not in the subjective violence seen in films like *El bonaerense* or *Elefante blanco*, but rather in the mangled body and tortured mind of Santi himself (Figure 4.2).

An aspect of *Nacido y criado* that is not particularly emphasized in the film but which is nevertheless significant within the context of Trapero's body of work is the fact that the State (or, perhaps more accurately, the Repressive State Apparatus) is, for all intents and purposes, entirely absent from both the film's narrative and its imagery. Every other film in Trapero's corpus, with the possible exception of *Mundo grúa*, features the State to some degree—it is the focal point of films such as *El bonaerense* or *Leonera*, and even a film like

Familia rodante, in which the State would not seem to have any significant presence, contains a scene where the police appear to inspect the family's truck and fine Gordo for having out-of-date vehicle registration. In *Nacido y criado*, however, no representative of the RSA appears on-screen at any point. This despite the fact that, throughout his time in Patagonia, Santi and his companions break numerous laws—drugs are consumed in public, Robert drives while intoxicated, even the sheep that the men slaughter and eat might be considered stolen property. This is uncanny considering the fact that one of the most significant thematic consistencies that can be found in Trapero's work is the dominant role the State plays in the lives of everyday people. In *Nacido y criado*, however, the State is conspicuous by its apparent absence. This might be explained by the remoteness of the location where the majority of the film's events occur—the area is so far from any population center that there is a sense that the characters exist in a space that civilization and society have yet to reach. The airport where Santi and his companions work is symbolic of this (meta-) physical distance. Superficially it functions as any other airport—passengers arrive for their scheduled flights, their bags are weighed and checked in and their tickets are examined. Yet, instead of boarding their flights, the passengers end up waiting entire days for planes that never come. While, in theory, the airport is meant to serve as a link connecting this outpost with the rest of the country, in practice it barely functions, a monument to what might be rather than what is. With this in mind it is, perhaps, plausible that the town of Veintiocho de Noviembre represents a sort of the last frontier, a twenty-firstcentury manifestation of the nineteenth-century pampa of Argentine folklore. And just as the pampa was an essentially lawless space so too is this tiny, easily forgotten corner of Argentina.

The state of exception as defined and theorized by Agamben is a specifically juridico-political circumstance that relates explicitly to sovereign power. However, Agamben's own writings allow for this strict definition of the term to be abstracted and challenged. Agamben explains, "[t]he state of exception is not a dictatorship . . . but a space devoid of law, a zone of anomie in which all legal determinations—and above all the very distinction between public and private—are deactivated" (2005, p. 50). What is critical for any understanding of how the state of exception functions within the context of *Nacido y criado* is not what role the sovereign plays but, rather, the fact that juridical power has been suspended. Puspa Damai contends that, in spaces where this has occurred, what is left is "a zone of anomie where law remains but only as a pure force of violence" (2005, pp. 256–7). Let us, then, focus less on the actions of the sovereign who declares a state of exception, and instead shift our attention to those living within this "zone of anomie." What becomes of them? Essentially, those living within a state of exception become bare life: *homo sacer*. Agamben himself explains that "together with the process by which the [state of] exception everywhere becomes the rule, the realm of bare life—which is originally situated at the margins of the political order—gradually begins to coincide with the political realm, and exclusion and inclusion, outside and inside, *bios* and *zoē*, right and fact, enter into a zone of irreducible indistinction" (1998, p. 12). Although Veintiocho de Noviembre does not exist within a state of exception in the same way as, for example, the *villa* in *Elefante blanco*, it is nevertheless a "space devoid of law," free from the RSA and the political reality of contemporary Argentina. And, surely, to live in such a space is to become a *homo sacer*, for in such a space, where there are no laws but only a "pure force of violence," what differentiates *zoē* and *bios*?

Writing about the aftermath of Hurricane Katrina in New Orleans and how images of the destruction affected Western (particularly American) society, Žižek states, "[a] fear permeates our lives that this kind of disintegration of the entire social fabric can come at any time, that some natural or technological accident—whether earthquake or electricity failure or the hoary Millennium Bug—will reduce our world to a primitive wilderness" (2009, p. 79). The car accident Santi lives through may not cause any sort of broad societal collapse but, in terms of his individual experience, it does function as a sort of apocalyptic moment, casting him out into the "primitive wilderness" (literally) of Patagonia. The fear that Žižek refers to in his text is the fear of being forced to live in a society without any sort of protections, a society in which anyone may be killed at any moment—the fear of becoming a *homo sacer*. Of course, Santi is not a *homo sacer* in the traditional sense; he has not had his identity stripped by law, nor is he being systematically persecuted by a government operating in a state of exception, a reality thousands of Argentines experienced during the *Proceso* dictatorship. However, the comparison with the *desaparecidos* that was made earlier in this chapter is particularly relevant here, for Santi has, as has been made clear, become a *desaparecido* himself. Of course, this is not the result of some sort of disciplinary action; he has not had this imposed upon him by others, as would be the case in the strictest interpretation of the *homo sacer*. Instead, Santi has become a sort of voluntary *homo sacer*—he has condemned himself to this role; he has willingly taken on the existence of a man whose life is reduced to the violence of bare life. This violence is not manifested through any sort of threat to his physical body on the part of the state or any individual, however. Rather, Santi commits violence against himself, as demonstrated by the severe psychological torment he puts himself through throughout his time in Patagonia.

Again, Agamben's own writings provide the context with which to challenge the strict understanding of the *homo sacer*. Agamben states that "in the body of *homo sacer* . . . [the world] finds itself confronted . . . with a life that . . . is defined solely by virtue of having entered into an intimate symbiosis with death without, nevertheless, belonging to the world of the deceased" (1998, p. 61). Santi embodies this figure precisely because he has experienced the rapidity with which violence can alter a life, because he is scarred, literally and figuratively, by his brush with death. The Santi that we encounter in Patagonia, then, is a personification of a certain type of *homo sacer*: a man whose life is haunted by death and dominated by violence, a man whose very existence is a state of exception.

With this portrayal of its main character, *Nacido y criado* marks a significant turning point in Trapero's career, as all of the director's subsequent films have incorporated this concept of the state of exception, all of his characters being, essentially, *homines sacri*. *Nacido y criado* is unique, however, in that it is the one work in Trapero's oeuvre where the film's protagonists do not need protection from the State but, rather, where they need protection from the psychological violence they inflict upon themselves. The Patagonian landscape that dominates so much of *Nacido y criado*—reminiscent of the dark, foreboding portrayal of the region found in Fabián Bielinsky's 2005 film *El aura/The Aura*—functions as a metaphorical representation of the state of exception that exists within Santi and the violence he continually commits against himself. The differences between how the region is portrayed in *Mundo grúa* and *Nacido y criado* are drastic: where the otherworldly desolation of the countryside of central Patagonia serves to highlight Rulo's frustrations in the earlier film, the mountains and forests of Veintiocho de Noviembre portrayed in *Nacido y criado* represent something altogether more complex. Andermann contends that in *Nacido y criado*, landscape as "space freed from eventhood" (Lefebvre) interrupts and suspends temporal continuity. But here it also . . . resonates with a state of mind, the sheer extremity and inhospitality of its ruggedness paradoxically providing spiritual refuge, a point of anchorage, for the character's state of immobilization by traumatic loss. (2012, p. 69)

Although it is unclear how long Santi spends in the region, throughout his time in Patagonia the ground is covered in snow, with snowstorms a frequent occurrence. Far from a stereotypical winter wonderland, however, the scenery is presented as harsh, uninviting, even dirty. Indeed, the audience's introduction to Patagonia, occurring immediately after the fateful car accident, sets the tone—as Santi's screams of agony fade, the black screen burns to a greyish white that is revealed to be a snow-covered field.

Contrasting sharply with the immaculate bright white of Santi's posh Buenos Aires flat from earlier in the film, the snow is pockmarked by dirt, rocks, and bald patches. Alternating between snowy mountains and discarded mining slag heaps where the earth has been torn apart, several more establishing shots of Patagonia are shown until finally we come across Santi and Robert walking quietly through a wood, Robert holding a shotgun as Santi follows behind. Far from the stylishly dressed interior designer with fashionable stubble and a clean haircut that we have seen prior to the accident, this Santi is wearing a utilitarian mustard-yellow jacket, has a scraggly beard, and long unwashed hair, his disheveled appearance mimicking his surroundings. The significance of this contrast is undeniable, Andermann pointing out that "the landscape in *Nacido y criado* turns from a mere scenic backdrop into an active bearer of meaning, its snow-covered wastes and dark, motionless forests echoing the sadness and silence inside Santiago's mind, his inability to come out of his state of shock and face up to an almost certainly unbearable loss" (2012, p. 69).

Patagonia and Rhizomes

Indeed, the metaphorical significance of the Patagonian landscape found in *Mundo grúa* is heightened exponentially in *Nacido y criado*, to the extent that the countryside assumes an active role in the film. Precisely because the weather is so terrible, the conditions so extreme, and the space so vast, the residents of Veintiocho de Noviembre are essentially forced to create a community. Santi, Robert, and Cacique end virtually every day by heading to "el riojano," a shorthand the men use to refer to the shop-cum-canteen where they eat dinner and, almost invariably, get drunk. "El riojano" (so called because the shop's owner comes from La Rioja province) serves as the village's focal point—whenever Santi and his colleagues enter the premises they are immediately greeted by people (usually old men) they know; Betty, a young woman who works in the canteen (and, it is implied, allows herself to be pimped out by the shopkeeper), brings her two sons to work with her, her elder boy ferrying plates from the kitchen to the customers. The three protagonists spend most of their waking hours together, discussing the challenges they face in their lives, commiserating with others and airing their own grievances in equal measure. Paz Escobar explains,

> las imágenes que predominan [en la película] son las de un muy pequeño grupo de trabajadores viviendo y trabajando en condiciones de extrema dureza y precariedad . . . se alternan las escenas de trabajo con las de descanso asociado a la solidaridad cotidiana y confraternidad entre trabajadores que se vuelven amigos. (2014, p. 127)

> [the images that predominate [in the film] are those of a very small group of laborers living and working under conditions of extreme hardship and precariousness . . . scenes of labor alternate with scenes of rest, these being associated with everyday solidarity and brotherhood between workers who have become friends.]

Although seemingly everyone in the town comes from somewhere else, and despite the fact that each individual in the story faces their own distinct set of challenges, a community forms through a sense of shared experience.

This community can be understood as an example of the Deleuzean rhizome in action—unique individuals with very little in common creating connections that are free of the hierarchical structures associated with arborescent relations (Figure 4.3). The film's title, *Born and Bred*, is representative of the rhizomatic nature of community in Veintiocho de Noviembre. Purported to be a phrase used by Patagonian natives to differentiate themselves from those who move to the region, Andermann finds that in the context of *Nacido y criado* the saying refers to a "double vision of Patagonia as space and as place . . . [Patagonia's] vast emptiness serving as projection surface for anxieties and desires, yet all the same representing for its inhabitants a place of lived experience" (2012,

Figure 4.3 *Nacido y criado* (2006). Rejecting rigid, traditional structures, Santi, Cacique, and Robert develop a kind of rhizomatic family.

p. 70). The great irony of the title is, of course, the fact that the film features a cast of characters who come from everywhere *but* Patagonia. They are left with little choice, then, to form bonds of friendship and community with the people they encounter in this unfamiliar space, rather than with people with whom they might have some shared characteristic or previous experience. Being born and bred in Patagonia matters little, for the region's population is so scarce that, while individuals may form smaller groups (as seen with the trio of protagonists), the community cannot afford to be exclusionary. In order to survive, therefore, the community must be rhizomatic in nature. This rhizomatic community can be understood as combating against the state of exception that has engulfed Santi and the other characters. The rhizome, in this case, helps Santi in particular as he struggles to come to terms with his new reality—no questions are asked of his past, no explanations are needed, and the extended periods of isolation that living in such a sparsely populated community offers him mean that he is able to reintegrate into society (such as it is) as he feels comfortable.

The shortcomings of the rhizomatic family, however, are made visible through the character of Cacique, the only one of the three main characters to have a traditional family in Veintiocho de Noviembre. Where *Familia rodante* and *El clan* portray the nuclear family in a fairly negative light, *Nacido y criado* approaches the family from a more ambivalent perspective, focusing on both its negative and positive traits. Santi's family pre-crash is central to the film's narrative, and the loss of that family sets the rest of the film in motion. Cacique's family, in contrast, almost never appears on-screen, even as the specter of his wife's illness predominates Cacique's narrative arc. Indeed, it is Cacique's narrative arc that perhaps best emphasizes the conflicted nature of the traditional family. The ambiguous relationship Cacique has with his family simmers throughout the film and finally comes to a boil on the night he accompanies Santi and Robert to Río Turbio. At times Cacique is quite positive about, if not his family in particular, the general concept of family; this is most noticeable when he encourages Robert to accept responsibility for the child his partner is carrying, telling him "un hijo siempre es bienvenido, Robert, trae un pan bajo el brazo." ("a child is a blessing, Robert, it brings good fortune.") Despite this, however, he spends very little time with his own family, much preferring the company of his friends in "el riojano." Indeed, he is so inclined to spend time in the canteen that his daughter must routinely fetch him at the end of the night, invariably interrupting his fun. While he normally goes with her, on the night of his trip to Río Turbio he waves her off. When she insists he explodes with rage, frightening not only his daughter but everyone else in the bar, as well. As the sun comes up and the men decide to head to the larger town, they stop at Cacique's house and again he is shown ignoring his daughter's pleas to remain at home, literally breaking free from her grasp as she attempts to pull him back into the house. As the men carry on drinking through the course of the next day in the nearby town of Río Turbio, their session broken only by a visit to the town's brothel, Cacique explains to his companions that he came to Patagonia to work a six-month contract and has stayed ever since, his children having been born and raised in the area. This statement is significant for it is the only moment in the film where Cacique offers any sort of interpretation of his own situation—the implication being that through having a family he has been forced to remain in Patagonia, where he now leads a deeply unsatisfying life centered entirely on caring for his dying wife and drowning his frustration in wine and coca leaves.

Whatever resentment he may feel toward his family quickly dissipates, however, when he returns home to find that his wife has died. Overcome with grief at the funeral, the emotion Cacique displays seems to force a realization in Santi. To this point in the film Santi has been trapped in a sort of Foucauldian prison of his own making—his grief and guilt are so overwhelming that they have served to individualize him, so that while he is a member of the Veintiocho de Noviembre community he is also isolated from it, unknowable to those around him and incapable of making lasting connections. In the aftermath of the death of Cacique's wife, however, Santi is confronted with the reality that everyone has challenges and difficulties, and while Cacique was perhaps burdened by his wife's illness, the love he felt for her outweighed that burden. The support and companionship Cacique received from his rhizomatic family, then, pales in comparison to the depth of feeling he has for his arborescent, traditional family. And it is this, ultimately, that leads to the film's final scene of Santi and Milli reuniting, acknowledging simultaneously the fragility and the importance of family.

Leonera

Taking a similarly ambiguous approach to both traditional and rhizomatic family structures, *Leonera* expands on many of the topics first introduced in *Nacido y criado*, while also sharing similarities to the films examined in Chapter 3. As with those films, *Leonera* portrays certain aspects of the traditional family unit in a highly critical light. Where no escape or alternative seems possible to the characters of *El clan* or *Familia rodante*, however, *Leonera*, like *La quietud*, presents an option that embodies the Deleuzo-Guattarian concept of relations of alliance (as opposed to filiation). Through its examination of the nontraditional family that is formed within a women's prison, the film provides a sympathetic examination of a facet of Argentine society that is often stereotyped negatively, something Trapero would repeat with his look at the *villa miseria* community in *Elefante blanco*. In its highly detailed examination of the female prison system, *Leonera* seems inspired by Dostoevsky's famous quotation that "the degree of civilization in a society can be judged by entering its prisons." The film questions the way in which inmates are treated, holding a mirror to Argentine society in the process; in doing so, Trapero carries on the tradition of social critique found in the works of filmmakers such as Mario Soffici (*Prisioneros de la tierra* [1939], *Héroes sin fama* [1940]) and, more recently, Hector Babenco (*Pixote* [1982], *Carandiru* [2002]). Much like its chronological predecessors *Nacido y criado* and *Familia rodante*, *Leonera* examines both the positive and negative aspects of the arborescent family; where it differs, however, is in its much more in-depth consideration of the rhizomatic community into which the protagonist is placed. In essence, the film functions as an extended meditation on the possibilities offered by the becoming-family, possibilities that are particularly beneficial in a confined, isolated environment such as the prison.

The film begins with a close-up of Julia (Martina Gusmán) as she wakes up one morning. Blood is visible on her pillow and her apartment is shown to be in disarray, though she does not seem to notice it or care. Julia remains either unaware or unconcerned as she makes her way to work and it is only at the end of the workday that she notices she is bleeding. Inspecting the bruises and cuts on her body as she returns home, she enters her flat to find two naked men lying on the floor, both of whom appear to be dead. Julia calls the police; when they arrive they manage to revive one of the men and, as they inspect the apartment, arrest Julia. She is swiftly processed by the police, charged with murder, and sent to prison to await trial. During the medical examination prior to entering the prison it is revealed that Julia is pregnant, although she is unsure of how many months along she is. She is placed in the maternal wing of the prison, along with other prisoners who are either pregnant or, as is the case with the majority of the women in the wing, have young children. Julia becomes friends with Marta (Laura García), the woman in the cell next to hers, who introduces her to other prisoners and in the process proves herself to be something of a power broker in the wing. The film chronicles her time in the wing as her pregnancy progresses—she and the other pregnant women take Lamaze classes, her friendship with Marta begins to form, and, most significantly, she is visited by a defense lawyer. Shortly after giving her statement to the judiciary Julia enters labor and gives birth to a son, whom she names Tomás. Upon returning to the prison, Julia is told that Tomás will stay with her in the maternal wing until he turns four years old, after which custody will be transferred to Julia's mother and Julia will be moved to the prison's general population to complete her sentence. Julia's initial period with Tomás in the prison is a difficult one, and Marta comes to her aid on several occasions, actions that cause the relationship between the two mothers to strengthen to the extent that they become lovers, despite Julia's initial resistance to Marta's advances. Julia's lawyer returns and explains that Ramiro (Rodrigo Santoro), the man from Julia's apartment at the beginning of the film whom the police were able to revive, has implicated her as the killer. As the years pass and Tomás grows, it becomes clear that Julia stands a very good chance of being convicted of murder, a fact that causes Julia's mother Sofía (Elli Medeiros) to attempt to remove Tomás from Julia's custody. Julia reacts extremely violently to this—even threatening to kill her mother—and is eventually locked in solitary confinement, where she suffers something of a breakdown.

After an unspecified period of time in solitary confinement she begins demanding to speak with the prison director, a demand she continues once she is released back to the maternal wing. One evening her demands become so disruptive that the other women in the wing leave their cells to ask why she is making so much noise. When Julia explains that her son is being taken away from her, the other prisoners begin to protest in solidarity with Julia, the anger within the group escalating so quickly that a full-blown riot breaks out. The prisoners eventually set fire to the wing, and this escalation finally gets the prison director's attention; he promises to try to have Tomás returned to Julia provided she attempts to quell the riot. Shortly after this, Julia's case concludes and she is found guilty of murder. Tomás, having reached the age of four, is taken from her and she enters the prison's general population. Time passes until, having completed enough of her sentence, she is granted a day pass to visit her son in Buenos Aires. While visiting him she manages to lock the guards who accompanied her in a room and escape the flat with her son. With Marta's assistance, Julia makes her way to the Argentina-Paraguay border, where she enters Paraguay on a false passport and escapes to a life of exile with her son.

Prison and Prison Films

Although not every film Trapero has made over the course of his career fits neatly within specific genre categories, many of his films can be understood as fulfilling certain broad generic tropes. *El bonaerense* is a police narrative, *Familia rodante* a road movie, and with *Leonera* Trapero offers his take on one of the more enduring genres in Latin American cinema: the prison film. What marks each of these films is the nontraditional approach Trapero takes in each case. In *El bonaerense*, for instance, Zapa is characterized by his incompetence rather than his ability as a police officer; at the end of *Familia rodante* there is virtually no catharsis and the family's divisions have only become more pronounced; and where most prison films focus on the male experience of incarceration—ranging from Latin American films such as Hector Babenco's films *The Kiss of the Spider Woman* (1985) and *Carandiru* to Hollywood productions such as *The Shawshank Redemption* (1994) or the HBO series *Oz* (1997–2003)—*Leonera* is focused on a group of mothers and their children attempting to approximate normality within a women's prison. (When it ended its seven-season run in 2019, *Orange Is the New Black* was Netflix's most-watched original series, suggesting that *Leonera* was something of a trendsetter.) In this sense, *Leonera* diverges significantly from the stereotypical female prison film. Judith Mayne explains that the genre tends to follow a series of highly specific tropes:

> A young woman either participated unknowingly in a crime; or participated in a crime because she was madly in love with a man who is a murderer or a thief . . . or is framed for a crime she didn't commit. She is sent to prison. There she encounters women (often in the requisite shower scene) who challenge her, try to seduce her, and make her life miserable. They include the prison warden, who is either kind and helpful or bitter and vindictive; the guard(s), who are also either kind or bitter . . . and of course the other prisoners. (2000, p. 115)

Most analyses of female prison films are centered on the women-in-prison exploitation films that dominate the subgenre. (And the type of film which Judith Mayne is describing.) In addition to the very specific tropes explained by Mayne, women-in-prison films also conform to one of the key tropes of men-in-prison films generally: the social hierarchy amongst inmates is determined through a synthesis of reputation and displays of dominance, the former earned as a result of the crime that led to incarceration and the latter displayed either through acts of violence or sexual assault. *Leonera*, in contrast, presents a significantly more sober examination of the incarceration experience for female prisoners, either avoiding the exploitative stereotypes of (women-in-)prison films altogether or, as shall be examined later in this chapter, turning them on their head. As a result, Trapero's film varies significantly from traditional (women-in-)prison narratives, providing a more realistic examination of how imprisonment (and the associated mandatory separation from her child) affects Julia's character.

While prison narratives are an important and popular component of many regional and national literatures and cinemas, they have played a particularly important role within the context of Latin American cultural production for

Figure 4.4 *Leonera* (2008). *Leonera* eschews stereotypical women-in-prison film tropes.

many decades. From novels such as Guatemalan Nobel Prize winner Miguel Ángel Asturias's *El señor Presidente* (1946) or Argentine Manuel Puig's *El beso de la mujer araña* (1976) to films such as Ruben W. Cavallotti's *Procesado 1.040* (1958), the Latin American *narrativa carcelaria* (prison narrative) often serves to emphasize the abuses, hardships, or neglect (or, quite often, a combination of all these things) committed by the State upon its population. As Rafael Saumell-Muñoz explains, "[l]os testimonios carcelarios narran como pocos el fracaso de los diversos proyectos políticos que se han querido implantar en Latinoamérica" ("prison testimonies narrate in a way few other things can the failure of the diverse political projects which have attempted to take hold in Latin America") (1993, p. 498). *Leonera* seems particularly inspired by the work of Argentine-Brazilian director Hector Babenco, especially his films *Pixote*, which tells the experiences of a group of boys who escape a youth penitentiary, and *Carandiru*, which chronicles the lives of various inmates in São Paulo's Carandiru prison in the lead up to the 1992 riot and massacre that occurred there. As Babenco did with *Pixote*, Trapero makes use of mostly nonprofessional actors in his film; in the same vein, just as Babenco shot *Carandiru* in the (then closed) prison in which that film is set, Trapero filmed *Leonera* on location in various women's prisons throughout Argentina (Figure 4.4). As such, while *Leonera* tells a fictional story it is nevertheless a fairly authentic representation of contemporary prison life for female wards of the State.

Saumell-Muñoz determines that the rise in popularity of the prison narrative in a Latin American context was first seen during the nineteenth century, stating,

A lo largo de esta centuria la prisión aparece con mayor frecuencia en la narrativa. El fracaso de los ideales independentistas, la entronización de largas tiranías, más la inagotable tradición de guerras civiles, han llevado a muchas personas a las salas de tortura, a las cárceles, al exilio y a los paredones de fusilamiento. (1993, p. 499)

[Over the course of the century prison appears with increasing frequency in narrative. The failure of independence ideals, the rise of long dictatorships, and the unending tradition of civil wars have all sent many people to torture halls, to prisons, to exile, and to the firing squad.]

Thematically, prison narratives in the twentieth century continued in a similar vein to those from the nineteenth century, largely because the social reality had changed relatively little. Dictatorships continued to dominate the region and state-sponsored violence was prevalent, although internal resistance (or subversive) movements might substitute for civil wars, and instead of facing the firing squad citizens who found themselves the victim of State violence were more likely to be simply disappeared.

In the Argentine context specifically, prison narratives have often been used as a form of social critique, particularly against whatever dictatorship happened to be in power at the time. Since the 1970s, however, prison narratives have come almost exclusively to be used within the context of commentary and reflection on the Dirty War. This is, perhaps, unsurprising when one considers that even before the *Proceso* dictatorship came to power, the mechanisms for mass incarceration that the government employed had been set in place. Mary Jane Treacy finds that, in the mid-1970s, government policies enacted during Isabel Perón's time as president meant that prisons in Argentina came to take on an added political significance, further complicating something that was already, by its very nature, highly problematic—"the ideological struggles that were once played out in a public arena through guerrilla and army violence were turned into a 'dirty war' fought in the hidden realm of clandestine jails and enacted upon the bodies of real and potential enemies of the junta-ruled state" (1996, p. 130). The prison-cum-torture facilities run by the armed forces during the *Proceso* dictatorship have been well chronicled, and the sinister legacy of those detention centers (and the period as a whole) is visible in films such as *La noche de los lápices* (Héctor Olivera, 1986), *Garage olimpo* (Marco Bechis, 1999), and *Crónica de una fuga* (Adrián Caetano, 2006).

While *Leonera* is set predominantly in a prison and, therefore, can be understood as carrying on certain aspects of the prison narrative tradition that runs throughout Argentine (and Latin American) cinema, the film differs in significant ways from those prison films that are explicitly focused on the dictatorship. For one thing, and in noticeable contrast to many recent Argentine prison films, *Leonera* is set in the present day, and whatever social critique is present in the film is a commentary on contemporary prison conditions and incarceration policies. Rather than functioning as a site where the state of exception exists explicitly—in a dictatorship's detainment center quite literally anyone under detention may be killed at any moment—the prison as it is portrayed in *Leonera* functions as a vision of total State violence. The women in the prison are capable of living fairly regular lives, yet their very existence is regulated and controlled by the constant presence of the State. As Michael Hardt explains, prison is "the site of the highest concentration of a logic of power that is generally diffused throughout the world. Prison is our society in its most realized form" (1997, p. 66). In contrast to the society of control portrayed in *Nacido y criado*, the prison community in *Leonera* is an archetypal example of Foucault's disciplinary society. Foucault describes the penitentiary as "an exhaustive disciplinary apparatus" (1991, p. 235), and finds that "[the prison] merely reproduces, with a little more emphasis, all the mechanisms that are to be found in the social body" (1991, p. 233). Any prison, therefore, simply reflects the very society from which its inmates are taken. *Leonera*, in its dual role as a family drama and a prison narrative, not only examines the violence that characterizes the Argentine state's treatment of its own populace but also how that violence affects individuals and their interpersonal relationships on the most basic level.

Rhizomatic Families

The concentrated violence of incarceration has an important effect on Julia's very nature. The more time she spends in the prison, the more institutionalized she becomes, accepting the ever-present violence of the prison as normal. Craig Haney describes institutionalization as "the process by which inmates are shaped and transformed by the institutional environments in which they live" (2003, p. 38). That transformation often manifests itself in a drastically altered personality, precisely because "[t]he various psychological mechanisms that must be employed to adjust (and, in some harsh and dangerous correctional environments, to survive) become increasingly natural—second nature in fact—and, to a degree, internalized" (2003, p. 39). Because the film follows Julia from the moment she enters prison until the moment she finally escapes, this evolution is most visible in the changes her character experiences. As the film begins, and through to the point that Marta first begins to make an attempt to get to know her, Julia is presented as being incredibly disconnected from the world, as if living in a trance. She wakes up covered in cuts and bruises but does not seem to notice them; she spends a day at work and does not seem to feel any aftereffects of the previous night's violence; she is arrested, charged, and sent to jail and, for the most part, puts up very little resistance, as if these things are happening to someone else and she is simply watching them occur.

For most of the film's first thirty minutes, Julia's dominant personality trait is passivity—her voice rarely rises above a mumble, she displays very little emotion beyond occasionally crying to herself, and she seems almost resigned to whatever her fate may be. This changes virtually the instant that she gives birth to her son Tomás. While recuperating with her child after the caesarean, Julia's mother Sofía, who lives in France, visits her in the hospital. Julia is quite reticent to display any sort of warmth toward her mother, even asking her "¿qué hacés acá?" ("what are you doing here?") As the two women speak, the camera frames the entire scene, with Julia lying down, her gaze rarely leaving her son who is cradled in her arms, and her mother sitting toward the foot of the bed. The camera then cuts to a medium close-up of Julia and her child, cutting out her mother entirely. As Sofía coos over the child off-screen she reaches out in an attempt to touch the child. Julia, however, raises her hand in a symbolic "don't touch" gesture and Sofía pulls her hand back and out of the frame. This moment is highly significant, for it represents not only Julia's mentality for the rest of the film—she and her child are conjoined, virtually one person, both people fitting within the close-up frame normally reserved for individuals—but also foreshadows the conflict between Sofía and Julia that will prove to be a key catalyst for Julia's ultimate decision to escape (Figure 4.5). Further, this action can be understood as the instant when Julia's rejection of her mother becomes fully realized and she is able to break free from the arborescent interpersonal relationships of her past.

Figure 4.5 *Leonera* (2008). Julia's subtle yet significant act of rejection.

Sofía, perhaps more than anyone else in the film (including Ramiro), represents the hierarchical, arborescent traditional family in which desire is channeled and limited. She continually acts upon Julia without Julia's consent—from hiring a lawyer whom Julia not only dislikes but also distrusts to, later in the film, removing Tomás from Julia's care, believing that her position as Julia's mother ensures that she is acting in her best interests. Despite an obvious tension existing in Julia's relationship with Sofía—upon first entering the prison Julia claims not to have any family—she remains fairly passive prior to Tomás's birth. Following her son's birth and her subtle yet potent rejection of her mother, however, Julia begins to exert herself much more forcefully. She begins to form stronger bonds with her fellow inmates, even entering into a sexual relationship with Marta. When Sofía attends Tomás' baptism in the prison and, while talking with Julia afterward, breaks down in tears, Julia's response is fairly shocking: she begins yelling at her mother, screaming, "¡BASTA! ¡Dejá de llorar! Haciendo este show delante de todo el mundo. . . . ¿Qué te pasa? Controlate." ("STOP! Stop crying! Making this scene in front of everyone. . . . What's wrong with you? Get a hold of yourself.") To a certain extent, this outburst represents the effects of institutionalization on Julia's personality. However, Julia's outburst can also be understood as an expression of her rejection of the hierarchical and traditional, and the freedom that rejection provides her. Paradoxically, imprisonment, a circumstance that frequently breaks down individuals (as Foucault makes quite clear), in this case provides Julia with the community she had been lacking in her previous life.

This is just one example of the many ways that *Leonera* goes against the conventions of the formulaic prison film. Perhaps more significantly, *Leonera* eschews the most stereotypical trope of prison narratives—that of forced sexual relationships based on rape and power dynamics—and instead presents the relationship between Julia and Marta as one which is positive in nature, entered into willingly and with consent from both women. While Marta is certainly a power broker within the maternal ward, her relationship with Julia is not one in which she is exerting her dominance or attempting to demonstrate her authority to the other inmates; it is telling that when Marta is released from prison and is saying goodbye to Julia it is Marta who begins crying first. Likewise, while Julia is at first reticent to begin a relationship with another woman, when she finally does, it is by choice and she is not in any way traumatized by the decision; in fact, just the opposite occurs: in Marta, Julia finds an ally, a person who approaches her free from any sort of judgment or ulterior motive. This is something she desperately lacks in all her other interpersonal relationships—as examined, the relationship she has with her mother is extremely complex and becomes, by the end of the film, adversarial. The lawyer Sofía has hired to represent Julia appears more concerned with keeping Sofía happy than with making any honest attempt at defending Julia; and Ramiro, a man who was her deceased bisexual partner's boyfriend and with whom she does not seem to have any particular shared past, is well aware of the fact that the only way he can exculpate himself is by shifting the entire blame of the murder onto Julia. As such, the healthiest relationship Julia has with any adult in the entire film is the one she has with Marta.

The significance of this fact within the context of Trapero's oeuvre is notable, for Julia's relationship with Marta is an archetypal example of the Deleuzian concept of the rhizome (Figure 4.6). Within the prison narrative that forms *Leonera*'s base, the film couches a family drama characterized by three different quasi-familial relationships. At the center of all three of these relationships is Julia herself. The relationship presented in the worst light is, without question, the one between Julia and Sofía. This is perhaps unsurprising given the conflicted representation of the traditional family throughout much of Trapero's work. The other two relationships are very different in nature from each other, but each is presented in a generally positive way. The first, the mother-child relationship between Julia and her son Tomás, is perhaps the most important of the three, for it provides Julia with a sense of meaning and

Figure 4.6 *Leonera* (2008). Julia and Marta create a becoming-family.

fundamentally changes her personality. Despite its importance, however, the relationship is not a particularly complex one: it is an arborescent, somewhat traditional family structure, but it is one in its (literal) infancy. The third relationship the film presents, the one between Julia and Marta, is the only true rhizomatic becoming-family that is seen in any of Trapero's films. With the becoming-family that emerges between Julia and Marta we can see how a rhizomatic understanding of the family concept allows for a situation that bears little resemblance to the arborescent family of general imagination. Julia and Marta's rhizomatic family begins to take shape immediately after Julia returns from the hospital and is unable to calm her crying son. With virtually the entire prison yelling at her to shut the child up, Marta enters her cell, takes Tomás, and begins comforting him. With the child still in her arms and while cursing quietly to herself Marta returns to her cell, telling Julia to fetch him once he has fallen asleep. A similar situation arises shortly thereafter, with Marta able to feed Tomás when the child refuses Julia's breast. In return for these favors (such as they are), Julia does things like washing Marta's clothes and arranging for things that Marta has requested—calling cards, towels, diapers—to be included in the care packages that Sofía brings with her when she comes to visit. As Julia becomes more experienced with motherhood, however, the relationship stops being one of trade and starts to become one of companionship, to the point that the two women and their respective children begin to form a large family. One scene, in particular, emphasizes the family-like relationship that develops— the two women are shown sitting on Marta's bed watching television, their children either in their arms or playing on blankets spread on the floor beside them, Julia lying against Marta as she falls asleep. This scene, so reminiscent of what one might expect to see in a traditional heteronormative relationship, portrays the two as a single unit undergoing the process of creating their own community within the cold walls of a prison.

What Julia and Marta form, over the course of their relationship, is a becoming-family. The significance of the becoming-family, especially within the prison walls, cannot be overstated. Deleuze and Guattari explain that "unlike trees or their roots, the rhizome connects any point to any other point, and its traits are not necessarily linked to traits of the same nature" (2013, p. 21), and the becoming-family that emerges between Julia and Marta demonstrates this. Theirs is a family that is created partially as a result of their forced proximity: they are, literally, prisoners of the Repressive State Apparatus, bound by a rigid set of rules and limitations that, in theory, attempt to ensure they remain subjects of the State. However, by forming their own rhizomatic familial unit, one based entirely on alliance rather than filiation, they are engaging in a subtle yet meaningful act of rebellion. Small acts of resistance against the RSA are portrayed at various moments throughout the film, perhaps most notably when the camera, cutting rapidly through scenes of the maternal ward's Christmas celebration, settles on the passionate kiss between one of the female prison guards and one of the inmates. The other guards, watching the festivities from the side, react with surprise but do not intervene, suggesting that this sort of defiance, where the all-important boundaries between guard and prisoner are disregarded, is permissible for one night of revelry. Julia and Marta's relationship differs from this in that theirs is not merely confined to carnivalesque moments but is rather something much more meaningful. The positivity and importance of the relationship is contrasted with the negativity inherent in the relationship that exists between Julia and Sofía. Indeed, Marta and Sofía can almost be understood as counterbalances to one another—where Marta cares about Julia's well-being (and understands that Julia having Tomás with her is fundamental to that well-being), Sofía is focused on removing Tomás from Julia's custody, regardless of what effect that will have on Julia's mental and emotional state; where Marta eventually helps Julia escape Argentina with her son, Sofía deceives Julia and refuses to return Tomás to the prison, something which sends Julia into an uncontrollable rage and results in her being sent to solitary confinement for a significant amount of time.

The events that occur immediately after Julia is finally released from solitary confinement are also quite significant. By this point in the narrative Marta's prison sentence has ended and Julia has, to a certain extent, taken over her role as a well-respected member of the maternity ward community. When Julia begins demanding to speak with the prison director in the middle of the night, explaining to the other inmates (all of whom, it must be remembered, are mothers themselves) that her son has been taken from her, the inmates rally to her support. Their own anger at Julia's treatment escalates to such an extent that they soon begin to riot, setting fire to bedding and banging pots and pans against the prison bars. While the inmates almost certainly take advantage of the situation, escalating what could be a simple protest into something violent, they are also demonstrating a degree of solidarity with one of their own. The mothers in the prison have an acute understanding of the emotional significance of having their children with them. This is something that both Ramiro and, particularly, Sofía fail to grasp. The rhizome of the prison community, then, is in this case far more positive and supportive than the mother-daughter relationship that we see with Sofía and Julia.

Though very different in many ways, *Nacido y criado* and *Leonera* tell somewhat similar stories and come to similar conclusions; for all that the films emphasize the possible benefits offered by the creation of alternative family units, neither film ends with the main characters rejecting the traditional family structure. Rather, for both works the primary takeaway from each narrative is the importance of the traditional family. Despite this, the two protagonists come to this realization in extremely different ways—Santi must witness Cacique's grieving process firsthand, shocking him into the realization that family is, in fact, of vital importance, whereas virtually from the moment she gives birth Julia defines herself in relation to her son. Where both films agree, however, is in stressing the permanence of the traditional family in contrast to the (relatively) ephemeral nature of the constructed one. At the end of both films, the main characters are confronted by the stark contrasts inherent between arborescent and rhizomatic families: Santiago is forced to acknowledge that, while the community he develops in Veintiocho de Noviembre has helped him to cope emotionally in the immediate aftermath of the car accident, he will never be able to truly heal until he returns to Milli and they attempt to process the loss of their daughter together. Similarly, Julia is posed with the very real dilemma of losing both her actual family—

Tomás has been removed from her custody and she has been moved into the general prison population—and her constructed family, since Marta has been released from prison and comes to visit only occasionally. While Julia does go about creating a new community amongst the other prisoners in the general population, she never loses sight of the fact that being with her son is far more important than whatever she may have built in the prison. Both films seem to suggest that family, despite its problems, is important and necessary. This is, of course, a more nuanced understanding of the family when compared to other films in Trapero's corpus, where traditional family structures are presented as something inherently negative and violent. *Leonera*, in particular, portrays the complex balance in which families exist—the film demonstrates how the collapse of one parent-child relationship is precipitated by the emergence of another. While it is true that by the time Julia escapes to Paraguay with Tomás her son has been taken from her by law, rather than through Sofía's efforts, at that point in the narrative the relationship between the two women has, for all intents, ceased to exist. Whatever emotional support Julia may receive from her rhizomatic family, when faced with the loss of her son she proves unwilling to accept the nontraditional prison family as a substitute. And this is perhaps the most telling aspect of both of the films analyzed in this chapter—whatever pain it may cause, whatever negative it may bring, the importance of family cannot be denied, for it is family that allows the characters to overcome violence.

Conclusion

This book has identified and analyzed the function of violence in the films of screenwriter-director Pablo Trapero. It has done this by examining different understandings of the concept of violence itself—with a particular emphasis placed on Slavoj Žižek's concept of objective violence—and how it is represented on-screen in Trapero's films. Each chapter has focused on a grouping of films from early and late in Trapero's career; in each case the earlier film introduces motifs and themes which the later films then expand upon and intensify.

In examining the entirety of Pablo Trapero's oeuvre, this work has tracked a period in which Argentina has, from a politico-economic standpoint, served as a sort of bellwether for the shifting trends that have affected societies across Latin America. The contraction and eventual collapse of the nation's economy in the late 1990s and early 2000s presaged (and, of course, was at least partially responsible for) similar events in neighboring Uruguay and Brazil, and the general experience of wide-ranging, culture-shifting economic crisis that Argentina experienced in 2001–02 was to be replicated across the world, to varying degrees, in the aftermath of the Global Financial Crisis of 2008. Further, for much of the twenty-first century the nation's political mood, from the left-wing populism of Néstor Kirchner and his wife and presidential successor Cristina Fernández to the return of neoliberalism in the form of Mauricio Macri, has often signaled broader tendencies throughout not merely the region but the world. Indeed, Macri's victory in 2015, widely understood as an explicit rejection of Kirchnerism, can now be seen as a harbinger of the widespread embrace of a new form of neoliberalism that occurred throughout the world in 2016. As evidenced by the Brexit referendum result, the impeachment of Brazilian president Dilma Rousseff (2011–16), and the election of Donald Trump in the United States, this neoliberalism more closely reflects Claudia Sandberg's understanding of the concept, as a system that "hinge[s] on repressive social and political measures . . . protects the interest of higher classes and promotes an accumulation of wealth, while converting citizens into consumers" (2018, p.4). It remains to be seen whether the return to Kirchner-era Peronism signaled by the election of Alberto Fernández will mark a similar watershed moment for global liberalism.

Trapero's films, the first of which was released in Menem's final year as president and the most recent of which was released several years into the Macri presidency, have portrayed Argentina throughout a period of profound change. In making films with such a clear political slant to them, and which are so focused on their criticism of the quotidian violence that dominates contemporary Argentine society, Trapero can, perhaps, be understood as focusing solely on the challenges that face Argentina. This would not be entirely fair, however, for although Trapero's focus has always remained firmly on his home nation, the violence that envelopes his characters—the violence that he portrays as having enveloped Argentine society as a whole—is universal in its reach and influence. In fact, the themes found throughout Trapero's corpus—the insidious manner in which violence is brought about by neoliberalism; the lasting negative effects of economic crisis on a nation's social structure; the pernicious role the State and its various apparatuses play in propagating objective violence against its own citizenry—are themes that are becoming ever-more central across global cinema, even in the so-called developed world. Though very different in tone and style, recent films that focus on the concepts of unemployment, social marginalization, and class conflict such as *Hell or High Water* (2016), *I, Daniel Blake* (2016), *Sorry to Bother You* (2018), or *Parasite* (2019) demonstrate that the issues Trapero has been critiquing in his films for nearly two decades have not simply gone away; indeed, society has not even made any real attempt to address them. Rather, as reflected in the recurring, increasingly violent nature of Trapero's own cinema, these issues have only become more acute, leading to a kind of self-perpetuating cycle in which the objective violence of quotidian life leads to acts of subjective violence which, in turn, further reinforce the structures which generate objective violence.

Despite their significant differences, Trapero's films do share much with the political films that emerged immediately before and immediately after the collapse of the *Proceso* dictatorship. Those films were laden with political symbolism and (especially once democracy was restored) were frequently quite explicit in their targeting of the government for criticism. At the other end of the spectrum is New Argentine Cinema, the cinematic trend to which

Trapero was most often associated at the start of his career. New Argentine Cinema featured a more disengaged aesthetic, one which cast a critical eye over society without necessarily offering solutions or even, for that matter, assigning blame. Trapero's films bridge the metaphorical gap between these two film styles by borrowing heavily from the observational style of New Argentine Cinema while nevertheless incorporating the more explicit political implications associated with traditional Argentine political cinema. As stated in the Introduction, by engaging with a hauntology of the failure of the future, Trapero stands at, or perhaps has even created, a crossroads of Argentine political cinema. Throughout his career Trapero has not only engaged with the topics that have traditionally been associated with political filmmaking, he has also forged a new path for political cinema, one which ignores the traditional markers of repression and, instead, examines the role we play in our own subjugation.

Familia rodante is particularly important in this regard, for it is in that film that Trapero scathingly recreates, on a micro level, the debilitating cycle of objective-subjective violence. Despite its seemingly innocent narrative structure, *Familia rodante* is perhaps the most significant political statement of Trapero's early career. By representing the process of subjugation, of creating "always-already subjects," that occurs within the traditional family structure, Trapero establishes the foundations for understanding virtually all of his films' characters, from Rulo in *Mundo grúa* to Mia Montemayor in *La quietud*. Although *Familia rodante* features an almost complete lack of subjective violence, the various family members are exposed to a seemingly unending barrage of bickering, nagging, criticism, questioning, and judgment. All of this combines to provide perhaps the most tangible example of what objective violence is, how it functions, and what effects it is capable of generating.

Of course, the negative portrayal of the traditional family structure that dominates *Familia rodante* or *El clan* is counterbalanced by the ultimate importance placed on it in both *Nacido y criado*, *Leonera*, and even, to some extent, *La quietud*. Despite the fact that those narratives place an emphasis on alternative family structures, in all three films the protagonists ultimately find salvation (or something approaching it) by embracing the traditional family. This, then, speaks to an underlying motif that runs throughout Trapero's cinema. Trapero rarely provides clearly defined endings to his films, instead preferring to leave his characters in a moment of ambiguity; the same can be said of his corpus as a bloc. Just as the family is capable of being exceptionally damaging, functioning as the entryway to a subjugated life, so too is it capable of providing essential support to individuals who have experienced the worst forms of objective and subjective violence. This duality extends to Trapero's portrayal of society as a whole—characters such as Sosa, Luján, and Padre Julián, who have been beaten down by the violence that surrounds them, nevertheless rely on the very society that generates that violence to provide them with purpose in their lives and, in some cases, loving relationships, relationships which often function as escapes from violence. And yet, as we see in *Familia rodante* and *El clan*, the family is perhaps the ultimate State Apparatus, more efficient in generating subjects inured to violence than any manifestation of the Repressive State.

That hardening to violence takes on an added significance when considered in the light of hauntology, particularly in the midst of the ongoing (at time of writing) Covid-19 pandemic. Fisher offers two understandings of the concept—"the first refers to that which is (in actuality is) *no longer*, but which is still effective as a virtuality.... The second refers to that which (in actuality) has *not yet* happened, but which is *already* effective in the virtual" (2012, p.19, emphasis in original). This binary—haunted both by what is no longer and by what is yet to come—is clearly visible throughout Trapero's work, and is a key aspect of the objective-subjective-objective cycle of violence that is so central to his cinema. In many ways, Trapero's entire corpus has served as a kind of hauntology of 2020, speaking to a state of permanent violence and death that had not yet happened when his films were made but which has now enveloped the world. The haunting by that which is no longer—as experienced by the likes of Santi and the Montemayor women—has been replicated in the world generally, as society is haunted by those lost due to the worst pandemic in a century. Similarly, the sense of dread and apprehension for that which has not yet happened that permeates *Carancho* and *El clan* is manifested in the constant threat of infection posed by the airborne coronavirus, invisible yet always (potentially) present. It will be fascinating to see how Trapero, whose films have often been considered overly violent and pessimistic, incorporates this essentially permanent state of violence into his cinema in the future.

Trapero's films are overcome with a feeling of violence that permeates every aspect of their narratives, and it is this feeling, this intangible concept made manifest, that most clearly defines his cinema. The experience of watching one of Trapero's films has always been a difficult one, with the sense of tension and apprehension that each film generates so palpable that the viewer is unwittingly brought into the same space as the narrative's protagonists. Upon watching one of his films, the viewer feels as if violence has been done to him or her. And this, perhaps, is the ultimate measure of Trapero's effectiveness as a political filmmaker.

Interview with Pablo Trapero

Matanza Cine Office, Buenos Aires, April 23, 2015

Douglas Mulliken: How has your work changed over the course of your career? Because, *Mundo grúa* is one type of film and... let's say *Elefante blanco* is another.

Pablo Trapero: Well... I have no idea! (Laughs) Let's see... It has changed as I have changed. But it's not a programmed change, nor was it planned. And when I say I have no idea it's a little bit of a joke because I never go back and watch my films over. So I've never watched *Mundo grúa* and then *Elefante blanco* in quick succession. So how I remember the difference is how I remember feeling when I made *Mundo grúa* and how I felt when I made *Elefante blanco*, for example. But I haven't undertaken a formal exercise of watching my films and doing an evolution, or an analysis of that evolution, so it's more the view of others, this type of question, that makes me conscious of the change. What I think *has* changed is that years have gone by, my lifestyle changed, and my way of thinking surely has, as well. What didn't change between *Mundo grúa* and *El clan* is the way I work on my films, that's to say my commitment to the story, my commitment to the universe that film portrays. There isn't much difference between how I filmed *Mundo grúa* and how I filmed *El clan* or how, in the period of postproduction, let's say, I keep working with the same enthusiasm with which I worked on postproduction of *Mundo grúa*. So what has changed is that I am a different person, I have more experience in some things, in others the same or even less experience, I realize I [thought] knew more and I realize that I know less.

There are evident differences: one is my first film, the other is my most recent, one had a certain budget, the other quite a different one. Those are differences that are easy to see. But I am always mobilized by the same things, despite the years. I'm mobilized to discover a universe, to discover a character or a group of characters. One of the most important things in the moment of making a film is what is going to remain when it is finished. Because you never know if the film is going to come out well or badly, if it's going to be good, average, very good, you just don't know. Because the process of making a film is a living process, one that changes a lot depending on the mood of the people who made the film, depending on a ton of factors that are distinct from the quality of the script, the quality of the director, the quality of the actors, or the budget. A director cannot always manage all of the different variables that change.

I'll give you an example—a crisis in Argentina arrives at a moment that you cannot predict, and that affects the film, or a family emergency happens at a moment when you've been planning a film for three years and suddenly the star actor's father dies, to give an example. Those types of things are part of the creation of a film and they are things we can't predict. Well, I like to work with those things. So things like the budget or your experience don't matter, because those other things are going to create the film as well. Living in a country like Argentina, where things change so quickly, in some other lines of work that could be a problem—change, surprise, the need to figure things out on the fly—but for me it's normal, normal to think that this country will actually help me to resolve my film with less stress, maybe, than in places where people plan what they are going to film for five years and then nothing happens during those five years. Here, anything can happen in those five years, and a film is that mountain of risk that you can't control but that must be controlled, that must be contained. So, going back to what I said earlier, one you start a film you don't know how it's going to end. Doing an analysis of the objective elements, like the experience of the actor, the quality of the script, the experience of the director, the money that, normally, the more there is, the more tranquility there is for the producer, all of those cold elements and objectives can be budgeted for.

What cannot be budgeted for is the mood, the feelings, and the situations that exceed any type of planning. So one can think a ton of things, like when I told you before, when I think about what will remain from a film, it's almost always the worst-case scenario—that the film won't turn out well, that nobody will see it, that it won't be accepted at any festivals, that the reviews will be bad... Just the worst-case scenario. And what's the only thing that has to survive all of those levels? That the film has something that someone, twenty years from now, can find outside of the context, the current situation, the historical moment in which the film was released. And what is important for me? The characters that remain and the universe of those characters. After that, everything else depends entirely on chance. At the moment of releasing a film... I'll give you an example—we're going to release *El clan* this year in August, which is the month of the primary vote here for the president after many tumultuous, volatile years. And really, it's not the best time to release a film, knowing that everyone is going to be thinking about who they are going to vote for president. But it's part of the rules of the game. And in its own way it's the best time to release an Argentine film for a number of reasons—the weather, the winter holidays; for a whole host of reasons it's the best date to release a film in Argentina. But it's also the most chaotic month in the last five years: the presidency will change, one cycle will end, and, presumably, a new one will begin. So those stories, or rather that universe that runs parallel to the film, and cannot be controlled, always inserts itself into the film.

I can't know what is going to happen when *El clan* is released in August; it could be that nobody will see it, maybe the critics won't like it, maybe the theatres will all close because Argentina will enter into a major crisis in August ... *Who knows?* But what will remain is that in that film there will be a universe with its own rules, that speaks to a reality that goes beyond the fiction of the film, that asks questions of the viewer, presents characters that the viewer should interrogate, and when one watches the film, in August in Argentina or in 2025 *somewhere else*, that film needs to offer something that wasn't there before the viewer chose to dedicate two hours to the film. That's my goal in all my films, and that hasn't changed between *Mundo grúa* and *Elefante blanco* or *El clan*. What has changed is that I have more experience, I'm older, and those things make me think about cinema in a different way. Like how at fifteen years old I had a different taste in films than at twenty-five, today I have a different taste than at thirty, and I'm sure it will be different when I'm fifty. And my way of making films is conditioned by my tastes as a viewer before anything else, because I come to cinema as a spectator. Of course there is a style that I enjoy that is very similar to what it was twenty years ago, but there are also new things that years ago I didn't have the curiosity to watch, and I've also found I now like films that I didn't like twenty years ago, and that films that I really liked twenty years ago I will watch now and say, "Hmm... Did the film age poorly or did it just age poorly for me?" So that certainly changes, my experience and my taste in cinema change.

DM: It appears to me that what has not changed in your work is that violence is something fundamental, that your films are, in general, studies of violence, from *Mundo grúa* up to, I suppose, *El clan*. The protagonists of your films try to understand violence, process it, and some, like Sosa for example, try to dominate violence. And they usually fail. Is that fair to say? That violence forms a key part of your work? And why does violence have such an important role in your work?

PT: Look, it could be. OK, for me that comes from something that is primary to drama—drama is violence. Drama is force A *against* force B. If there isn't that clash of forces, there isn't drama. That's what classic drama is—it's an advancing force against a defending force, and the drama exists within that encounter. And that drama isn't a product of fiction, it's the product of observation of reality, of our reality. Good drama, classic drama, is the representation in fictional form of reality. And reality is pure violence, from the violence of trying to survive in nature to the violence of society, trying to find a place in a society that is, let's say, more modern than primitive, to say it crudely. In the individual, in the group, in the social, violence is like a silent war that is lived every day. Your social class matters, because you want to change class but cannot, you don't have anything and you want to have something, or you have very little and you want a lot, or you have a lot and you want even more. It's a permanent tension between what you are and what you want to be.

And that violence is manifested in many ways: in physical violence, in emotional violence, in moral violence, in ethical violence. Therefore the same question is always formed, which is: Does one let oneself? Let's take a person on the street... I'll give you an example, ok? An example which is applicable to different places. A person has to cross the street. If that person crosses the street, this is a stereotype but if that person crosses the street in Switzerland, or a Nordic country, probably he will step into the road and the vehicles will stop so that he can cross. There are distinct forces on the same action, the same situation. If that situation were to happen here, that person would have to look to make sure that he could cross the road without being hit. And if it were to happen in India, for example, probably, if it were a Swiss person that wants to cross, he's going to burst into tears because he's going to be unable to, the necessary elements to cross the road in India aren't there, it's impossible. So, confronting the same situation, three distinct events are created, each one more violent than the next, because the code is different. The code in your place is: you take a step and the world stops so you can cross. Here it's: you take a step but you double-check because you could get run over, regardless of whether the light is green or red. And in India, or somewhere like that, it's *run* and if you fall as you're trying to get to the other side . . . Good luck! The three circumstances generate different things from the same situation. Now, in the case of the guy who crosses in Switzerland, probably the person who is going to feel violence is the man who is late for work and has to stop so that the other person can cross. One man feels more violence than the other. On the other extreme, the person who feels violence is the man who has to cross the street amidst a sea of cars that aren't going to stop. Surely that man feels more violence than all of the people who are committing that violence. So, the fascinating thing about working with violence is that it's subjective; it's subjective depending on where you are. It's subjective for the actor, but not for the spectator. For us, if we see that scenario on the street, if we see that in a film, we can evaluate who between the two characters experiences the violence. But it would be very different if the camera were inside the car in India, inside the car in Switzerland, or inside the car in Buenos Aires. Every character inside that vehicle would have a different dramatic context.

Having said all that, for me violence, what it does, it's a catalyzer, it's something that accelerates a reaction. It's a narrative tool, it's an element of the narration that I like to use because I feel that, above all in our societies but also in nature, I think the need to survive, to overcome violence, is innate. If you get hit what do you do? Do you defend yourself, do you hit back harder, do you run away? An example: right now there's a volcano erupting in Chile. What does one do when facing that violence of nature? Run, hide. That type of link fascinates me, and above all in capitalist societies where the rules are so unfair, which just generates more violence. That is to say, violence just leads to more violence.

DM: But, what you've just said is very interesting because you said that the world is violence. Do you think that perhaps that's an Argentine mentality, a

Latin American one, a Third World one? Because the guy in Switzerland that crosses the street isn't going to say that the world is violence. He's going to say that the world is mountains and snow and chocolate!

PT: It could be that it's the view of a person who was born in a country that is the product of that violence. Don't forget that Latin America was the product of the killing of lots of people. Of one colonization, and another colonization, and another. Then again, there were Vikings in Scandinavia. They are different histories. Vikings weren't *soft* or *nice*. But the Spanish who came here weren't *nice*, either. So I think that societies are founded on that violence, because it's simple. Like, I saw this very clearly when my son went to kindergarten for the first time. I understand that it's very similar in many parts of the world, I'm not sure how it is everywhere, I would have to do some research, but I imagine it's something natural for human beings. When my son went to his first class two years ago, two-year-olds hardly talk; they speak very little. One says, "gato," another wants to say, "gato" but says, "pato," the other says, "meow" when he means "gato," the other says, "michimichi," and every kid has their own way of speaking. What really made an impression on me was that every single two-year-old knew how to say *"mine," "mío,"* that's mine, this is mine, every one could say "mine," regardless of what else they could say. That was really heavy for me! (Laughs)

DM: Yeah, that is really shocking!

PT: Really shocking! Because they are kids with different educations, even if they are from the same neighborhood, a similar social context. That's part of violence. When you think about, I don't know, primitive people. There's a small bird, who's going to eat it? The person who runs the fastest, the person who hits the hardest, whomever has that tool to survive. So I think that could have something to do with Latin America. Because in Latin America it's very difficult to survive. My production company is called Matanza (Slaughter) for that reason—first, because I grew up in a neighborhood called Matanza, but also because our history is constructed upon slaughters of different types, some more bloody some less so, some explicit some less so, some overt some hypocritical. But I think the corruption, for example, which is so graphic in Latin America, exists in the same way in Europe and now you're seeing that—what's happening in Spain—what happens is that different cultures have distinct ways of addressing the subject. But that's also something I learned very early with my films, when I was making *Mundo grúa*, I thought that it was just a local thing, that the film was talking about a very Argentine world and that it would generate only minimal interest abroad. And abroad the impact was bigger than here.

When I made *El bonaerense* it was the same: a film about a cop that . . . How much of that are people going to understand? And I'll never forget that when I premiered *El bonaerense* in France, people came up to me and said, "Thank you for helping us understand the reality of the police in France" and I would say to them, "What are you talking about? It's not like that here." And they would say, "No, it's not like that, but the root of the problem is the same, or it's very similar." They told me, for example, that it's not the corruption of someone who wants such and such a thing in order to get money to pay their bills at the end of the month, but rather it's the corruption of someone who joins the police so they can exercise their neofascism in uniform. But the problem is similar, the way they utilize force for private gain and not to serve the community. So it's something I learned very quickly, which is that even if in Switzerland they are going to see the situation of the guy crossing the street differently, they probably will see it differently, but the dilemma that is created by those two forces that encounter one another of the person who, if he doesn't brake, will kill the person trying to cross, it generates a different reading . . . no, I'm sorry, it's a different situation here compared to Switzerland or India, but the readings of those three distinct situations are going to create the same type of reflection.

And who is right? The one guy steps into the street and the other brakes, but if that guy is going to the hospital and his wife is dying then by letting the person cross, the violence against the first man is greater than the violence against a guy who can't cross the street in India because 200 cars a minute go by. And that man is as justified as the other man who can't cross the road and on the other side his wife is about to give birth. This is an illuminating but exhausting exercise for a writer or director, because the multiplicity of viewpoints and potential options is infinite. And it leads to exasperating situations, because when I write a story I have to think about that situation and all of the contexts of that situation, and also the context of who is watching the story, and how it could be viewed in Switzerland or India, and how it is viewed in Argentina. And that's something extra, that *is* different from the *Mundo grúa* period. When I made *Mundo grúa* I was completely unaware of what a film could provoke outside of my world. And the years and the films obligated me to reflect on something: that it's good to have a certain unawareness as a filmmaker, it's good to not understand some things. Because the excess of control and understanding can often transform into an excess of formalism, of formality, everything becomes too diligent, everything is too measured, overly ordered, the narrative can no longer surprise you.

And that is something I have to work on more than before: my own ingenuousness of the story I want to tell, my own unconsciousness, how to give myself space for a surprise, how to surprise myself with the story I'm going to tell, how to make sure that the actor can still be surprised ten weeks into filming, how to make sure that the viewer is surprised after reading a positive review, or a middling review, or who has seen so many Trapero films that they already expect what world they are going to see. That's also complicated. It's harder to make a film now than before, despite it being easier to acquire the resources needed to make a film. Because the viewership is diverse, because the average viewer is different and therefore in that sense it's harder and it's what I'm saying about starting over. It's not entirely different from how I felt when I made my first film and I had no idea of who was going to see it. Well, now I have an idea but that doesn't make it any easier. And, an example that's going to happen very soon: *El clan* is a film that's going to have a very different reception outside of Argentina than in the country. Because *El clan* has a structure that contains a ton of things that we know about here but that abroad they won't have that information, that background will be missing. That isn't to say that it will do better here or that it will do better abroad, it's just to say that there will be two very different readings. Because, with it being a true story that references very specific things, there are fewer elements that translate to the local reality in Switzerland or India or Italy or France. Because the translation is very localized, that is, Arquímedes Puccio is the result of a very particular Argentine story, a very violent, unique, extreme story, and without that information, which can be conscious or unconscious, it could be that for somebody from Buenos Aires or from a Latin American culture who knows what it was like to live in one of those countries during the 1970s, there's a lot of information that doesn't need to be given. But for other places that information isn't in the film, the film doesn't explain that, but it works on a collective unconscious. So that is a challenge of new films, as well—what films to make?

For me, between *Mundo grúa* and *El clan* another thing that changes is there is a bigger public. What am I going to continue doing? Films for the people of *Mundo grúa* or the people of *El clan*? Or do I have to go out and find a different type of public, or find a different style of film? That is certainly something I ask myself as a filmmaker. I don't go back and watch films and say which is better and which is worse, so then what is the next step? My view as a filmmaker is always toward the future and, well, what am I going to do? Am I going to film another true story? Am I going to adapt a novel? Am I going to start from scratch again and describe every detail of a character who never existed? Am I going to direct in Spanish, in English, in Italian, in French? Those are the things I evaluate—towards the future. Looking backwards it's more about what I intuit or what gets back to me from someone like yourself or from a viewer.

And so to finish with the violence idea—I understand that in all those films violence is latent because I understand that violence is latent out in the streets. When someone is born, the birth is painful for the child. Air entering into the body of a baby is painful. For a mother the happiest moment, at least if we are using stereotypes, the happiest moment is giving birth and it's the most painful. So the things I get asked about—the sweat, the blood, the grime—they are very present in my films because I believe it's part of nature, of life, let alone the grim of the city. Because when an animal is born in nature, its skin is covered by the earth on the ground. When someone is born in the city . . . That violence, naturally, is the result of a concept that is curiously vital, no? Growth is painful; when a child grows his bones hurt. Of course, growth is good, it's not a bad thing, so my films ask the question: to what point is violence tolerable, to what point can an individual stand that violence and apply that violence, because violence is on a scale in which you both receive it and apply it. So what my films set out, and this is a little . . . a formal decision to question a certain hypocritical perspective of the viewer . . . . The viewer always feels a little bit distant from those dark worlds, other things are always happening to him or her.

I'll go back to the example of my films. In the European view Latin America is seen as corrupt because the corruption (in Europe) is at another level; it's manipulated at different levels. It is a society that has advanced more and in which corruption is used in a quieter way, until it explodes and appears in the cases we all know. Now for a European citizen it's easier to see the violence and corruption on the streets of Colombia, but it's simply a different way of representing the same thing. It's a kind of permanent fight for survival, above all, without talking about the nature of a society that has unjust rules that generate violence and where a lot of people are responsible for ensuring that those rules don't change. The people who are charged with keeping us safe—that is our governments or the people who really have power—appear to be doing very little to make that injustice disappear. Rather, they appear to be profiting or benefitting from that injustice. Of course, there are lots of exceptions, and there are also cases of exceptional people who dedicated their lives to combating injustice and making the world a little more fair. And you see that in my films. But in synthesis, as none of my films deal with nature, they deal more with society; those films narrate or have that violence inherent in them because unjust societies generate that violence, no? And probably in Latin America that type of contrast is seen more clearly, that need to survive is seen more graphically than in other places, where other paradoxes exist. I remember when I was just starting to make films and people said to me, coming from Latin America, "How jealous I am of you"; they said, "Because you, in that country and that context, you have the chance to move up, you can make films at twenty-five." And I would look at them like the world was upside down, because here we were saying, "No, but you guys have unemployment benefits, and the state pays for your studies, and you don't have to go out and work until 10 PM to be able to study." And of course, sometimes all those things create the opposite of what you think it would provoke: it leads to a life that is *flat*, with less risk, less possibility to explore, because you know that in that scheme you aren't going to direct your first film until you are forty-five, because there are a lot of steps and levels that you have to go through in order to make your first film.

So, I go back to the same example of the street—what might be for a Latin American the dream of the welfare state, for someone who enjoys the benefits of that welfare state he or she might feel the weight of what that signifies and might look with romanticism at someone who makes-do, and has to pay for their studies and has to hustle to make contacts or find a job or whatever it is. And that's the amazing thing about cinema: converting quotidian stories into fiction. When I see a French or Korean film, I don't need to know the idiosyncrasies of

Korea, in fact I know very little about Korea, maybe I know a little about Spain because my grandparents were Spanish, but I don't know anything about Korea, and when I watch those films I have to watch them and understand them as Pablo. Obviously if I live in Korea I would watch more, I would understand more, but the marvelous thing about cinema is that it can excite us, like you said, twenty-five, thirty, forty years later, it doesn't matter when you see a film. And that concept of violence I think is universal, maybe that's why my films travel so well, because it seems like they go beyond the borders of Latin America.

DM: Speaking of that, and keeping in mind some of the scenes from your films, it reminds me of Grupo Cine de la Base and Grupo Cine Liberación, all of that from the 1960s and 1970s. For example, *Carancho*'s first scene reminds me so much of the opening scene of Gleyzer's *Traidores*. And obviously, well I would say obviously but maybe not, it appears that you have been influenced quite a bit by some Argentine filmmakers. Are you influenced by any Argentine filmmakers from the present or the past or whenever?

PT: Sure. An example to follow with your suggestion would be Solanas, also Aristarain, whose cinema is more academic, but which reflects on things very . . . It's a very classic cinema, very different from Solanas, let's say, but which is constructed on very solid pillars. Birri is another example, on the other extreme, the opposite of Aristarain you might say.

DM: Well, not necessarily . . .

PT: Well it's a cinema that appears to be more improvised, more open, freer, less clear.

DM: In fact, if I can interrupt you, that has to do with my next question, which is about political cinema. Birri was, in his day, a political filmmaker. Aristarain began, especially in the 1980s, making political cinema; obviously Getino and Solanas made political cinema. It's often said that this, let's call it, Nuevo Cine Argentino doesn't deal with politics, but your cinema is very political.

PT: Cinema is political by definition. The omission of an idea is a political manifesto. I'll give you an example to go with this idea—directors who influenced me in different moments and for different reasons. Chaplin is the same—his is a cinema that appears to be one thing but has much more to it than on initial viewing. Fellini could follow in that line, Herzog, Scorsese, all comparable directors but who all have a vision and a commitment to the stories they tell, which makes their films popular. If you watch, to bring up Scorsese, *Raging Bull* and then you watch *The Aviator*, I see the same director. Scorsese fanatics would say no, the real Scorsese is the guy who made *Mean Streets*, but I watch *The Aviator* and I see the same guy reflecting on things, the same guy but forty years later. But I see a line that connects all the points. I watch a Herzog film, the remake of *Bad Lieutenant* with Nic Cage . . . I wanted to give an example of how all those directors have a political viewpoint because I believe that cinema, naturally, is born as a political act. I'll give you an example that's a little basic and stereotypical, about the supposed first projection of the Lumiere brothers, when the train comes and all the people in the theatre ran out, it's not just the effect of entertainment, it's not the effect of introspection that happens to the viewer of the work. It's an effect that affects your daily life. Those people who ran out in a panic away from the train saw their lives differently out in the street than they had before they entered the theatre. Like Godard said, the camera is a weapon, to put a point on it.

So I think that hoping for an apathetic cinema, a cinema that tries to distance itself from a political ideal creates the idea of a world, a political idea of a world. So I think that cinema is political, but I don't believe in militant cinema, which is something different. Militant cinema has a problem, which is in its militancy. Because cinema, for me, is not propaganda; Soviet propaganda cinema lost all of its cinematographic value. A couple of auteurs survived due to their cinematographic value, not for the value of how they applied propaganda to cinema. American propaganda cinema loses value from one year to the next; the famous official mainstream Hollywood cinema that is so popular is a bunch of films that history forgets almost immediately. And it's the same with the militant cinema of the 1970s. A lot of militant cinema was only seen by militants in shadowy rooms. That cinema is valuable for reasons that are not necessarily the same as what I find valuable in cinema, which isn't about cinematographic value. It's a propagandistic value, a pedagogical value, a marketing value; in other words it is valuable for reasons that are distinct than what I consider cinema to be, which is cinema for its own ends.

But I also think that politics are one of cinema's ends, that is, for me politics are intrinsic to cinema. But I don't believe in militant cinema. I believe that militant cinema only speaks to a group of people who already know what they are going to hear, or only hear what they want to hear from what they are watching, without any critical value, and probably with less aesthetic value since the ideas are more important than the aesthetics. So it's very contradictory, because I like political cinema, but the politics that I can do are through the aesthetics of a politics, a politics of the poetics of a film, if you like.

DM: That does strike me as contradictory . . .

PT: No, it could appear contradictory, but for me, my politics is my poetics, let's say. It's a somewhat artificial saying, because it could sound pretentious, but it seems that the cinema that I like, the cinema that excites me, is the cinema that excites me for its cinematographic value. And that makes me reconsider the crisis in New York in the 1930s or, I don't know, the invasion in Iraq, whatever it might be that I am watching. But first it's the cinematographic value, first it's the aesthetic definition, the commitment by the person making that film with that story. Then there's a lot of pseudo-political cinema. They take an important theme that is opportunistic, they determine what they think the public needs to see regarding a specific subject, and they take advantage of that to construct their film. That is terrible, it's terrible and it can be felt in the films, opportunistic films, directors who are not committed to what they are telling, but rather see themselves projected into that universe.

DM: What you've just said, about how you value the cinematographic most of all interests me because you are a writer and I would suppose that as a writer the narrative matters to you. But you are saying that maybe the technical aspects of a film matter more to you than the narrative.

PT: The script is an instrument to manifest the ideas of the film. The ideas always come before the story. The story is a consequence of the thesis statement of a film, such as, to give an example, a film is going to be about motherhood. Before the jail, before Julia's mother, much before any of that. Then comes the script, and the girl is the representation of that idea. But what really represents those ideas are the words on the paper, the images on the screen. So for me writing is a very difficult process. Because half of what I write is simply a reference for what I'm going to film later. I'll give you an example, to continue with the question about *Carancho*. In *Carancho* there is a block that is the heart of the film, which is the three long tracking shots that go from when they break the man's leg until when he dies, which changes the whole feel of the story. Those are three shots that, when someone sees them, says, "Oh that's just one shot" because they don't see the moment when it cuts. How do you write that? It's a tracking shot, which is to say that it's very difficult to write because then it would be what we call a "technical script"—the camera enters into the ambulance while Sosa blah blah blah, the camera zooms in on Luján, this thing or another, then it turns and pans.... If someone were to write a script like that, it would be the least exciting script in the world, there's no way to be excited about that script. Therefore, the script is an intermediate step between the idea and the film. The script is a spiritual guide, like a manual. Going with the idea of the manual—when someone has a TV manual, the manual says, "Press this button for more contrast or more brightness," but it doesn't say, "If you want it really bright, press ninety-five, if you want a lot of contrast press whatever." It says, "This is what you have to do. If you want to change the picture of the film go to the menu and then image, and then press bright and blah blah blah." Then it's up to me if I make it more or less bright. That's an extreme example of the script, but a very graphic one. The script says, "Sosa breaks the man's leg, blah blah blah, he goes to the car and waits." That can be in five shots or in one tracking shot. The writing is completed by the technical.

As a director, I am obsessed with that. If I could, I would film more than what I do. Because from one year to the next there is a new camera with a new gel and a new CCD or a new lens with an apparatus that moves differently or who knows what.... I have a thing that for some might be an advantage and for others might be a disadvantage, even I view as a positive or negative, depending on the day. I like to write, I like to direct, I like to edit—I've got an editing room here in my office, I edit images, I edit the dubbing because I want to hear the dialog that the actor has dubbed, I use ProTools to edit the dialogs that I want the sound mixer to use. I like to have my hands in everything. That's got a good part to it—I save time, although it might seem absurd, working twenty hours a day, but I save the time of having to explain to someone else what it is that I want them to do. But the bad thing is that my style is in everything. So if my style is good, if I'm lucid, then it will be good for the film. If I'm a little off, the film is going to be worse. So for me the writing of the film ends with the last day of coloring in the lab, the last day of sound-editing in the lab, when the film's at "the end," it's closed, it's saved, it's gone from negative to disc, ready, that's when the film is finished. The script is fundamental, it's very important, it's a process that takes a lot of work for me because, in my mind, I feel like I write too little for what I imagine I will want to film, but at the same time if I write everything exactly as I want to film it, the script becomes unreadable. So there are rules of writing that have to do with how a story is presented but that doesn't necessarily reflect in detail how it's going to be filmed. But I think the script is . . . . I think it's very difficult to make a good film with a bad script.

Now, with a good script you can make good films or even excellent ones, but it's very difficult to do it the other way. I think a very good film necessarily has a good script as a base. When I say script I don't just refer to the story but also the characters, the universe, the script is all those things, it's not just when people who know about cinema say, "What a good script because . . . I don't know, it's got a lot of plot twists, because the character had lots of adventures. . . ." A good script is one that allows for, not just the *twists* of the script but the universe it presents, the world that the story presents. All of that is very important, but it's a transition phase. The script by itself doesn't have value. If you read scripts, they don't have literary value. They're boring to read, they are . . . they don't have any metaphor, because you can't put in a script "the actor is sad." What does sad mean, how is sadness seen? How must one explain how to behave in order for someone else to understand that this signifies that someone is sad? So, it's a phase that I enjoy quite a bit, but also as time has passed I began to enjoy reading other people's scripts, which before made me feel something like "if I didn't write it then I couldn't make the film." I still have not made a film from someone else's script, but I read them at least. Before they would send me scripts to read, and I wouldn't read them.

I feel that for a good film to be born the script is fundamental, but also that the writing of a film, the true writing of a film, is in the direction. A film can be very bad with a good script, but the reverse is more difficult. A good script can be destroyed by making it poorly, and there are lots of examples where you watch and say, "It's well-acted, the story is incredible, it's a story about some thing in some period, etc." and you watch it and it didn't excite, nothing happened, because the direction, which is the real writing in cinema, didn't work. Some screenwriter somewhere would hate me if he heard me say this, but the thing is real scriptwriters know this beforehand. Scriptwriters, not writers, know that the script is a tool that can then be converted into a film. So the really good scriptwriters share this mentality. . . . Well, not all of them!

DM: And they all have a really dark sense of humor. . . . Like you said, scriptwriters know their place in the world, let's say, the world of cinema business.

PT: Of course, because a lot of it depends on the films themselves. There are formula films; I don't mean that as disrespect, I just mean that style of filmmaking, where there's a script, a producer takes the project, then they look for a director, then they find the financing and lots of times the films they make are brilliant, but in proportion to the number of films made that way the number of great films is pretty small. In general, the interesting films are the films that maintain that spirit of a type of self-creation (autogestión). I don't mean to say self-creation, like the director wrote the first draft and if he didn't write it then he isn't the real director. Rather it's a mode of production, and that's where I go back to what we talked about earlier: what Scorsese keeps doing at his age or, for example, the most recent films to come out of Hollywood, the directors who enter into Hollywood and are making films in English but are from . . . (inaudible) . . . This year, the most similar case to this would be *Gravity* or films like that, where you can recognize the director there. It's not the other way, it's not some guy thought up a film, found Alfonso, then called up the star. . . . It took years to make that film, the appearance would be that: the first film to do it!

DM: I want to talk to you about the process of creating your own production company, the process of finding money, generally, in order to make your films. Because you are talking about the script and how the script itself is very boring and, obviously—I suppose, I don't know, everybody has a different system—but I imagine that, at some point, when you are speaking with someone who has money, you have to show them the script. So the entire process of, when you were making *Mundo grúa* and you had to speak with the Hubert Bals Fund, or now that you are doing *El clan* and you're going to speak with, I don't know, Fernando Suar or someone from Canal+ or something. The whole process of finding money seems very important to me, and I have some questions, but the most important would be: Would it have been possible to do what you wanted to without establishing Matanza Cine?

PT: (Laughs) No, simple as that.

DM: And what was the process of its creation?

PT: Let's see ... The quantity of films would not have been possible. It probably would have been a different amount. The fact that I produced those films allowed me to take risks that others didn't want to take. Looking at how they turned out, it's easy to imagine that there were people who wanted to produce my films. But at the time that wasn't the case. *Mundo grúa*, like you said, nobody wanted to produce that, I had to finance it using funds from all over. And I'll give you an even more extreme example—my first script was *Familia rodante*. When I took my first script, *Familia rodante*, to people, including for example a contest by the INCAA for *opera prima*, I didn't win the contest. Producers looked at me saying, "Trapero, this film is enormous, it's really expensive, it can't be your first film, nobody is going to finance it." So in the wake of this rejection of my first film, which was going to be *Familia rodante*, I thought about what I should do. I didn't win the INCAA contest, producers didn't want to finance me, what do I have to make a film? First, I've got lots of desire, and that in itself is a type of capital. It seems foolish to say so, but it's important because in lots of cases filmmakers have more desire to be a director than to actually make a film and there is such a big difference between the two that it's important to acknowledge it. And I see it now, even in some famous directors—they like being directors more than they like making films.

Getting back to *Mundo grúa* in order to get to Matanza—*Mundo grúa* was a film that I could do so naturally I became my own producer. I began to send letters, I spoke with this person and that person, trying to convince people. I asked them, "Will you accompany me on this? It will be like this, it will film in that place, I'm finding actors." So I was my own producer. Once filming was finished, after I secured the help from the Hubert Bals, and the Fine Arts fund, from various places, I had my completed film. Filmed, edited offline, and in that moment I felt that I couldn't do any more than I already had. But it was that I couldn't do any more, it was that I didn't know what to do next,

I didn't know how to release a film, how to finish it on 35 millimeters, it still requires a lot of money to finish a film. And then I met Lita Stantic and she accompanied me and we finished the film together. But even at that point, when I was twenty-six years old, when I spoke with Lita I said, "But I'm the producer. We are partners, but I made this film."

DM: You said that?

PT: Yes, and Lita was very . . . You can see it in the credits, it's very clear. Now, luckily, I was dealing with Lita, perhaps if I had been dealing with someone else they would have said, "*I don't care.*" But I've defended that from my very first film, that I manage the film, if I acquire the money, if I do all that, for me the money in the best case is as valuable as all the rest. It isn't worth more. In the best scenario of the partnership, the guy who brings the money isn't any more of a producer than the person who made the entire film. In every case they are equals because, well, without the money you can't make the film, but your money without my work or my story won't make a film either. So it's a bit classic in that sense, classic in the sense where the director was considered the author of the film despite the fact that, in the credits, the producers were, let's say, omnipresent.

DM: Like in the 1970s with the New Hollywood . . .

PT: Exactly. To me, producing is a way of writing. Why? Because, for example, if I had made *Mundo grúa* with a different production system probably the producer would have told me, "No, wait, to get our money back we need to have [Ricardo] Darín in this." Then it wouldn't have been *Mundo grúa* as we know it. It would have been something else. And myself, as the producer, I was faced with needing to cast Ricardo, but in a different film, in a different context, in another moment, another story. So producing is what ends up giving you the tools to write. Because there are lots of films, for example, where you can tell that decisions were made not because of the script but because of the production, the co-production of this or that. So those things affect the film, and I have at times suffered as a viewer and as a filmmaker. Let's say I have to go to France for two months to work, and I'm not sure if that puts me in the best mood at that moment. Because of co-production I have to go there for sound-editing, and despite the fact that the editor might be objectively really good and the lab is great, maybe in the moment of my life it was torture to be away from my 45-day-old child. Is that good for the film or bad for it? So production really does write the film.

Now, it's a very tiring job doing all of this, especially the production, so I learned as I went along over the years. Before, I used to do everything from Matanza—finance, production, production design, executive production, resource administration plan, contracting—back when Martina and I started Matanza in 2000-whatever. But I learned over the years. I still want to maintain the part that I like about producing, and the part that I feel is important for the film, but I changed: I don't hire the crew anymore, I have no clue about organizing the, who knows, technical stuff, I don't know those values in detail these days, despite still being involved in production. I'm involved in more general decisions now, like "OK, let's go with this partner because this partner will help us with the financing part or the artistic part or because they're going to offer an amount that we can't cover," or different things like that. But I'm not like how I was before, ten or fifteen years ago, when I was "OK, how much does the catering cost for the film, and how many days . . ." It was hell!

DM: That leads to my next question, which is: a lot of people have written about this idea that if you, as a director/filmmaker from Latin America, Argentina, wherever, let's say Latin America, if you receive money from Spain or France or a festival, the Hubert Bals or whatever, then there is a pressure from that to make a film that those people like. Do you think the country of origin of the money influences your working process, or the working process of Latin American filmmakers in general? And you have to produce something, like I was explaining to someone yesterday who said, "Every Argentine film has dirt roads in it, and this and that and . . ." and I responded, "That has to do with the fact that, whomever, the French, the Spanish, the Americans, the British, they want to see dirt roads, violent men, whatever it might be." No? So, do you feel that pressure to produce a work that corresponds to European expectations, or imagined European expectations?

PT: It's a good question and I'll tell you what happened going back to *Familia rodante*. After making *El bonaerense*, my next film was going to be *Elefante blanco*, which was called *Villa* at that point. And I had the sense, I had done

Mundo grúa about the world of labor, *El bonaerense* about the world of police, and I had the sense that if I made *Villa* at that moment, this movie about priests, it wasn't going to be good. Because I didn't want my work to always be related to the social world, or with a predetermined question. And it was a difficult decision, in fact, because I lost a lot of producers. When I decided I wasn't going to make *Villa*, that I was going to make *Familia rodante* instead, they told me, "You're crazy, you've got a brilliant film—the slums, the grime, Third-World priests. Strike while the iron is hot!" And I felt that no, the iron wasn't hot. I thought it was the moment to show that I wanted to do other things, as well. Certainly *Familia rodante*, in many aspects, generated less interest than what was expected after *El bonaerense*. Don't even mention *Nacido y criado*! "An introspective film? No, we don't want to see an introspective film from Trapero about a middle class guy with problems. We want to see something else."

There is pressure, but it is a pressure that any director must know is going to exist. That is, it's better to have that pressure than not have it, it's better to feel like there is somebody demanding something from you rather to feel like nobody wants to produce your films. The question is how you, as a director, are able to manage yourself with it. And the proof is there to be seen. Films that grab poor people and put them in the dirt and whatever else tend to fail, because if you don't have anything else to say then you won't go anywhere. In other words, that can't be the motive. Going back to what we were talking about before: if someone asks you to do that, and you are someone who wants to direct a film, you want to be a director so you say sure, it makes no difference to me, if I have to have dirt roads I'll have dirt roads, if I have to have poor people I'll have poor people. The film ends up a disaster, it doesn't say anything, it just ends up being a lot of . . . A mosaic could be made about Latin American films that take advantage of those funds, and producers who live off those funds, because it's a completely perverse scheme. There are lots of producers who only produce that type of film because they live in the world of the *lobby* for that type of cinema.

So it's very important to be able to say no, or accept that rule and still make a good film. It's the same rule as when an American producer approaches you and says, "Look, I have all this money to make a film, but you have to do it with this amount. Do you want to do it?" And you evaluate the proposal, and if you believe that with that you could make a good film, it's a valid way to do it. It's not bad to make a film that someone expects if the film is good. It's as valid as any other scheme, such as when a French person says to a French director, "I want to make a film about the history of France. I have money from the ministry, I have blah blah blah . . . Do you want to make it?" And the director looks at the film and says, "Maybe so . . ."

DM: Have you had to change your films because of . . .

PT: (interrupting) No. No.

DM: Well, for example, in *Elefante blanco* you have a Belgian actor, Jeremie Renier, who, the first time I saw the film I was thinking, "Why does this film have a Belgian?" Not only that, a Belgian who looks a lot like Guillermo Pfenning. Why does that film have a Belgian and not Guillermo Pfenning, for example? You have the habit of always using the same actors, so I thought maybe it had to do with the fact that . . .

PT: That France was involved.

DM: That France was involved, or that some producer said, "Look, you need to put this guy in your film . . ."

PT: No, it was, in that case, in the specific case of *Elefante blanco*, no. Because in that case the character was called "the gringo priest." We wanted someone kind of blonde, kind of foreign, who had no idea about the reality of Argentina or Latin America. And in the specific case of *Elefante blanco* a lot of it has to do with the world of Third-World priests, these guys who travel the world. When I made that film I had the idea in my head that I wanted a Polish or German priest; I didn't want someone Spanish, we even had production from Spain and they were absolutely insistent that we get a Spanish actor because it would have served the Spanish co-production. Jeremie is Belgian, not French. Fine, he's European but the important co-production for *Elefante blanco*, the important money, came from Spain not France. The producer was Morena. And when I went to Morena and said, "Look, I want," from the possible actors there was Jeremie and the others that we looked at, they said to me, "He can't even speak Spanish, Pablo." But it didn't matter! That's exactly the point, a gringo priest. In other cases it can happen, but specifically with

Elefante blanco it wasn't the case, because it corresponded to the script. In fact, we looked at Germans, we looked at other French actors. The hardest thing there was telling the Spanish producer no to all of the Spanish actors they proposed.

I'll give you an example that corresponds to that . . . I have responded to a co-production scheme that the script didn't really call for, but I could have responded in a different way, with *Leonera* for example, [Rodrigo] Santoro's character is a character who comes from Brazil. That character could have come from Brazil, China, or Mataderos, because in the story the important thing is that he was a guy who was living on Julia's house temporarily; he was her lover. So he didn't necessarily have to be Brazilian; he could have been from San Luis, or Ushuaia, or Italian or something. But because of the co-production it was helpful to do it with Santoro. It doesn't necessarily make it better, but it did have to do with a production scheme. In Jeremie's case, it was much better to have Jeremie rather than a Spanish actor with his Spanish accent in the slum. Because that could have hurt the film much more. I wanted someone with a gringo accent, since in the script he's called the gringo priest; in fact in the movie they call him the gringo priest. So . . . but there are ways, even so, that the production has an effect, because afterwards the producer has an opinion about things so you, as the filmmaker, have to condition yourself for that opinion. For example, I'll give you an example that I lived through with the editing of *Carancho*: I had producers from France, Korea, and Spain, I think. The notes I was getting from France, Korea, and Spain could not be more different. So naturally I, as the filmmaker, have to listen to the three and give an answer to each one. "Yes, I'm going to try that; no, that seems like a bad idea; no, that seems like a bad idea but I'll show it to you anyway." In other words, the director, part of his job is to dialog with the producer. That happens to Malick, you understand, who apparently gets money from all over to make whatever he wants; you watch his films and they change depending on who has given him the money, based on who knows what. It happened to Fellini, and nobody said, "Why Anita Ekberg?" Because he had to put a gringa, and there was somebody there, and afterward nobody said, "Oh, that's bad." But what happens is lots of times, it does end up badly. Lots of times it doesn't work.

DM: But that also has to do with the fact that if a European does it, it's a relationship of equals whereas, with the way the world is today, if a European or American is telling, ordering, a Latin American, "You have to do that," then it's clientelism.

PT: Yes, but I think the most important responsibility falls on the director. Because the producer is always going to ask for things. That's how it is. What's Warner [Bros.] going to tell you? "Make a film with lots of stuff, lots of music, whatever else so that it sells tickets." That's fine, and there are lots of films that Warner produces with good directors and then some films that aren't so great. It *is* tough, and it's something I have had to go through and which I think I came out of well; I still have my producers and I've set my boundaries. My films have set a lot of boundaries in this regard, and I think they function as a reference point for people who might think that if they don't do that they can't make a film. No, that's a lie. The director is like . . . One time a journalist told me, "Your characters are like the things that a director has to go through, no? Fighting all the time against different pressures." I think it was *El bonaerense*. And sure, but who is making you direct? Directing is withstanding all types of pressures. There's not enough money, there's not enough time, there's a producer who is asking you to do such and such a thing and you don't know if you can do it or not. The director is obligated to struggle with these things. So clientelism exists because there are people who allow it to exist.

If you have . . . I had producers who asked me things and I told them, "No, look, I can't." That's why I gave you the example of *Familia rodante*. Because in that moment I lost half my producers. When I chose to make a Latin Americanist film, with dirt roads, but red dirt and picturesque countryside and it wasn't the same thing, it wasn't what was wanted. Both *Familia rodante* and *Nacido y criado* were films that cost me a lot of work to make. Because I had to make them with fewer producers, with less money, and also with less curiosity from the festivals. But then *Born and Bred* had an incredible reception in England, which couldn't be said for France, for example. Now, I can't make films always thinking about the same people. What I mean is, I said it at the start, I can't with that; I wanted to make *Nacido y criado* and luckily there were a lot of people who loved it when it came out, particularly in England, where they praised it more than *El bonaerense* was praised when it came out in France, for example. Or, it had the same type of praise, the same euphoria that I had felt when *El bonaerense* premiered in France was what I felt when *Nacido y criado* came out in England. Even more so, because the reviews there were incredible, and I remember when *Nacido y criado* premiered there what I felt was really strong, really beautiful, because it confirmed what I was saying to you—"I can't keep working with producers who ask me to do this." Because I believe that *Nacido y criado* has a lot to say, despite what the French public might think. I mean, what do I know? [The film] just didn't speak to the French that time.

So, I lived that, and those are two concrete examples of my films. And later, when I made *Leonera*, my most important producer was Korean, not even European!

DM: And how did that go?

PT: It was part of that same process, of saying, "OK, what do I admire in cinema today?" I love Korean cinema. It's irreverent, new, violent; it doesn't have any prejudice; it is capable of solidly mixing commercial elements with auteur elements. So that's how I met the producer Suh Young Joo, and actually we made a very strange film, the first was *Leonera* which is a melodrama, but also partly action, and it appears to be a prison genre film but isn't. So producers *do* matter. Because that dialog exists with someone who thinks that way. Mine was *Carancho*; *Carancho* is a very strange film—for auteurist cinema it's very commercial, for commercial cinema it's very strange, and it was a great experience because it did really well at the festivals, commercially it did really well. Curiously, it was a film that seemed to be too *arty* to be commercial but which did really well in England; in the United States, it did incredibly. There's talk of a *remake*, so my career, that is, my international career became much more solid because of a film that is very *arty*, very strange.... So yes, producers do matter. I learn from producers when I do my work, and the work of producing is very noble... When the producer is good! Then there are those producers who, what they do is *fundraising*. That's the word, right? Go out and find money, all of it *soft money*, where nobody runs any risk, and everything goes from subsidies to reimbursement subsidies, and that's not producing. That's managing funds. Producers are those people who have a conception of cinema and from that same logic are going to exert a pressure on the director.

But it seems important to me that the director can speak as an equal. If not, the responsibility is shared. I mean, if there are people who ask that you put dirt roads in your film, and half-naked guys, and you do it... You're kind of like Zapa. You're kind of... The guy who lets himself be corrupted for personal benefit.

DM: Yeah... Mendoza is the corrupt one.

PT: Right, and for corruption to exist there has to be someone who allows themselves to be corrupted. So if clientelist films or cinema does exist, it's because there is someone on the other side who allows it to happen. Of course, we can all make mistakes. What happens is you make a decision, you put something in because you didn't know what else to do, it's your first film, that desperation of a director who wants to make his first film, and I don't want to sound omnipotent but... I could have made an easier film than *Mundo grúa* when I made my first film. Nobody forced me to make *Mundo grúa*, and it would have been easier to make a different film. So those decisions that you make, over the course of the years, have value.

You can also be hired to work on a film that's already commissioned, because that's how you make a living, and slowly, like Aristarain did with the films that he had to make during the dictatorship—it's clear that, OK, this is a job, this is my job and this is the film I want to make. But the problem is when you are mixed, when it's "OK, I want to make a film and therefore I do this whole *mélange* of things that I don't identify with, that don't represent me, but it's an opportunity to make a film." You can do that once, twice. I wouldn't do it ever, I've never done it. But suppose that your necessity forces you to do it. You do it one time. Fine, there it is, you can't do it again. When you see a director who has followed that line, it's because that director wants to play in that league and those are the rules. I think it's the responsibility of the producers, but the responsibility falls as much on the producers as it does on the directors who do that. As a Latin American director, my life would be much easier than it is now if I made a different type of film. Big ones, with big budgets, they probably would have won more prizes at the festivals. *Carancho* isn't a typical Latin American film, neither is *Leonera*. Yes, OK, the jail part could be because the jail, the overcrowding, but that's not the valuable part of that film, nor is it the center of it.

Now, I live in a country where I cannot forget the street I live in. It could be *Carancho*... *Carancho* can be seen in the blackness of the street and, well, that's how it is. So it's a very delicate balance.... In fact soon you will be seeing all the publicity that will come out for *El clan*. Because it seems to me that *El clan* is not a film that much is hoped for outside of the country. It's a film that's going to work better in some places than in others. Because it's a period piece, very formal, very theoretical. So yeah, it's an interesting question, and we'll have to see what happens a year from now when we are in the middle of everything with *El clan*. But it is interesting. It's very difficult as a director, because you have to say no to things that you want. I want to film more than I do, I would like to try a ton of things that I have to say no to. Doors get closed, no? I'll give you an example in reverse: for several years I've had an American agent who brings me things in English. The number of times I've said no to projects that people have wanted me to do in English, it's astonishing! In fact, I had to change agents, because he said to me, "Look, how many years has it been that you've been saying no?" To say no to that . . . If you're going to make a film in English, really, you'd probably have much more money, but it's a lot of stuff that I would have to do that I wouldn't feel I could do well. Basically it's that, if I feel like I could do it well, I'll do it. Afterwards I might be wrong, but when I feel like a number of factors would lead to me doing it poorly, I would prefer not to do it. But that's not the romantic discourse of a romantic artist, because a film director cannot have that discourse. Because you're working with money, with producers who pressure, with theatres that have to be full so that you can keep making films. It's not that I'm giving you the artiste: "I don't want to make films that corrupt me, blah blah blah." Because cinema is made with compromises, and directors need to know how to deal with that pressure.

But if I definitely know that I'm going to make a bad film, it would probably be more difficult to make the next one, and that's even more damaging than making a bad film. I want to film, it's the thing I most enjoy doing, so what sense is there in making a film where I believe I'm going to fail, where before I even begin I know it's not good? It could be in English, it could make a lot of money, I could end up in places I never thought I would . . . I said no to that, as well. So it's a very interesting question because, in general, it's not talked about much. The director seems like an artist who is free to create his ideas and his vision of the world and not struggle with those problems, but it's a lie!

DM: Money influences everything in this world . . .

PT: Yes, and take a director who is a master and a permanent influence—Buñuel. When Buñuel goes to Mexico, did he want to make those films in Mexico? Of course not! He would have preferred to stay in Spain. Now, what did he do? Did he stop filming? No, he figured out a different way to keep filming however he could. Did that make him less Buñuel? No, it made him more Buñuel. Those are the examples that should be followed, or that I follow at least. And also: Did moving into the Mexican production system worsen Buñuel's films? No! Look at him, see how he isn't finished. No, the idea is to overcome those production problems, and learn from them to build your work. That's a cinema director. So there's no justification for why Latin American films all seem the same. . . . Don't do it! As a director, choose something else! Make a different film!

DM: You refer a lot to festivals. Here we have this trophy cabinet filled with prizes, and the walls and everything, so it's obvious that festivals matter to you. But, what importance do they have? Beyond the fact that it's always nice to receive a prize, what importance have festivals had in your career?

PT: Well, that also a good question, because the thing about festivals is somewhat similar to the thing about producers. That is, festivals can become your editors, as in editors who edit your book, like they mark your destiny. And that's tremendous. Because it can be as damaging as a bad producer. That is, filming for a festival is just as questionable as filming to make a producer happy. Now, the other way it's great! I mean, when you make something that's selected for a festival, it's the best. And that's somewhat strange because, at least this is what I believe, my films are not the typical festival specimen, they aren't the films that aim for . . . in general festival films have a scheme, a rhythm, a theme. And a *performance* in the theatres that is the opposite of the festivals. In fact, these are the usual conversations with the film distributors. Sure, putting the Cannes Palme or the thing from Venice is nice, they say, but every year they make it smaller, because a lot of those films don't work in the theatre. So then people start to associate festivals with boring or inscrutable films. And I, as a director and as a viewer, don't have any problem with an inscrutable or "boring" film. But for a theatre owner, who wants people to come into his theatre, sometimes it's better to have the festival logo be very small.

And that's interesting because for me obviously festivals are important for lots of reasons. The first is because when you are just getting started, you need your work to be seen, and it's much more likely that your work will be seen at a festival than in commercial cinemas. Then, again when you are just getting started, meeting colleagues, and watching their films you learn a ton. The problems where you feel like you're the only one who these terrible things happen to, they happen to 200 or 1,000 people at the same time. At a festival, when you meet another kid from Palestine with his film or, I don't know, Korea or France, and you say, "No, but in France things are great," you encounter someone with their first film and he says, "I've been making this film for fifteen years," it helps you to think about your own cinema and reflect on the cinema of your contemporaries. What they are doing in France? What they are doing in Italy? What's happening in Mexico? As long as you're a curious person, right, if you just make films for fun, which is also a reason, then probably this stuff won't matter to you. But if you really have a passion for cinema and for films, all of that is part of your education. And it's part of my education even now. When they invited me last year to be a judge at Cannes, and the other year to judge at Venice, I am there like a child. I watch fifteen, twenty films at Cannes, Venice, wherever else; they show the sixty most important films of the year. And watching a third of the most important films of the year without the pressure of filming, without the pressure of premiering a film at the festival, since when you go to Cannes with a film you don't have much time to watch films. So festivals serve lots of functions. As a director, above all when you are just getting started, it's very important. Now the Dardennes, who already have a Palme d'Or, still go to Cannes. And Kosturica is hoping that his next film will go to Cannes, or Venice, speaking of festivals . . .

DM: Or the Berlinale or San Sebastián . . .

PT: The Berlinale, exactly. San Sebastián is on another scale, but in those three or four festivals those are very important names. So it's not just for when you're starting out, but what it represents is different when you are making your ninth or tenth film, if you've been lucky to be on that path, but there are also directors who have made eight or nine films and have never been on that path. So if your ninth film is the one that is accepted it has the same value as if they accept your first film, no? What I mean is that your first festivals are not necessarily your first films. Your first festivals have a very pedagogical function, like film school. Seeing how it's done in the rest of the world at that moment, of course over time things change because it's much easier now with the internet, watching films however you want, but it's not the same as going to a cinema, being there, talking to the cinematographer from a Spanish film, whatever it might be . . . I travel everywhere. I saw what it was. . . . I saw different things about my own films depending on the public that watched them. It was one thing in Norway and another in Poland. Now, I can't keep doing the touring I did with my first film; if I did I wouldn't be able to film at all. Above all, with first and second films there is a type of category at festivals, which is kind of a protected category, it's the critics' week at Cannes or Venice, which is a competition for first and second films. In the festivals you have the official competition where you have prizes for drama, and then for "opera prima." That's to say, it's a very guarded category, the one for your first two films, which in general is normal.

I won more prizes with *Mundo grúa* than with any other film, but only because I won a lot of "opera prima" prizes. So that's pretty normal, that a director wins more prizes with his first film and then doesn't repeat that. Because of the "opera prima" festivals at festivals. Rotterdam is a prime festival for first and second films. When I went back to Rotterdam, I went back to a showing of something, but I didn't go back to the Tiger Award competition because it's not for my films. So above all, if you go to a festival of first and second films it's really good, it's incredible. Beyond everything I experienced, beyond the conversations about cinema, beyond all of that, you meet producers, you meet people with money, you meet a world that's very good to know. Afterwards, depending on your path, it becomes your only objective. I know directors who film thinking only about Cannes and if they don't get into Cannes it's the end of the world because they have no other space. Maybe other festivals, but Cannes is the clearest example in this sense. Festivals are very important, even now, but the importance has changed in relation to before.

DM: Well, when you say that, I think about the Hubert Bals, part of its requirement says that the film must be national cinema, or it has to have something to do with the nation of the director. And that is an example of a festival conditioning the cinema of another country, more or less, because you, as a young director, if you would have said, "I want to make a film that is about..."

PT: Russia...

DM: Sure, wherever but not Argentina, they wouldn't have given you the money.

PT: Probably not.

DM: So that is very interesting.

PT: Yes, it is interesting. It's interesting but that's why I'm telling you that it's as important as the discussion about producers. Because producers can damage your work, or they can be the mentors for your work. Your patrons. It could be that, thanks to this producer, you were able to make a great movie. So it's the same, Hubert Bals helping you means that you made your first film, or winning in Rotterdam or Venice means that your next film will probably be easier to make. They are scenarios, they are places where you need to speak without prejudices. Because the festivals don't like it when you say that. Cannes doesn't like when you say, "Well, Cannes likes a certain type of cinema." Or "Rotterdam likes a certain type of cinema." But that's how it is! What I mean is, the films that don't go to Cannes, despite being very good, and the films that don't go to Rotterdam just because of the situation where it's your third film, that doesn't mean that the film isn't good, that if it doesn't go to Cannes or Rotterdam or Venice it's not good. It just doesn't work with their editorial line. But that's very difficult when you've just started. Because if your film doesn't blow up in theatres and it doesn't go to festivals you've got a problem, and you really do have a problem. Because, what do you do in order to keep making films? You won't find any help from abroad and you won't find any help domestically. So it's very important to reflect on that without prejudice.

DM: Speaking of marketing a bit, because obviously if you win something at Cannes or if you've got, if your film is in the Cannes Film Festival, that helps with marketing. That category of New Argentine Cinema—I suppose that at the time it helped a lot but, what do you think of New Argentine Cinema?

PT: Well, I think it's a category that was defined by critics and academics. But it isn't. . . . There wasn't a formal movement here where four or five of us met and said, "OK, we're going to make a cinema that speaks to all of these things, and doesn't speak to these other things, and everything will be filmed like this, or like that." Dogmas are . . . I find dogma ridiculous, those types of definitions. Films create their own rules. I couldn't even tell you that directors, even though I, as a director, have thought about this. . . . The rules of every film are different depending on each film. That might sound extreme but for me it's reality. What I mean is, what it is that makes "New Argentine Cinema?" Not a whole bunch of rules but a group of films. They've been given uniformity, but is there that much uniformity between Rejtman, Trapero, and Martel? You can see, the films are very different. What is it that unifies them? A moment unifies them, a window of time; they are unified by being distinct from other types of cinema. It's what Borges said: "we aren't united by love but by fear." What unifies us? Everything that we don't like, everything that we reject. And I feel proud to be a part of that generation and of having provoked everything that we provoked, but twenty years have passed. Many years have passed and it seems absurd to me that we keep talking about New Argentine Cinema.

And, really, that just highlights something else which is that there still has not been another rupture or another. . . . That is, directors who have come up after us continue to be comfortable with that definition instead of creating their own definition, their own break, or their own fight with us. I don't know. But on the other hand what Rejtman is doing now remains very different from what I'm doing; it's not like we keep doing the same things that we were doing back in that period as a group or in our individual careers. I might be the one who has shifted the most in that sense but . . . It seems like those definitions help, in the moment, but that all of those definitions can end up surpassing the filmmaker. That's to say, Latin American cinema: What is Latin American cinema? Does it depend on birth? Iñárritu's latest film, is that Latin American? There are people who continue to refer to the Latin American director. He is, obviously, a Latin American director. That *gaffe*, the commotion over Sean Penn's comment, is very symbolic in that sense. Because he's a Latin American director, but the film doesn't seem very Latin American. What defines that?

But that's a very extreme case. Let's go to a less-extreme case. What do *Tropa de Elite* and *Mundo grúa* have in common? What do I know!? Sure, it could be that they are from the same region, more or less, maybe *Tropa de Elite* has more in common with *El bonaerense*, that could be. But that's like saying that all cop films, yes or like saying, "All Vietnam [war] films." And, well, *Platoon* is not the same as *Apocalypse Now*.

DM: Or *Leonera* and *Carandiru*, for example.

PT: Exactly. For me, the definition of Latin American cinema . . . Going back a bit, obviously I feel like I have my roots in, or I feel more affinity for certain things that happen in Brazil compared to things that happen in Russia. But I have no idea what affinity a Spaniard has with a Pole, speaking about European cinema. A Spaniard and a Pole probably have more things in common with each other than either of them do with Argentine cinema, but I think there's more in common between Argentine cinema and Romanian cinema than between Romanian and French cinema, for example. Those kinds of definitions work to theorize, but they work at a certain time and generally the same thing always happens—those who benefit the most from them aren't necessarily the protagonists, let's say. Because now, for me, when *Carancho* premiered, people didn't go to see a new film from the New Argentine Cinema, they saw something else. However, that label of New Argentine Cinema did help for other, younger directors, but I think that is a mistake, actually. What I think they need to do is create their own hole and climb out of it and . . . I don't know. I think it's good that what New Argentine Cinema represents is everything that unites us, in relation to that which we don't like, and that is very important because it was very important to say, "Everything that we had been doing, we're not going to do it anymore." It was a way to break [with the past], which gave us unity. What I also think happened in that moment was, there were a lot of people who coincided in their passion for the cinema, which was a change, because there are people for whom cinema seems fun, it seems interesting. The universities of cinema right now are filled with people who are studying it to see if they like it. It wasn't like that back then, when we were filming in that period it was . . . I had to explain to my parents what it meant to be a filmmaker and they didn't understand what it was. So it seems like that passion, which Rejtman still has in his own way and Lucrecia still has in her own way, was very important. It really helped to re-think how to produce, for example, that there isn't just one way to make films, there isn't just one way to know cinema. So that *was* very important. But what happens is, that was almost twenty years ago. Something new has to happen . . . soon.

DM: Going back to your own work, what I postulate in my book, or what I am going to postulate over the length of the book is that your work has been very cyclical to this point. What I mean is, obviously, I haven't seen *El clan* but if we have eight films, not including *7 días en La Habana*, then we have four pairs—*Mundo grúa* and *Carancho*, *El bonaerense* and *Elefante blanco*, *Leonera* and *Nacido y criado*, and *Familia rodante* and *El clan*. In *Mundo grúa* and *Carancho* we have a man trying to survive in a generally antagonistic world, let's say. *El bonaerense* and *Elefante blanco* deal with the State and the various manifestations of the State—police, police and church. *Leonera* and *Nacido y criado* we've got loss, the loss of the self, that idea of mental as much as physical incarceration. And then, with *Familia rodante* and *El clan*, the concept of the family, and the difficulties of the family, because *Familia rodante*, although it might not seem like it, is a rather violent film.

PT: Yes, and hard!

DM: Hard, and it's the violence of the family. Look, generally when people talk about Trapero's career they say that *Familia rodante* is like, it's somewhat out of sync, it's not like all the rest. But for me it's exactly like your work in general! And the difference between each film within those four pairings is that the second film, with the possible exception of *Nacido y criado* and *Leonera*, the second film is always much more violent. And I suppose, since you've gone from a family that goes on a holiday to a family that kidnaps people and kills them, I suppose that . . .

PT: (Laughing) It's going to happen again!

DM: It's going to happen with *El clan*. So, why do think that's the case? Because always, take *Carancho* and *Mundo grúa*—Rulo is a lovely guy, sympathetic, and completely incapable of doing anything. Doing anything against the system that oppresses him. Sosa tries to do something, but there's that impotence that, in the end, results in him failing, let's say. And if we look at *El bonaerense*, you're talking about the police, and Zapa is a very interesting character, super interesting, and then we have Darín as the priest in *Elefante blanco*, and that film is even more violent than *El bonaerense*, which is already a really violent film itself. Why do you think that is, that there's this escalation of the violence in your work over the years?

PT: Look, I have no idea, I've never thought about it. But it's probably got something to do with how, the older I get the more I am bothered by injustice! (Laughs) Either it's affecting me more or the world is becoming more unjust, I don't know which of the two, but . . . Maybe both. I'll give you an example of something personal. When I was younger, I was really naïve. In fact, the particular neighborhood where I come from, I never was worried about insecurity, I never thought that anything could happen to me. Nobody was going to rob me, nobody could do anything to me. Even just a few years ago my neighbors rang my doorbell and said, "Pablo, you left your keys in the door!" There was a level of *relaxation* that, over the years, has changed. It began to change when I became a father, precisely, but every year that sensation of violence, or maybe insecurity, becomes sharper. No? Injustice generates violence, it generates insecurity, it generates a kind of silent societal war, where everyone is trying to figure out what they must do to survive. And maybe I'm more conscious of the insecurity that I didn't feel before. It's probably either that I am more conscious of it or that it's become worse. I lived in a neighborhood like the one in *El bonaerense* and I definitely feel like it's more violent now than it was when I was twenty. I think my view of this, or my analysis, is an objective one. And I don't think that what I am feeling is necessarily a reflection of just the local situation in Argentina. When I read the news from the last year, or two or three years, I see that the level of violence is atrocious. There are a ton of examples, and each of them taken in the abstract might be somewhat banal, but from the airplanes that crash, and we don't know if they crashed or they were shot down, to the Islamic State which has lost all logic of the number of deaths and the violence and torture and the grotesque of those deaths, the boats that sink in the Mediterranean and every time the number of deaths doesn't even surprise you anymore, everything feels like it's at a level that demonstrates a state of things in collapse, like the whole system is collapsing. And obviously the system doesn't stop generating injustice; it's just lived with more clarity in Latin America and less clarity in other countries. And, going back, it's a question of scale, right, Latin America is in the middle, but look at Africa and you say, "What about that?" I mean, it's inhumane what you read, what you see, the news that comes in, that little boat, the *gomón* as we called the Cuban boatpeople, compared to what's happening in the Mediterranean it's like Disney, and what they both represent is just ridiculous. Therefore, perhaps what is happening is that reality is becoming more and more violent, and my own being is more and more a victim of that violent connection, you understand?

But I don't know if it's that . . . I remember my dad saying thirty years ago that "things have never been worse." And I think my dad would say the same today. He said, "Where is it going to stop? It can't be worse. The world is more violent than ever, the world is out of control." More than thirty, forty years ago, I must have been . . . yeah, I was fifteen so thirty years ago. I remember that moment really clearly, that the 1970s were the most violent years in Argentina, that there could never be years worse than those. However now, thirty-something years later, I think it might even be more violent now than before. It's different, it's changed . . .

DM: But, here in Argentina? Or in the world? Because, obviously you said in the world but when you say, "There is more violence," are you referring to Argentina?

PT: I think it's mutated into something else. That is, there is less explicit violence like the violence of the dictatorship, the disappearances and the death of people, but there is much more quotidian violence. The product of international circumstances, probably, the product of an internal question about the changes within Latin America, lots of things that don't solely have to do with the government itself. But there is a kind of violence in the street, a dispassion, I'm not sure if you understand that word. It's not a coincidence that the most successful film in the history of the Argentine box office would be *Relatos Salvajes*. They put things in that film and then they came out in the news! Someone was killed by a gunshot in the street, an airplane is shot down, those things might seem a little stereotypical in the film, but then you encounter them in real life! I think there's something about that that isn't actually coincidence, because it's not just a film about living in Argentina. It's a film that came out in a moment when this could have been replicated in other places. So I definitely think the world is more violent, that Argentina is more violent, and I believe . . . From my reading, which is a very limited reading because I'm not a theorist, I'm not a sociologist, nor an anthropologist, for me it's like something growing, it's a symptom of a more unjust world, more unjust every day. Now, following that line of thought, is this era more unjust than the feudal period? I don't know if it is more unjust than the feudal period. It's different. More unjust than the time of slavery? More unjust than . . .? I don't know. But it depends on what we compare it to. I don't want to compare against something that was worse, I want to compare with what it should be, not with the worst of the past.

It seems to me that something like that is happening. Maybe it's that, despite having a very critical view of things, I am quite optimistic and I have an optimistic outlook on life. I believe people overcome, we have the ability to learn, I'm not a pessimist. I don't see things. . . . Even if my diagnosis is quite dark, even black, I feel like there are new possibilities to learn and change. Like what I said about what my dad was saying forty years ago, I prefer the violence that manifests itself today over the violence where they went around killing people on the street. You understand? I'm saying this is better than what was happening forty years ago in that context. Is it more violent, do more people die because there are more homeless people, do more people die because of narcotrafficking, do more people die because they don't have anything to eat? It could be, but that's different than having the State killing people deliberately. So in that sense it's better. It's more distressing, because the problem is harder to solve, it's harder to understand, we have a government with a very progressive message but in practice their actions don't always match that; it's more complicated. So, as much as I consider myself an optimistic person despite having an outlook that is very hard on reality, and I feel that probably this moment of crisis, or this sensation of "che, this can't keep happening" will probably create something new. After those 700 people sank in the Mediterranean, they're going to have to sit down and say, "Guys, what are we going to do? Are we going to watch people drown?" I suppose that will generate something . . . I hope.

Works Cited

Agamben, G., 1998. *Homo Sacer: Sovereign Power and Bare Life*. Translated from Italian by D. Heller-Roazen. Stanford: Stanford University Press.

Agamben, G., 2005. *State of Exception*. Translated from Italian by K. Attell. Chicago: The University of Chicago Press.

Aguilar, G., 2008a. *Estudio crítico sobre El bonaerense*. Buenos Aires: Picnic Editorial.

Aguilar, G., 2008b. *New Argentine Film: Other Worlds* [e-book]. Translated from Spanish by S. A. Wells. New York: Palgrave MacMillan.

Aguilar, G., 2015. *Más allá del pueblo: Imágenes, indicios y políticas del cine* [e-book]. Buenos Aires: Fondo de Cultura Económica.

Aldana Reyes, X., 2013. "Violence and Mediation: The Ethics of Spectatorship in the Twenty-First Century Horror Film." in G. Matthews and S. Goodman, eds. *Violence and the Limits of Representation*. London: Palgrave MacMillan. pp. 145–160.

Althusser, L., 1971. *Lenin and Philosophy and Other Essays*. Translated from French by B. Brewster. New York: Monthly Review Press.

Amado, A., 2009. *La imagen justa: cine argentino y política (1980–2007)*. Buenos Aires: Colihue.

Andermann, J., 2012. *New Argentine Cinema*. London: I.B. Tauris.

Arendt, H., 1970. *On Violence*. New York: Harvest Harcourt Int.

Ban, C., 2016. *Ruling Ideas: How Global Neoliberalism Goes Local*. New York: Oxford University Press.

Batlle, D., 2008. "Las Grúas del Mundo Rulo" in BAFICI, ed. *Cine argentino 99/08*. Buenos Aires: Gobierno de la Ciudad de Buenos Aires. pp. 147–150.

Beauregard, L.P., 2018. "*La quietud*, la telenovela de Pablo Trapero." *El país*, [online] September 3. Available at: https://elpais.com/cultura/2018/09/03/actualidad/1535977467_268728.html [Accessed May 21, 2020]

Bourdieu, P., 2001. *Masculine Domination*. Translated from French by R. Nice. Cambridge: Polity.

Buchanan, I., 2008. *Deleuze and Guattari's Anti-Oedipus: A Reader's Guide*. London: Continuum.

Busso, A., 2016. "Neoliberal Crisis, Social Demands, and Foreign Policy in Kirchnerist Argentina." *Contexto Internacional* 38(1), pp. 95–131.

Caruth, C., 1996. *Unclaimed Experience: Trauma, Narrative, and History*. Baltimore: The Johns Hopkins University Press.

Comolli, J-C, and P. Narboni, 1971. "Cinema/Ideology/Criticism." Translated from French by S. Bennett. *Screen* 12(1), pp. 27–36.

Connell, R.W., 2005. *Masculinities (Second Edition)*. Berkeley: University of California Press.

Copertari, G., 2010. "Far from Heaven: On *El cielito*, by María Victoria Menis." in C. Rocha and E. Montes Garcés, eds. *Violence in Argentine Literature and Film (1989-2005)*. Calgary: University of Calgary Press. pp. 111–124.

da Silva Catela, L., 1998. "Sin cuerpo, sin tumba. Memorias sobre una muerte inconclusa." *Historia, Antropología y Fuentes Orales* 20, pp. 87–104.

Damai, P., 2005. "The Killing Machine of Exception: Sovereignty, Law, and Play in Agamben's *State of Exception*." *CR: The New Centennial Review* 5(3), pp. 255–276.

De Vedia, M., 2014. "Denunció la Iglesia que la Argentina está 'enferma de violencia'." *La Nación* [online] May 10. Available at: http://www.lanacion.com.ar/1689386-denuncio-la-iglesia-que-la-argentina-esta-enferma-de-violencia [Accessed September 20, 2014.].

Deleuze, G. and F. Guattari, 1983. *Anti-Oedipus: Capitalism and Schizophrenia*. Translated from French by R. Hurley, M. Seem, and H.R. Lane. Minneapolis: University of Minneapolis Press.

Deleuze, G. and F. Guattari, 2013. *A Thousand Plateaus: Capitalism and Schizophrenia*. Translated from French by B. Massumi. London: Bloomsbury.

Deleuze, G., 1979. "The Rise of the Social." in J. Donzelot, ed. *The Policing of Families*. London: Hutchinson & Co. pp. ix–xvii.

Deleuze, G., 1992. "Postscript on the Societies of Control." *October* 59, pp. 3–7.

Denissen, M., 2008. *Winning Small Battles, Losing the War: Police Violence, the Movimiento del Dolor and democracy in post-authoritarian Argentina*. Amsterdam: Rozenberg Publishers.

Derrida, J., 1994. *Specters of Marx: The State of the Debt, the Work of Mourning and the New International*. Translated from French by P. Kamuf. New York: Routledge.

Documento final de la junta militar sobre la guerra contra la subversión y el terrorismo, 1983. Buenos Aires: Fuerzas Armadas.

Donzelot, J., 1979. *The Policing of Families*. London: Hutchinson & Co.

Dyer, R., 1999. *Stars*. London: British Film Institute/Palgrave Macmillan.

Edgerton, A. and I. Sotirova, 2011. "Sex and the Barrio: A Clash of Faith in Latin America." *World Policy Journal* 28(4), pp. 34–41.

Escobar, P., 2014. "Escenas de la Patagonia neoliberal: Las representaciones de las actividades económicas en películas argentinas filmadas en la región (1985–2006)." *Revista Estudios del ISHiR* 4(8), pp. 118–129.

Falicov, T.L., 2003. "Los hijos de Menem: The New Independent Argentine Cinema, 1995-1999." *Framework: The Journal of Cinema and Media* 44(1), pp. 49-63.

Falicov, T.L., 2007. *The Cinematic Tango: Contemporary Argentine Film.* London: Wallflower Press.

Fischer, A. and S. Vaz, 2018. "O lugar da morada no cinema de Lucrecia Martel e de Pablo Trapero." *Rumores* 23(12), pp. 221-241.

Fisher, M., 2012. "What is Hauntology?" *Film Quarterly* 66(1), pp. 16-24.

Foucault, M., 1983. "Preface." in Deleuze, G. and F. Guattari. *Anti-Oedipus: Capitalism and Schizophrenia.* Translated from French by R. Hurley, M. Seem, and H.R. Lane. Minneapolis: University of Minneapolis Press, pp. xiii-xvi.

Foucault, M., 1990. *The History of Sexuality, Vol. 1: An Introduction.* Translated from French by R. Hurley. New York: Vintage Books.

Foucault, M., 1991. *Discipline and Punish: The Birth of the Prison.* Translated from French by A. Sheridan. London: Penguin Books.

Foucault, M., 2006. "28 November 1973." *Psychiatric Power: Lectures at the Collège de France, 1973-1974.* Translated from French by G. Burchell. J. Lagrange, ed. New York: Palgrave Macmillan. pp. 63-92.

Gabriel, T., 1982. *Third Cinema in the Third World: The Aesthetic of Liberation.* Ann Arbor: UMI Press.

General FAQs, 2015. "Hubert *Bals* Fund" [online]. Available at: https://www.iffr.com/professionals/hubert_bals_fund/faq/general/#1 [Accessed February 17, 2014].

Ghio, J.M., 2007. *La iglesia católica en la política argentina.* Buenos Aires: Prometeo Libros.

González, H., 2003. "Sobre *El bonaerense* y el nuevo cine argentino." *El ojo mocho* 17.

González, T., 2012. "The Gothic in Cristina García's 'The Agüero Sisters.'" *Melus* 37(3), pp. 117-39.

Gordon, A., 2008. *Ghostly Matters: Haunting and the Social Imagination.* Minneapolis: University of Minnesota Press.

Gorelik, A., 2003. "Mala época: Los imaginarios de la descomposición social y urbana en Buenos Aires." in A. Birgin and J. Trímboli, eds. *Imágenes de los noventa.* Buenos Aires: Libros del Zorzal. pp. 19-46.

Grimson, A. and G. Kessler, 2012. *On Argentina and the Southern Cone.* Translated from Spanish by M. Westwell. New York: Routledge.

Hall, S., 1982. "The Rediscovery of 'Ideology': Return of the Repressed in Media Studies." in M. Gurevitch, T. Bennett, J. Curran, and J. Woollacott, eds. *Culture, Society and the Media.* London: Routledge. pp. 52-86.

Han, B-C., 2019. *What is Power?* Translated from German by D. Steuer. Cambridge: Polity.

Haney, C., 2003. "The Psychological Impact of Incarceration: Implications for Postprison Adjustment." in J. Travis and M. Waul, eds. *Prisoners Once Removed: The Impact of Incarceration and Reentry on Children, Families, and Communities.* Washington, DC: The Urban Institute Press. pp. 33–65.

Hardt, M., 1997. "Prison Time." *Yale French Studies* 91, pp. 64–79.

Heise, T.S. and A. Tudor, 2013. "Dangerous, Divine, and Marvelous? The Legacy of the 1960s in the Political Cinema of Europe and Brazil." *The Sixties: A Journal of History, Politics and Culture* 6(1), pp. 82–100.

Hinton, M.S., 2006. *The State on the Streets: Police and Politics in Argentina and Brazil.* Boulder: Lynne Rienner Publishers.

Holmes, A., 2017. *Politics of Architecture in Contemporary Argentine Cinema.* New York: Palgrave Macmillan.

Hortiguera, H. and C. Rocha, 2007. "Introduction." in H. Hortiguera and C. Rocha, eds. *Argentinean Cultural Production During the Neoliberal Years (1989–2001).* Lewiston: The Edwin Mellen Press, pp. 1–20.

Ingoldsby, B., 1991. "The Latin American Family: Familism vs. Machismo." *Journal of Comparative Family Studies* 22(1), pp. 57–62.

Jones, S., 2013. *Torture Porn: Popular Horror After Saw.* London: Palgrave Macmillan UK.

Kairuz, M., 2010. "La ley y la calle." *Página12* [online] May 2. Available at: https://www.pagina12.com.ar/diario/suplementos/radar/9-6116-2010-05-02.html [Accessed July 11, 2017].

Kantaris, G., 2016. "Pablo Trapero y el elefante blanco de la razón populista." in B. Chappuzeau and C. von Tschilschke, eds. *Cine argentino contemporáneo: visiones y discursos.* Madrid: Iberoamericana. pp. 83–106.

López-Vicuña, I., 2010. "Postnational Boundaries in *Bolivia*." in C. Rocha and E. Montes Garcés, eds. *Violence in Argentine Literature and Film (1989–2005).* Calgary: University of Calgary Press. pp. 145–62.

Lorraine, T., 2005. "Oedipalisation." in A. Parr, ed. *Deleuze Dictionary.* Edinburgh: Edinburgh University Press. pp. 194–6.

Lukes, S., 2005. *Power: A Radical View.* 2nd ed. New York: Palgrave Macmillan.

Marks, J., 2005. "Control Society." in A. Parr, ed. *Deleuze Dictionary.* Edinburgh: Edinburgh University Press. pp. 55–6.

Matheou, D., 2010. "Poet of the Everyday: Pablo Trapero." in *The Faber Book of New South American Cinema.* London: Faber and Faber. pp. 259–84.

Matthews, G. and S. Goodman, 2013. "Introduction: Violence and the Limits of Representation." in G. Matthews and S. Goodman, eds. *Violence and the Limits of Representation.* London: Palgrave MacMillan. pp. 1–11.

Mayne, J., 2000. *Framed: Lesbians, Feminists, and Media Culture.* Minneapolis: University of Minnesota Press.

Morello, G., 2015. *The Catholic Church and Argentina's Dirty War*. Oxford: Oxford University Press.

Natanson, J., 2015. "Empezar por el conurbano." *El dipló/Le monde diplomatique* [online] September. Available at: http://www.eldiplo.org/index.php/archivo/195-los-nudos-de-la-economia/empezar-por-el-conurbano/ [Accessed July 11, 2017].

Onuch, O., 2014. "'It's the Economy, Stupid,' or Is It? The Role of Political Crises in Mass Mobilization: The Case of Argentina in 2001." in C. Levey, D. Ozarow, and C. Wylde, eds. *Argentina Since the 2001 Crisis*. New York: Palgrave Macmillan US. pp. 89–113.

Oubiña, D., 2013. "Footprints: Risk and Challenges of Contemporary Argentine Cinema." in A. Fernández Bravo and J. Andermann, eds. *New Argentine and Brazilian Cinema: Reality Effects*. New York: Palgrave Macmillan US. pp. 31–41.

Oxford English Dictionary, 2017. *Oxford Living Dictionaries* [online]. Oxford: Oxford English Dictionary (UK). Available at: https://en.oxforddictionaries.com/definition/white_elephant [Accessed July 13, 2017].

Oyarzabal, S., 2017. *Nation, Culture and Class in Argentine Cinema: Crisis and Representation (1998-2005)*. Suffolk: Tamesis.

Page, J., 2009. *Crisis and Capitalism in Contemporary Argentine Cinema*. Durham: Duke University Press.

Pew Research Center, Nov. 13 2014. "Religion in Latin America: Widespread Change in a Historically Catholic Region." Available at: https://www.pewforum.org/2014/11/13/religion-in-latin-america/ [Accessed December 19, 2020].

Pinazza, N., 2014. *Journeys in Argentine and Brazilian Cinema*. New York: Palgrave Macmillan US.

Ricoeur, P., 2010. "Power and Violence." *Theory, Culture & Society* 27(5), pp. 18–36.

Rocha, C. and E. Montes Garcés, 2010. "Introduction." in C. Rocha and E. Montes Garcés, eds. *Violence in Argentine Literature and Film (1989-2005)*. Calgary: University of Calgary Press. pp. xi–xxxiii.

Rocha, C., 2010. "Barbaric Spectacles: Masculinities in Crisis in Popular Argentine Cinema of the 1990s." in C. Rocha and E. Montes Garcés, eds. *Violence in Argentine Literature and Film (1989-2005)*. Calgary: University of Calgary Press. pp. 93–110.

Rocha, C., 2012. *Masculinities in Contemporary Argentine Popular Cinema*. New York: Palgrave Macmillan US.

Sanchez R.M., 2006. "Insecurity and Violence as a New Power Relation in Latin America." *The Annals of the AAPSS* 606, pp. 178–195.

Sandberg, C., 2018. "Contemporary Latin American Cinema and Resistance to Neoliberalism: Mapping the Field." in C. Sandberg and C. Rocha, eds. *Contemporary Latin American Cinema: Resisting Neoliberalism?*. New York: Palgrave Macmillan. pp. 1–23.

Sarlo, B., 2003. "Plano, repetición: Sobreviviendo en la ciudad nueva" in A. Birgin and J. Trímboli, eds. *Imágenes de los noventa*, Buenos Aires: Libros del Zorzal. pp. 125–50.

Saumell-Muñoz, R., 1993. "El otro testimonio: Literatura carcelaria en América Latina." *Revista Iberoamericana* 59(164–5), pp. 497–507.

Schaumberg, H., 2014. "Argentina since 2001: From Spontaneous Uprising to 'Transition,' or a Crisis Intermezzo?" in C. Levey, D. Ozarow, and C. Wylde, eds. *Argentina Since the 2001 Crisis*. New York: Palgrave Macmillan US. pp. 135–54.

Schindel, E., 2014. "Ghosts and *Compañeros*: Haunting Stories and the Quest for Justice around Argentina's Former Terror Sites." *Rethinking History* 18(2), pp. 244–64.

Scorer, J., 2011. "Trigger-Happy: Police, Violence and the State in *El bonaerense/The Policeman*." in C. Rêgo and C. Rocha, eds. *New Trends in Argentine and Brazilian Cinema*. Bristol: Intellect. pp. 163–76.

Selimović, I., 2019. "Unorthodox Homes in Pablo Trapero's *Leonera* (2008) and *El clan* (2015): Shattered Lives, Political Selves." *Chasqui* 48(2), pp. 34–52.

Solanas, F. and O. Getino, 1973. *Cine, cultura y descolonización*. Buenos Aires: Siglo Veintiuno.

Springer, S., 2016. "The Violence of Neoliberalism." in S. Springer, K. Birch, and J. MacLeavy, eds. *The Handbook of Neoliberalism*. New York: Routledge. pp. 153–63.

Stagoll, C., 2005. "Becoming." in A. Parr, ed. *Deleuze Dictionary*. Edinburgh: Edinburgh University Press. pp. 25–7.

Standing, G., 2011. *The Precariat: The New Dangerous Class*. London: Bloomsbury.

Strønen, I.A. and M. Ystanes, 2018. "Introduction." in M. Ystanes and I.M. Strønen, eds. *The Social Life of Economic Inequalities in Contemporary Latin America: Decades of Change*. London: Palgrave Macmillan UK. pp. 3–35.

Sturzenegger, F., 2003. *La economía de los argentinos: Reglas de juego para una sociedad próspera y justa*. Buenos Aires: Planeta Argentina.

Treacy, M.J., 1996. "Double Binds: Latin American Women's Prison Memories." *Hypatia* 11(4), pp. 130–45.

TV Pública Argentina, 2012. "¿Qué fue de tu vida? Pablo Trapero—14-12-12 (1 de 4)" [video online]. Available at: https://www.youtube.com/watch?v=b3tBiGw0D_I [Accessed July 11, 2017].

Urraca, B., 2010. "An Argentine Context: Civilization and Barbarism in *El aura* and *El custodio*." in C. Rocha and E. Montes Garcés, eds. *Violence in Argentine Literature and Film (1989–2005)*. Calgary: University of Calgary Press. pp. 125–42.

Urraca, B., 2011. "Transactional Fiction: (Sub)urban Realism in the Films of Trapero and Caetano." in C. Rêgo and C. Rocha, eds. *New Trends in Argentine and Brazilian Cinema*. Bristol: Intellect. pp. 147–62.

Urraca, B., 2014. "Rituals of Performance: Ricardo Darín as Father Julián in *Elefante blanco*." *Revista de Estudios Hispánicos* 48(2), pp. 353–72.

Vezzetti, H., 2014. "Archivo y memorias del presente. *Elefante blanco* de Pablo Trapero: el padre Mugica, los pobres y la violencia." *A Contra Corriente* 12(1), pp. 179–90.

Wayne, M., 2001. *Political Film: The Dialectics of Third Cinema*. London: Pluto Press.

Weber, M., 2015. "The Distribution of Power Within the *Gemeinschaft*: Classes, *Stände*, Parties." in T. Waters and D. Waters, translators and eds. *Weber's Rationalism and Modern Society: New Translations on Politics, Bureaucracy, and Social Stratification*. New York: Palgrave Macmillan US. pp. 37–58.

Williams, R., 1983. *Keywords*. London: Fontana Paperbacks.

Wolkowicz, P., 2014. "Escenas del *under* porteño. Experimentación y vanguardia en el cine argentino de los años 60 y 70." *Imagofagia: Revista de la Asociación Argentina de Estudios de Cine y Audiovisual* 9.

Zamostny, J., 2015. "Ricardo Darín and the Animal Gaze: Celebrity and Anonymity in *El aura*." *Confluencia: Revista Hispánic de Cultura y Literatura* 30(2), pp. 154–66.

Zavarzadeh, M., 1991. *Seeing Films Politically*. Albany: SUNY Press.

Žižek, S., 2009. *Violence: Six Sideways Reflections*. London: Profile Books.

Films Cited

Bad Lieutenant, 1992. Directed by Abel Ferrara. USA: Bad Lt. Productions.
Bolivia, 2001. Directed by Israel Adrián Caetano. Argentina: INCAA.
Camila, 1984. Directed by María Luisa Bemberg. Argentina: GEA Producciones.
Carancho, 2010. Directed by Pablo Trapero. Argentina: Matanza Cine.
Carandiru, 2002. Directed by Hector Babenco. Brazil: HB Filmes.
Crónica de una fuga, 2006. Directed by Adrián Caetano. Argentina: K&S Films.
El aura, 2005. Directed by Fabián Bielinsky. Argentina: Patagonik.
El bonaerense, 2002. Directed by Pablo Trapero. Argentina: INCAA.
El caso María Soledad, 1993. Directed by Héctor Olivera. Argentina: Aries Cinematográfica.
El clan, 2015. Directed by Pablo Trapero. Argentina: Matanza Cine.
El mismo amor, la misma lluvia, 1999. Directed by Juan José Campanella. Argentina: JEMPSA.
El secreto de sus ojos, 2009. Directed by Juan José Campanella. Argentina: Tornasol.
Elefante blanco, 2012. Directed by Pablo Trapero. Argentina: Matanza Cine.
Familia rodante, 2004. Directed by Pablo Trapero. Argentina: Matanza Cine.
Garage Olimpo, 1999. Directed by Marco Bechis. Italy: Classic.
Goodfellas, 1990. Directed by Martin Scorsese. USA: Warner Bros.
Hell or High Water, 2016. Directed by David Mackenzie. USA: Film 44.
Héroes sin fama, 1940. Directed by Mario Soffici. Argentina: Argentina SonoFilm.
Hiroshima Mon Amour, 1959. Directed by Alain Resnais. France: Argos Films.
Historia de un clan, 2015. Directed by Luis Ortega. Argentina: Telefe.
I, Daniel Blake, 2016. Directed by Ken Loach. UK: Sixteen Films.
Juan sin ropa, 1919. Directed by Georges Benoît and Héctor Quiroga. Argentina: Quiroga Benoît Films.
Kamchatka, 2002. Directed by Marcelo Piñeyro. Argentina: Patagonik.
La ciénaga, 2001. Directed by Lucrecia Martel. Argentina: 4K Films.
La historia oficial, 1985. Directed by Luis Puenzo. Argentina: Historias Cinematográficas Cinemania.
La hora de los hornos, 1968. Directed by Octavio Getino and Octavio "Pino" Solanas. Argentina: Grupo Cine Liberación.
La noche de los lápices, 1986. Directed by Héctor Olivera. Argentina: Aries Cinematográfica.

La quietud, 2018. Directed by Pablo Trapero. Argentina: Matanza Cine.

Leonera, 2008. Directed by Pablo Trapero. Argentina: Matanza Cine.

Los traidores, 1972. Directed by Raymundo Gleyzer. Argentina: Grupo Cine de la Base.

Miss Mary, 1986. Directed by María Luisa Bemberg. Argentina: GEA Cinematográfica.

Mundo grúa, 1999. Directed by Pablo Trapero. Argentina: Lita Stantic Producciones.

Nacido y criado, 2006. Directed by Pablo Trapero. Argentina: Matanza Cine.

Negocios, 1995. Directed by Pablo Trapero. Argentina.

Nueve Reinas, 2000. Directed by Fabián Bielinsky. Argentina: Patagonik.

Orange is the New Black, 2013–2017 (Television series). USA: Tilted Productions.

Oz, 1997–2003 (Television series). USA: HBO/Rysher Entertainment.

Parasite, 2019. Directed by Bong Joon-Ho. South Korea: Barunson E&A.

Pixote, 1980. Directed by Hector Babenco. Brazil: HB Filmes.

Pizza, birra, faso, 1998. Directed by Bruno Stagnaro and Israel Adrián Caetano. Argentina: Palo y la Bolsa / Cine.

Prisioneros de la tierra, 1939. Directed by Mario Soffici. Argentina: Pampa Film.

Procesado 1.040, 1958. Directed by Rubén W. Cavalloti. Argentina: Argentina Sono Film S.A.C.I.

Rapado, 1992. Directed by Martín Rejtman. The Netherlands: A.K. Films.

Silvia Prieto, 1998. Directed by Martín Rejtman. Argentina.

Sorry to Bother You, 2018. Directed by Boots Riley. USA: Significant Productions.

Sur, 1988. Directed by Fernando "Pino" Solanas. France: Canal+.

The Four Horsemen of the Apocalypse, 1921. Directed by Rex Ingram. USA: Metro Pictures Corp.

The Kiss of the Spiderwoman, 1985. Directed by Hector Babenco. Brazil: HB Filmes.

The Shawshank Redemption, 1994. Directed by Frank Darabont. USA: Castle Rock Entertainment.

The Wild Bunch, 1969. Directed by Sam Peckinpah. USA: Warner Bros./Seven Arts.

Tiempo de revancha, 1981. Directed by Adolfo Aristarain. Argentina: Aries Cinematográfica.

Tire dié, 1960. Directed by Fernando Birri. Argentina: Instituto de Cinematografía de la Universidad Nacional del Litoral.

Training Day, 2001. Directed by Antoine Fuqua. USA: Warner Bros.

Index

Agamben, Giorgio   158–60, 169–71, *see also* homo sacer; state of exception
agency   29, 43, 61, 66, 83–4
Aguilar, Gonzalo   10, 57, 69, 72, 94
Alfonsín, Raúl   1, 127, 135–8
Alianza Anticomunista Argentina (Triple A)   74, 93–4
alliance   104–7, 154–6, 176, 187
Althusser, Louis   19–20, 64–7, 74, 90, 103–9, 156–7, *see also* interpellation
Andermann, Jens   2, 4, 5, 7, 69, 109, 113, 171–3
Arendt, Hannah   13, 17, 58, 61, 65, 98–9
argentinidad   29, 62, 112–14
    national symbols   75–8, 92, 114
Asturias, Miguel Ángel   180

Babenco, Hector   176, 179–80
Bechis, Marco   2, 181
becomings   141, 155–6, 177, 186–7
Bielinsky, Fabián   171
Bonaerense, la   64, 68, 72–8, 80, *see also* police
Borges, Jorge Luis   113, 225
Bourdieu, Pierre   59
Brazil   89, 114, 190, 216, 226
Buchanan, Ian   154
Buñuel, Luis   221

cacerolazo   1, 13, 14, 55, 62
Caetano, Adrián   5, 35, 181
Campanella, Juan José   2, 48
Catholic Church   1, 21, 24, 64–8, 89–95
    Argentine Episcopal [Bishops'] Conference   1, 90
Cavallotti, Ruben W.   180
Chile   9, 14, 44, 77, 89, 161, 199
Ciudad Oculta   10–11, 86–99, *see also* villa miseria

class   3, 8–10, 31, 32, 58, 118, 167, 190–1, 198, *see also* precariat
    middle class   2, 7–9, 18, 31, 46, 49, 53–8, 62, 71, 112, 118, 125, 162, 214
    upper class   125, 141, 161–2
    working class   3, 18, 30–1, 33, 36–9, 41, 43–9, 53, 55–9, 162, 167
Comisión Nacional sobre la Desaparición de Personas   127, 135–6
community   37, 64, 79, 87, 90, 95–9, 154, 172–4, 176–7, 182, 184–5, 187–9, 201
Connell, R.W.   32–3
control   25, 58, 67, 75, 82, 95, 104–6, 117–20, 124–5, 132, 157–9, 182, 202
conurbano   70–4, 88, 160
corralito   2, 13, 39
crime   1, 22, 23, 48, 66, 72–80, 126, 132–6, 143, 149, 159, 179
curas villeros   90–6, *see also* Mugica, Carlos; *villa miseria*

Damai, Puspa   169–70
da Silva Catela, Ludmila   164
de la Rúa, Fernando   55
Deleuze, Gilles   107–8, 157–9, 173, *see also* control
Deleuze and Félix Guattari   10, 13, 24–5, 104–13, 117–18, 124–31, 147–55, 176, 187, *see also* filiation; Oedipus; rhizome
    Anti-Oedipus   107–8, 117, 154
    Capitalism and Schizophrenia   154
Derrida, Jacques   11, 141
desaparecidos   135, 138, 144–5, 164–6, 170, 181
desire   10, 25, 108–9, 114, 117–19, 124–5, 132, 149–50, 154–6
    desiring-production   108, 110, 117–18, 128, 147
Dirty War   2, 36, 132, 165–6, 181, 184

Donzelot, Jacques   106–7
Duhalde, Eduardo   73, 75
Dyer, Richard   56

economy(-ic)   1, 5, 9, 16, 22, 31, 39,
    73, 109, 112, 167–8, 190, *see also*
    neoliberalism
  collapse of   1, 3, 30–1, 49, 55, 159
  crisis   2, 4, 8, 13–14, 23, 29–30, 33, 48,
    54–5, 62, 73, 112, 163, 190–1, 230
employment   31–3, 37, 40, 46,
    59, 191, 204
environment   156, *see also*
    conurbano; Patagonia
  rural   44, 68, 79, 120–1, 161–2, 169
  urban   9, 43–4, 58, 79–80, 113–14,
    121, 138
Escobar, Paz   173
Escuela de Mecánica de la Armada
    (ESMA)   74, 143–4

Falklands/Malvinas War   2, 127
family   13, 21, 24–5, 29, 33, 67–8, 90,
    117, 138–9, 152–3, 174–6, 183, *see
    also* becomings; rhizome; sexuality
  arborescent structure   115, 117–18,
    121, 124, 150–1, 155, 175, 183–9
  breakdown of   121–3, 144, 147–8, 183
  as site of violence   125, 129, 135–6
fear   97, 167–8, 170, 225
filiation   107, 154–6, 176, 187
Fisher, Mark   11, 145, 193, *see also*
    haunting(-ology)
Foucault, Michel   104–7, 113–17, 124,
    156–8, 175–6, 182–4, *see also*
    alliance; panopticism; sexuality

Gabriel, Teshome   21
gatillo fácil   73–4
gaucho   43, 113–14
Gewalt   88–9, 93
González, Horacio   79
Gordon, Avery F.   139, 141, 144
Grimson, Alejandro and Gabriel
    Kessler   8, 9, 31, 49, 112

Hall, Stuart   19–20
Han, Byung-Chul   95–7
haunting(-ology)   10–12, 23, 139–45,
    150, 192–3

Henn, Jorge   137
hierarchy   5, 9, 80, 154, 173, 179, 184
  of Catholic Church   89–91, 99
  of family   104–7, 118, 131, 155
Hinton, Mercedes S.   72–4
Historia de un clan   136–7
homo sacer   159–60, 170–1
horror films   49–52, 59–60
Hubert Bals Fund   4, 210–11, 213,
    223–4

identity   8, 29, 32–3, 40, 54–5, 70–2, 112,
    121, 145, 158–9, 170
ideology   13, 18–21, 31, 66–8, 104,
    106, 151, 157, *see also*
    State Apparatus
impotencia   29–30
incest   140, 148–51
insecurity   22, 30, 32, 71, 72,
    137, 228, 235
Instituto Nacional de Cine y Artes
    Audiovisuales (INCAA)   2, 4,
    211
interpellation   104, 156

Kirchnerism   9–10, 190

Latin Americanization   22–3, 29, 40
Lukes, Steven   13, 65–7, 76, 78, 81,
    85, 95

machismo   68, 120–4
Martel, Lucrecia   5, 139, 146, 225
masculinity   29, 32–3, 40–1, 120–1, *see
    also* machismo
Matanza, La   2, 68–71, 79, 200
Matanza Cine   195, 200, 211, 213
Mayne, Judith   179
Menem, Carlos   2, 3, 8, 9, 16, 18, 24, 30,
    35, 39, 78, 167, 191
micro-societies   111
Misiones   110, 120, 124
Mugica, Carlos   93–4, 97–8

neoliberalism   3–6, 8–13, 18, 21–2, 30–3,
    45, 62, 112, 167, 190–1
  and globalization   18, 66
neurosis   129, 131
New Argentine Cinema   2, 3, 5, 10, 12,
    35, 44, 69, 191, 192, 205, 224–6

objective violence   5, 14–17, 21, 24–5,
    30, 32, 46, 58, 60–1, 64, 66–7, 80,
    85, 91, 93, 99, 103, 109, 125, 156,
    166, 190–3, 196, see also subjective
    violence; violence
Oedipus(-al)   13, 24, 107–9, 124, 128–9,
    147, 154–6
Olivera, Héctor   181
Oyarzabal, Santiago   111

Page, Joanna   4, 5, 37, 42, 44, 69, 112
pampa   70, 113, 120, 169
panopticism   157
Paraguay   178, 189
Patagonia   32, 34, 37, 39, 42–6, 57, 161,
    164, 166, 168–75
    Comodoro Rivadavia   34, 40, 43
    Veintiocho de Noviembre   161–2,
        169–76, 188
Perón, Juan   1, 35
piqueteros   7, 13, 55
police   22, 24, 47, 50, 58, 64, 136, 140,
    156–9, 167, 169, 177–8, 201, 214,
    227, see also Bonaerense, la
political film   4–8, 10–12
postcrisis   17, 55, 58, 112, 138, 163
precariat   32, 35–46, 49, see also class
Proceso dictatorship   1, 2, 4, 14, 21, 24,
    73, 89–93, 125–7, 132–44, 159,
    170, 181, 191
    *Documento final de la junta militar
        sobre la Guerra contra la subversión
        y el terrorismo*   132–3
    Secretaría de Inteligencia
        (SIDE)   126, 133

rage   17, 46, 47, 53–6, 58, 61–2, 129,
    131, 175, 187
Rejtman, Martín   2, 5, 35, 225–6
repression   24, 61, 67, 74, 107–10, 117–20,
    124, 129, 135, 141, 148–50, 156–7, 192
Resnais, Alain   48–9
rhizome(-atic)   25, 150, 152–6,
    173–7, 185–9
Ricouer, Paul   65
Rocha, Carolina   3, 8, 33, 44, 62, 69

San Martín, José de   75, 77, 78, 114
Sarlo, Beatriz   8, 33
Saumell-Muñoz, Rafael   180–1

Schindel, Estela   145
schizophrenia   128–32
Schmitt, Carl   159
Scorer, James   69, 75, 83
Scorsese, Martin   133, 206, 210
Selimović, Inela   146
sex   40, 82–4, 117–18, 122, 140,
    148, 184–5
sexuality   105–6, 118, 122, 140
    deployment of   105, 116–17
Soffici, Mario   4, 176
Solanas, Fernando "Pino" and Octavio
    Getino   4, 10, 19, 205
Springer, Simon   31
stand   76–7, 81, 85
Standing, Guy   31–2
Stantic, Lita   212
State Apparatus
    ideological   19, 20, 67, 68, 90, 99,
        104–6, 156
    repressive   67–8, 74, 78, 81, 84–5, 93,
        97–9, 153, 156–7, 168–70, 187, 193
state of exception   158–60, 169–71,
    174, 182
Sturzenegger, Federico   22–3
subjective violence   5, 9, 15, 16, 22,
    24–5, 30, 32, 46–7, 49–53, 56,
    58–62, 66–7, 74, 88, 89, 93, 98, 109,
    120–6, 152–3, 155–6, 163, 167–8,
    171, 191–3, 198, see also objective
    violence; violence
subjugation   37, 43, 109–10, 124, 146–7,
    157, 192–3

Third Cinema   4, 19

Urraca, Beatriz   90, 111, see also
    micro-societies
Uruguay   9, 70, 190

villa miseria   10–11, 86–99, 170,
    176, 213–14
violence, see also objective violence;
    subjective violence
    introduction of   18, 30, 116,
        128, 163, 168
    and power   17, 38–9, 53, 61,
        64–7, 77–8, 81, 84–5, 89, 93–7,
        99, 139, 185
viveza criolla   35–6, 80

Wayne, Mike 5
Weber, Max 64–5, 74, 76–7, 88, *see also*
    Gewalt; stand
White Elephant 10–12, 87–9, 96–7
Williams, Raymond 14, 66

Zapatista movement 30
Zavarzadeh, Mas'ud 20
Žižek, Slavoj 13–17, 32, 58,
    61, 66–7, 77, 80, 170,
    190

Printed in the USA
CPSIA information can be obtained
at www.ICGtesting.com
LVHW012255030224
770781LV00001BA/146